PARTY SHOES TO SCHOOL AND BASEBALL CAPS TO BED

The parents' survival guide to understanding kids, clothes, and independence

Marilise Flusser

Photographs by Steve Moore
Additional Photography by Bruce Laurance

A Fireside Book   Published by Simon & Schuster
New York London Toronto Sydney Tokyo Singapore

FIRESIDE
Simon & Schuster Building
Rockefeller Center
1230 Avenue of the Americas
New York, New York 10020

DESIGNED BY BARBARA MARKS
Manufactured in the United States of America

10 9 8 7 6 5 4 3 2 1

Library of Congress Cataloging in Publication Data
Flusser, Marilise.
    Party shoes to school and baseball caps to bed : the parents' survival guide to understanding kids, clothes, and independence / Marilise Flusser ; photographs by Steven Moore.
        p. cm.
    "A Fireside book."
    Includes bibliographical references and index.
    1. Child rearing. 2. Children's clothing. 3. Autonomy in children. I. Moore, Steven, 1954- . II. Title.
HQ769.F547 1992
649'.1—dc20   91-34861
                                                                   CIP

ISBN: 0-671-74722-3

Dear Abby Letter taken from the *Dear Abby* colum by Abigail Van Buren. Copyright 1991. Universal Press Syndicate. Reprinted with permission.
"Samantha's Suitcase" excerpted with permission from *Mothering*, volume #58. All rights reserved.
Excerpts from *The Difficult Child* by Stanley Turecki, M.D. copyright © 1989 by Stanley Turecki, M.D. and Leslie Tonner. Reprinted with permission of Bantam Dell, division of Bantam Doubleday Dell Publishing Group, Inc.
The Hurried Child, David Elkind, © 1988 by David Elkind. Reprinted with permission of Addison-Wesley Publishing Company.
The Ordinary Is Extraordinary, Amy Laura Dombro and Leah Wallach copyright ©1988 by Amy Laura Dombro and Leah Wallach. Reprinted with permission of Simon & Schuster Inc.
Freed Your Kids Right copyright © 1979 Dr. Lendon Smith. Reproduced with permission of McGraw-Hill, Inc.

The First Five Years: The Relaxed Approach to Child Care copyright © 1973, 1984 by Virginia E. Pomeranz, M.D. and Dodi Schultz. Reprinted with permission of St. Martin's Press, Inc.

Additional photographs by Bruce Laurance, pp. 45, 69, 129, 132, 135–36, 139, 146, 158, 187, 193, 201, 210, 214, 224
Photographs and drawings styled by Marilise Flusser.
Drawings by Debby Albenda.

Ten percent of the author's proceeds from this book's sales will go to **PARENT ACTION**, an organization founded by T. Berry Brazelton, M.D. and Bernice Weissbourd to encourage parents to take action to insure that government, communities and workplaces have policies and services that support and strengthen families. **PARENT ACTION** is located in Washington D.C.

To Alan, who is "the best"! for all those make-do dinners at Nick's, and to my girls, Skye and Pipey, who will always be my inspiration— thank you for all your ideas and help, and for lending me your accessories, clothes, and shoes whenever I needed them, even if they were new.

To Mom, who introduced me to the joys of Paris and K-Mart and who always led the way with humor, persistence, and an open mind, and to Pop, Suzie, and Nicky for all their support and for always listening.

My gratitude to the following professionals for their help and inspiration: Barbara Lowenstein, Angela Miller, Carla Glasser, Debby Albenda, Bruce Laurance, Kathy Friedman, Jan Miller, Helen McClatchy, R.S.C.J., and Bill Cunningham.

With special gratitude to: Kara Leverte, my editor, who nurtured this book twice over, who inspired me, put up with me! and made my dream a reality; Deborah Chase, my literary mentor and friend; Lesley Logan, my cowriter and long-distance runner of wit and patience; and Steven Moore, who through rain, sleet, and snow always got the shot.

CONTENTS

INTRODUCTION

By the time we had our first child, my husband and I had worked in the clothing business for years. Alan was known for his elegant designs for men while I specialized in junior and children's wear and was known for my colorful sense of style. None of our expertise prepared us for the very specific questions about the infant layette. What on earth was a "stretchie"? Why did we need a "receiving blanket"? "Bunting": I knew the word from the nursery rhyme but there was no way I could have identified one. I had all the child-care books on hand, but they just didn't have the kind of details and advice on children's clothing that I wanted. I suppose that the seed of this book was planted way back then, and the need for such a book came up continually as my two girls grew.

By the time my oldest daughter was three, I knew that children's clothing not only required shopping expertise, but was one of the great underground issues of parenting. My oldest daughter was so determined about what she would and would not wear, even at the age of two and a half, that she'd often throw a fit if she didn't want to wear something. I couldn't understand it, I thought it was me: I was a terrible mother, I didn't know how to handle my child, I couldn't even get her to perform the simplest task of dressing. Then, on her third birthday, things came to a head when I brought out a new French cotton dress for her to wear and "look pretty." She had an all-out tantrum two hours before her party and still ended up wearing the same t-shirt dress she'd been practically living in for the past four months. It was then that my own attitudes about dressing my kids started becoming more thoughtful. What was going on? I realized if I wanted to avoid constantly laying down the law but still enjoy a harmonious home life, my parenting skills needed to become more progressive.

When my kids were young, I spent a lot of time with other mothers. What would start out as a casual conversation about my fashion tips for their kids seemed to always evolve into a broader and often surprising discussion of the "clothing problem." I learned from their experiences and my own observations that clothes actually are a pivotal childhood issue. Preceded only by food, clothing is a child's earliest opportunity to exercise personal autonomy and

"My mother was on top of me all the time. It was the fifties—she liked us dressed very Junior League and proper. I didn't mind how the clothes looked, I minded how critical she was. She attached so much importance to it. If I lost a white glove, I felt like I was a bad person. I have boys now, and I determined from the beginning that as long as they were clean and the colors didn't clash too much I'd be happy."

"Any time I got a uniform of my own, it was thrilling for me. I was one of four brothers and somehow belonging to something outside my family made me feel special, independent. The first three or four weeks I got my first Little League uniform I proudly sat on the bench. I wasn't quite good enough to play yet. But after each game I used to slide around the bases so I'd come home dirty."

"I remember being very young, and having horrible fights with my mother over wanting to wear the same dress every day. I couldn't explain it then, but now I distinctly remember having the feeling that if I didn't wear that same dress all the time, no one would know who I was."

then to experience the results. Children are not verbal—they can't tell you how they feel—but they can spit out the spinach, or smile contentedly in response to certain clothing. Even a very young baby who cries every time an undershirt is pulled on over her head is making her first choice about what feels comfortable. And when you substitute for those over-the-head shirts the more comfortable (but less convenient) side-snap ones, you are sending a message back of understanding and love.

Until I started talking with my parent friends specifically about the clothing issue, I never read about it or heard it discussed. It seemed as if these kinds of daily worries—infants who outgrew all their shower presents in the first week; arguments over what to wear; three-year-old girls who wouldn't keep their clothes on or boys who wouldn't take off their favorite hat, even for bed; parents who went broke keeping up with shoe sizes—were considered too petty to discuss in the grand scheme of "parenthood." Well, I know that even though I had been a "fashion expert," I had needed all the help I could get in clothing my kids. And I believe that most modern parents do.

In today's society, the tightly knit family and community structures that effortlessly and automatically passed on gems of child-rearing wisdom to each generation are no more. Families are more likely connected by a long-distance telephone call. Many parents are trying to develop parenting skills in isolation, from scratch, and are more adept at reading a financial spread-sheet than interpreting the language of layette. Shopping for kids' clothing might be done on the run at lunch hour, or from a catalogue, rather than in the orderly seasonal approach of the past. With our busy lifestyles and tight budgets, parenting in the nineties is an incredibly intricate balancing act. And dressing, just like feeding your child, is a daily, unremitting responsibility. Everyone knows the eight A.M. day-care deadline can challenge the patience of everyone in the household and sets the tone for everyone's day.

What parents don't know is that clothing can be a teaching tool and source of communication to help us raise creative, independent children. My kids don't have much to say about their school, their bedtime, or their safety, but I can encourage them to express themselves with their own choices in other ways, like letting them choose what they want to wear (or at least let them actively participate in dressing themselves). And if we listen to our children's clothing preferences—instead of making them wear what *we* want them to wear—we can learn a lot about them. For instance, I have noticed that some kids repeatedly choose knitted fabrics, such as sweatpants, over stiffer woven fabrics, such as jeans, just as my own daughter did with her t-shirt dress. And like me, parents are often bewildered and frustrated by these seemingly arbitrary choices. They have no idea how a clothing preference could give them clues to their child's personality. Stanley Turecki, M.D., author of *The Difficult Child,* has conducted much research on young children and their temperament, and finds that choice of clothing is often related to temperament. He explains: "Some children have a low sensory threshold due to their temperament. This explains their preference for the more comfortable, less scratchy clothing or even for bizarre outfits they may like to wear. They're not being willful. They are responding to the dictates of their sensitive skin. This choice should be understood and respected." If a parent understands his child has this temperamental trait of "low sensory threshold," he'll not only know to avoid certain uncomfortable clothing (turtlenecks!) and cut out "scratchy" labels, he'll have clues to understand his child's behavior in other areas, e.g., screaming in pain from minor bumps and bruises (the child's not "overreacting"—they really do hurt that much to him), or finding fault with certain foods (he's not "spoiled"— they really do taste disgusting to him).

The more we see what makes our child an individual, the more we can view him or her as an individual, totally separate from us, and the better we can parent. I hope especially to take a lot of pressure off first-time parents who don't have the experience of having other children for comparison and don't know where the boundaries are between them and their child, and that there are other factors influencing their child's behavior besides their own parenting skills—and that most behavior is normal. I've amassed lots of input from educational specialists, teachers, doctors, and even a nutritionist. They have many fresh opinions and suggestions on how to use the clothing issue as a parenting tool.

From a "fashion" viewpoint, looking over the choice of children's clothing offered at most stores, many parents have complained to me about the "too grown-up" looks for their little girls, or the "too expensive" designer outfits that overpower their child and their budgets. And I have to agree. To confuse matters, kids' clothing advertisements and editorials show kids wearing perfectly coordinated outfits. They're great to sell to adults who are buying them (and show off the manufacturer's designs perfectly!) but are rarely possible or appropriate to duplicate on real-life kids.

Besides any shopping problems, something to consider is the fact that clothing sends a message out into the world—even on kids. When we dress our kids in a too-adult style or too expensively, that clothing can actually add stress to their lives. Dr. David Elkind, author of *The Hurried Child*, says that in the past, when children dressed in more babyish clothing, set apart from adults, "it signaled adults that these people were to be treated differently; made it easier for children to act as children. The pressure for early academic achievement is but one of many contemporary pressures on children to grow up fast. Children's dress is another." In our fast-track age we rush children through childhood as if they were in a race to adulthood. We know even as parents of our own kids that when we dress them like miniature adults, it's hard for us to avoid that visual message we receive ourselves: we tend to believe the package and expect

. . . .
"When I see pictures of myself as a kid, I wonder how my mother could stand it! I had a real love for totally clashing, rather horrible patterns and I wore this kind of ensemble always. I was the fourth kid in a large family, and I guess she just didn't have the time or strength to argue me out of whatever hand-me-downs I took a shine to!"
. . . .

. . . .
"I remember the struggle with my parents about my tight blue jeans when I was thirteen. That's why I'll let Steven wear his surfer look and not say a word, even if it means he'll wear his t-shirt down to his knees."
. . . .

. . . .

"My mother preferred only tailored clothes. She dressed me in overalls and pants. She really disliked ruffles and frilly clothes and so I grew up with a real anti-girl thing. It took me until my late twenties to come out of my clothing shell and stop looking like I walked out of a TV commercial for a kitchen product. Today, my style is a lot wilder, but her training saves me from becoming a total fashion victim."

. . . .

the children to think and act like adults—and judge them on that level, too. And if we've invested in an expensive piece of clothing, it's hard not to get really angry if it gets lost and not to take our anger out on our child. But a young child isn't thinking about taking care of a special piece of clothing. His or her agenda is to play, learn, and have fun.

What results may often be a low-level tone of irritability on the part of the adult who is constantly expecting grown-up behavior a child can't deliver or maybe even understand. For instance, there's much confusion about how soon to expect a child to actually be able to dress herself or himself. I have often seen harried parents telling their three-year-old "Hurry up, hurry up. You always make us late," while the child is struggling to try to button her jacket. Or a parent will say to me, "He always wants me to tie his shoelaces—I'm afraid I'm spoiling him," when the child is only five years old. First of all most young children don't understand the concept of "being late": they can't tell time yet and often view being hurried as a rejection of them as a person.

Secondly, if parents understood more about nature's underlying timetable, they'd put far less pressure on their kids *and* themselves and enjoy each other a lot more. The whole physical process of getting dressed is ordinarily only mastered at about age six, and the skill of tying shoelaces usually comes last. It may be hard to reconcile the facts that a child who picked up how to read at age four still can't dress himself at five. I feel that if that little girl struggling with the buttons of her stiff designer jacket were dressed in a Shirley Temple dress above the knees instead of her body-hugging bike pants, or if that little boy were dressed in short pants and knee socks instead of his aviator jacket and cool haircut, the signal might be different, and the parent would unconsciously expect less grown-up competence and treat the child with more patience. Of course, we can't turn the cultural clock back when it comes to our kids. What we can do is learn as much as possible about nature's general developmental timetable of mastery of skills, and relax about whether our kids are behind or ahead of the norm. This will give us the confidence to encourage each of our children to develop at his or her own rate. Instead of confusing a child by expecting her to do things ahead of time, we'll be able to enjoy her accomplishments as she *does* master them—one by one.

After sixteen years working in the clothing business, and through the years of being a parent and talking to many other parents and experts, I've uncovered many problem-solving parenting techniques and fashion tips to help dress your child. They range from clothing in relation to key behavioral issues such as toilet training and getting out of the house in the morning, to managing a finicky dresser, to tips on how to help your child look his or her best and have the most fun with his or her clothes for the least amount of money.

Each chapter includes many colorful anecdotes from parents. Ranging from poignant to hilarious, they are a wonderful chorus of advice and encouragement. My wish is that with their wisdom and my efforts, *Party Shoes to School and Baseball Caps to Bed* will be a source of fresh, new information that encourages and reassures all parents committed to raising a happy, self-confident child.

. . . .

"One of my earliest memories is from when I was three. I had gotten all dressed up in my favorite, pink-striped sunsuit, which my mother had just ironed perfectly. (Our poor mothers, having to actually iron all our clothes!). I went over to my little friend David's yard, feeling very lovely indeed. He was watering the garden or something, and he turned to me and completely drenched me and my pretty sunsuit with the hose. You know, I can remember that sunsuit more vividly now than I remember my maternity clothes from two years ago!"

. . . .

Appreciating differences. Children from the same family may look their best in very different colors. Alison, on the left, looks better in muted tones. Karen, on the right, looks better in brighter tones. Both sisters are each wearing their favorite dresses. Children often gravitate toward the colors best suited to them, if allowed the choice.

COLOR

The carefully gendered color-coding of blue and pink we use to distinguish our otherwise identical-in-clothing infant boys and girls tells volumes about the importance of color. As early as the baby shower, when the expectant parents receive all those sleepers and receiving blankets in shades of yellow, white, red, and unisex blue, color is an issue.

Color is *the* building block of style for kids' clothes. Kids love color and color loves kids. To use color effectively you don't need to know any complicated rules or decipher a color wheel. I can help you understand your child's coloring and give you some easy, effective ways to enhance his or her beauty and personality. With the plethora of upbeat colors available to choose from—at all prices—any child can look great, no matter how little or much money is spent. The trick is to know what colors flatter your child.

Wearing the latest fashionable looks and spending a lot on them doesn't guarantee your child will look his or her best. For example, when I was working on an ad for children's jackets that required a "romantic" look in the model, the perfect young girl came in. She had hair like Alice in Wonderland and a pale, doe-eyed freshness. Unfortunately, she was clad in an eye-jarring black sweatshirt outfit accented with high voltage neon green and hot pink appliqués. Apparently, she or her mother thought this expensive outfit would make her stand out and get her the job. However, her naturally soft look was completely overwhelmed by these clothes and my clients dismissed her, unable to see her real beauty. A simple inexpensive pastel sweatshirt from the five-and-ten or discount department store would have been more effective. According to Ann Runyon Evans, color specialist, "The eye will avert if a person is not dressed in harmony with his or her looks."

The whole color analysis industry is based on the premise that correct use of color can improve your appearance. There are two general—and I emphasize general—color types. Finding your child's type is as simple as comparing the color of the hair to the tone of the skin. A child with muted coloring is one whose face and hair hues are similar: there is little contrast between skin and hair color. This color group looks best in more toned-down color combinations. For instance, if your little boy has brown hair and olive skin, you should look for combinations that blend together, such as dark green, brick red, navy, and soft yellows. Avoid the bright primary shades that could overwhelm him.

The other group is one whose face and hair tones are in contrast with each other: these children need colors that have "pop." They should be clearer and

. . . .

"When Ian was three, all he ever wanted to wear was pink—pink shorts, pink shirts, pink socks. It didn't really bother me, but my husband was uncomfortable with it. We finally figured out that he wanted to be like his daddy, who often wore pink oxford shirts to work."

. . . .

brighter and contrast with each other as the hair and skin of your child do. So, if your daughter has dark brown hair and peaches-and-cream skin she's going to need strong contrast in her clothing to support the contrast between her skin and her hair. Muted colors will dull her vibrant looks. If she's drawn to the pinks and purples as most little girls are, look for strong pastels that are clear rather than dusty. Your boy with black hair and paler skin will look best in rugby-striped shirts with lots of clear colors, not grayed down muted ones.

As for black and brown-skinned children, these two color groups also apply. For instance, a black child with lighter black hair and a peach-tone skin would look better with softer, more blended colors, whereas a darker-skinned black child with very dark hair has a stronger look and will need stronger, clear bright colors to complement her coloring. Asian children may have gold skin or pink skin tones, and in each case different colors are needed to enhance them: the former would be clearer, brighter, the latter more blended.

Nutrition and Skin Coloring

Have you ever found that your daughter "looks so pale" you want to put blush-on on her for a special family photo? My mother did! Or find that most colors overwhelm your son whether they're clear or muted?

Dr. Lendon Smith, author of the classic *Feed Your Kids Right,* believes that the skin reflects bodily health, and that nutrition is a major factor in a pale complexion. Ruling out colds and flu, temporary lack of sleep, anemia, or lead poisoning, etc., the circles-under-the-eyes look is often due to an allergy, usually to homogenized, pasteurized cow's milk. "The children (or adults) with this syndrome usually are fair people with blue or green eyes, so the dark-blue lower eyelids are in sharp contrast to the pale cheeks. Some parents believe that since the whole family looks like that, it is hereditary. Not so. The allergy is hereditary, but not the washed-out look.... It usually takes about two to three weeks of avoidance of all dairy products, or whatever particular food they are allergic to, to clear up the syndrome."

"My daughter, who looks best in bright colors, gravitated toward a tiny floral pastel print one day when we were shopping. I thought it would look wrong on her but she was so determined that I suggested she take the print dress she liked, and the one that I had selected, by herself and hold them both up to check out how they looked against her face in the mirror. I stood aside and resolved to stick with her decision. After a minute or two, she ended up picking the more flattering dress. She's now in fifth grade and when in doubt, she still uses this same method to pick her clothes."

Children usually get their permanent coloring around age 13, so be flexible. And don't forget to use your own visual instinct. My younger daughter looked wonderful in high contrast colors for her first four years—especially reds, yellows, and bright blues. Then I noticed her face was becoming lost in the same clamor of color that had once framed it so well. Her coloring was growing gentler, and even she herself began to gravitate to softer colors. I began to adjust her wardrobe accordingly. From then on, we bought only the more muted versions of those brights. In contrast to the color analysis industry which tends to pigeonhole people into rigid color types and suggests they exclude certain colors from their wardrobes, I agree with color specialist Ann Runyon

Evans, who says: "No color is wrong. In fact any child can wear just about any color. It's the clarity or clearness of the color versus the toned-downness or mutedness of the color that enhances or detracts from the appearance of a child." If you find that many of your child's clothes aren't as flattering as they could be, don't think you have to dump his whole wardrobe. Start by putting the right colors near his face, using the existing clothes elsewhere. As a fashion stylist, a trick I use that always helps a child look great is to add a flattering accent color near the face, such as a bright turtleneck or a colorful hair accessory.

So, what's the payoff? When you know what your child's best colors are, it won't matter so much where you shop or how much you spend. You can be sure that whether your child is dressed from a discount store or an expensive specialty store, he or she will look great. Shopping will become more efficient as you cut down on time-consuming indecision. Choosing clothes with confidence will make the whole shopping experience more enjoyable for both you and your child.

Appreciating differences. These six-year-old identical twins have different styles of dressing which their parents encourage. Raber likes his clothes tucked in; Taylor likes his clothes loose. Piper Smith is a mother of boys who has never given in to a predictable route when it comes to her sons' clothing. She offers them color constantly: fuchsia, turquoise, and purple. If they say: "That's a girl color," she'll counter with a walk to the window for a view of their garden. "Now there's every kind of color out there. Does it make sense that only girls can have pink? Pink is for everyone." Her tip for cool weather: Buy turtlenecks big, so the neck doesn't bind. Layer them in cool weather to stave off a jacket for a few more weeks. For a lively casual color accent, use the longer one underneath in a different color.

One color development in children's fashion that distresses me is the use of black. When I see an infant wearing a mostly black coverall or a five-year-old girl in an oversize sweat top with black leggings, it seems that an important part of childhood—the innocence and the lightness—has been lost. Instead we have children looking like miniature teenagers and adults. Of course, I have many friends who think black is contemporary and practical (stains don't show). These days moms and dads themselves wear a lot of black, a trend since the early eighties. It's guaranteed their preschooler girls going through their symbolic dressing phase (see the School Days chapter) are going to want to wear black too, to "look like mommy." After offering clothing choices to build the autonomy in their kids that parents feel they never had, nineties moms may have a hard time finding a reason to say a sudden decisive "No, honey. This is a color for mommy's wardrobe. You can wear it when you get older." These mothers may not even want to restrict black or other adult looks: they think it's cute and ask, "What harm?" And if their child is Asian, or has contrast coloring, physically she or he may look just fine in black.

I know I'm in the minority on this issue but personally I can't help thinking that wearing black is an age-old Western symbol of mourning—inappropriate to the promise of childhood. And when it comes to parenting, opening the door early to black (perceived by both boys and girls to be a grown-up color) and to other adult looks makes it difficult to close that door and set limits in other areas. ("Why can't I watch MTV?" will perhaps be the next question from a younger six-year-old sibling.) Children are "hurried" enough. Why not institute some family clothing markers? For example, one friend of mine restricted her daughter from wearing black in too grownup a way by saying, "You can wear black, but only from the waist (leggings, etc.) down, till you're such-and-such age." Another parent friend of mine says that black per se doesn't bother him; it bothers him only when the general impression the color creates is too adult-looking. And he evaluates this criterion with his kids as they go along. (This might be one way to avoid black becoming the "forbidden" color.) Markers, though often frustrating to kids, give them structure within a very unstructured world. With more digestible goals, kids better understand their progression from childhood to adulthood, and there is less stress on everyone. One way to make black look young is to keep it away from the face: the black velvet party dress that has the relief of its cream-colored lace collar is a classic example. Or always juxtapose the color black with bright colors as athletes do. Avoid solid expanses of black in any outfit, and always use colors to accessorize.

Another pitfall of children's design is that clothing is often over-designed and looks contrived. A boy's outfit, for example, might have a shirt with bright stripes on the collar, pocket, and cuffs. This will coordinate with matching pants that have the same stripes on the pockets, kneepads, and cuffs. There's so much going on that all you see is the outfit, not your child. Or, a five-

"When my older girl Maggie reached seven, all of a sudden she wanted anything with black. I wear black all the time, plus I think she identifies with teenagers. She'd say pointedly to Claire, her four-year-old younger sister, 'I hate pink and purple' as if to separate herself from her 'baby' sister. But, I didn't want my seven-year-old walking around in outfits that looked too grown-up. So we started at the bottom with black leggings and bright skirts."

year-old girl might be dressed in an adult-scale cabbage rose print blouse and skirt in bright fuchsia. It may be an adorable copy of the Parisian original and quite expensive, but because the scale of the design is for an adult, it is totally overwhelming. My suggestion is to break up over-matched sets. Think of each piece as a separate item, not as part of one outfit. Then, add or take away color or design for a more natural-looking outfit. Think in terms of replacing a patterned piece on the top or bottom with a solid piece in a complementary color. So use plain sweatpants to go with the busy shirt from the outfit, or a plain t-shirt or sweatshirt to go with the busy pants. (See School Days, photo on page 79). Now what about surfing looks that are loaded with color from top to bottom? These eclectic mixes—however wild they look—are usually chosen by your child. His or her emerging personality shows through, not a designer's fixed idea.

Forgetting about black, little girls' clothing may often end up looking too adult merely because not enough color is used. It's not the shape of the clothes, since except for some bathing suits (and *some* gym gear) girls' clothing is usually modest. For example, two-color outfits like black and white, or colors that are European in feeling, such as mustard and navy, look sophisticated on a grown person, but dull on a vigorous four-year-old. As a fashion stylist, I discovered that adding a *third* color—even a *fourth!*—as an accent, such as yellow, turquoise, red, or even white, will always remedy this. Whether it's just a contrasting collar on a shirt or a turtleneck, belt, barrette, suspenders, tights, or socks, the addition of the extra color injects spontaneity, making the outfit younger and more childlike.

Most of us don't need studies to tell us that certain colors can enhance a person's appearance or create moods. But few experts can explain why some children at various stages in their development become obsessed with wearing one particular color. If your child has this fixation it's a definite sign that he or she has a talent for persistence and probably a rich imagination. So often the underlying reason for a child's tenacious grasp on a color is much more logical and persuasive than we adults understand. Be a detective and find out what that reason is. It's another opportunity to learn more about what makes your child tick.

"Eddie has red hair. He looked really cute with a lavender or pink t-shirt with his khakis. I got away with it until he was five and said, 'That's a girl shirt.' The next time I got to see him in those colors was when he got into surf colors, hot pink was 'cool' —in that context."

Color Tips for Shopping and Styling

➤ Sale items usually consist of the *colors* that didn't sell. Don't be persuaded by the price until you're sure the color is right.
➤ Each season, manufacturers push the "new" color. Don't be influenced by the ubiquitous displays and the subtle pressure to buy something whose value lies merely in being the latest, not the most flattering.
➤ Color translates differently to different fabrics. Evaluate every piece of clothing. A color in one fabric may look great (a bright fuchsia in a cotton

t-shirt) but too overpowering or harsh (a purple in an acrylic sweater) because of a different dye, yarn, or finish.

➤ Bright socks are the easiest quick color accent. Bright yellow is always a good stylist's unisex fail-safe accent. If you can't find a good yellow, turquoise is a new accent color that flatters any child.

➤ Buy t-shirts with a good background color. Even a plain navy is better than the white background ones of a synthetic blend that yellow or gray with washing and then drag down your child's coloring. This applies even to novelty shirts with pictures of popular cartoon characters on them.

➤ Those pale pinks and pastels your preschooler girl craves are often difficult to find in department stores—they are not always "in." However, you can always find these pales in three places: catalogues, discount department stores and traditional stores specializing in classics. In fashion stores, paler pinks are usually available in November and December, at holiday time. If your child just doesn't look good in *pale* pink, move toward mid-tones—she probably won't notice as long as it's pink. Pink or other soft colors are often accented with black for a trendy, teenage look. To keep the look young, avoid accenting the outfit with accessories or hair clips in black. Always go for color.

➤ A third, or even a fourth, accent color assures a youthful appearance in a child's outfit—adult clothing is usually two-color. If you use the accent color more than once, keep distance between it so the child is not overpowered by color. For instance, use the color on socks and headband or shoelaces and t-shirt.

➤ A "cool" surfer answer to lost socks: When you lose one of a pair of socks, use two different colors together for a fun fashion look. The same goes for winter gloves. This works especially well if your child has those one-size-fits-all (even an adult) type of gloves that you can wear on either hand.

➤ Neons have become the number one summer theme, as well as fall-winter accent. But not all kids look great in full-fledged neons. Evaluate. Your child may be satisfied with neons on a white ground, instead of a denser black or chartreuse. If your child still craves an overpowering look, respect that choice, and offer a cap or headband in a lighter color to offset it.

➤ The color black attracts heat while white repels it. Avoid buying a solid black t-shirt to be worn in the high heat of summer. After the first wearing, it will stay in the drawer. Compromise with a hat or socks.

Color Tips for Parenting

➤ Use a multicolored skirt or t-shirt to teach your toddler and preschool child the names of colors when he or she wears it. Increase the child's vocabulary and artistic taste by describing the colors accurately, such as emerald green versus mint green. You'll be surprised how they pick up on it, and proudly name very specific colors.

. . . .

"Rachel had dressed herself in a long-sleeved red shirt and pink corduroy overalls for day camp on a day when the temperature was supposed to reach ninety. Somehow, that morning, I managed to say calmly 'Oh, you're wearing a red shirt and pink overalls,' instead of 'You're going to die of the heat in those clothes—hurry up and change.' Rachel looked up at me proudly and said, 'Don't I look great? I'm Strawberry Shortcake today.' I was so glad I hadn't criticized her. I believe in letting my kids learn by consequences, so instead of arguing, I decided to let her go to camp as she was. The next day she was happily ready in shorts and a tank top."

. . . .

> Bright, unusual colors can be a useful identifying flag. A bright t-shirt can help you spot your kid in a crowd, or a bright fabric-covered elastic around your girl's ponytail can help you track her whereabouts in the pool or lake.
> Kids look great in colorful clothes. You may not look good in acid yellow, but your child just might. Keep an open mind.
> Start teaching your children fashion autonomy early (even at age three or four) by teaching them to find their own best colors. Take time once in a while to have them hold up different colored t-shirts to their face, look in the mirror, and then choose. Stick with their decision. You'll be surprised how young kids can pick their most flattering colors.
> Be prepared for pink, and all hues of it, to be generally the Number One color choice for the preschool girl. Psychologists say the developmental issue of symbolically identifying with "female" occurs at this age and that the pink obsession may be part of this, similar to the preference that many little girls have for skirts and dresses at this age. Boys' color preferences are less predictable.

"When my older son was five, he loved anything with black in it. Certain things he liked really surprised me. It could be an ordinary pair of socks that happened to have black and white stripes or a surfer bathing suit with black in the print. Now, with my second, he could care less about black. He's dying for a purple sweatshirt. Again it was surprising. What's the big deal about purple? I finally decoded it. Black was for Darth Vader when Star Wars was popular, and now purple is for the Joker in Batman."

Using Color to Parent

"I read once how the acting coach Stanislavski taught his actors to use clothes to dissect a role. He said sometimes if you can't understand a character, you have to dress 'outside in'—you have to wear a kind of uniform, the clothes that character would wear—to help you create the character. Other times, he said, an actor can feel a character so easily, he can dress 'inside out'—as if he were that person. This reminds me of the way my own daughter, Jessie, uses clothes. She's six years old and not particularly open about her feelings—it's like pulling teeth to find out what's going on day to day. But when I observe what colors and styles she chooses for clothing every morning and think of Stanislavski, it really helps me. If she's feeling a little uptight about a fight at school with her best friend or is plain tired, she'll dress 'outside in'— she'll reach for a white top and a navy skirt or sweatpants. In my mind it's her neutral power look—she's not feeling 'up' enough to stand out, she wants to be 'okay.' Other times, when she's feeling ebullient—she's just read her first chapter book, had a great time on the weekend, or is well rested, she'll reach for neon bike pants, a multicolored sequin sweat top—a trendy look—totally different from the other. That's 'inside out'! With the first, I know to be gentler after school and get her to bed a little earlier with more time for hugs and talk."

Onesie or Bodysuit.
By Mothercare.

LAYETTE

Waiting for the first baby is one of the most exciting times of expectant parents' lives. It can also be one of the most vulnerable. Some parents may have waited a long time for this event and even if they're usually very savvy shoppers, they can't help going wild when buying a layette. Many parents have had little or no experience with children. First-time parents seem to buy either too much or too little. They need help! While they may read that they need something called a receiving blanket, or know that undershirts and sleepers are standard baby garments, they're more focused on the event of the birth and on what cute outfit to bring the baby home in.

Usually the hospital or birthing center will provide you with a list of the absolute essentials, but sometimes this is even more confusing. A layette has a new, strange vocabulary that needs to be translated. Even though I was in the clothing business, I was baffled by the list we got in our birthing class. This chapter is devoted to the new parent who needs to understand the language of layette to know what to buy.

See the general list on the opposite page for a basic layette that I've drawn from top designers of layette, professional nannies, and my own and other parents' experience. For cold weather layette needs see the Outerwear chapter.

Many first-time parents have been told by professional caretakers or experienced friends that it is necessary to hand-wash newborn clothing to avoid germs that may be left in commercial washer-dryers in their building or neighborhood. Katherine Karlsrud, M.D., a practicing pediatrician and clinical instructor in pediatrics at Cornell Medical College in New York City, disagrees. "This is absolutely not necessary. The only problem for your baby may be the residues of other detergents and softeners left in those washers. Putting the machine through a double rinse cycle before use will take care of any residues. When hand-washing may be beneficial for the really young baby is if you have a long history of allergy in your family. After several months, reevaluate if you feel it's still necessary. As for soaps, Ivory and Dreft are the gentlest but don't always seem to clean as well as other stronger brands. If you choose one of those stronger types, use less of the detergent than you would for older children's clothes." Hand-washing infant clothing has been a traditional activity for centuries but it is not a necessity for your new baby's health. Wouldn't you rather get an extra nap?

. . . .

layette . . .n
[French] a
complete outfit of
garments, toilet
articles, and
bedding for a
newborn child.
—*Webster's New Twentieth
Century Dictionary*

. . . .

Basic Layette

4–8	all-cotton side-snap undershirts in white for sizes 6 and 12 months (only 3 for size 3 months)
4–6	all-cotton slip-on undershirts in white for sizes 6 to 24 months
4–6	onesies or bodysuits (one-piece crotch-snap undershirts), short or long sleeves, up to size 24 months
4–6	drawstring gowns—for newborn
3–6	coveralls (for fall and winter) or creepers (for spring and summer)
6–10	stretchies in sizes S, M, L (more for a fall–winter–spring baby than a summer arrival)
2–4	pairs of booties (with drawstring) or slipper socks
2	drool bibs
1	all-cotton cap and/or outside hat
1	sweater
4	all-cotton flannel receiving blankets—they also come hooded, and can replace the cotton cap indoors
2	hooded terry bath towels
2–4	baby washcloths
1	lightweight flame-resistant blanket
3	dozen cloth diapers (see box on page 50)

The key question to knowing how much clothing to buy is: *How often are you going to do wash?* The answer to this question has a great deal to do with the accessibility of your washer and dryer. *Where is it?* Is it right in your home? Is it down in the basement of your apartment building? Or down the street? If you have a washer and dryer at home, no doubt you can get along with fewer items. If you do laundry only once or twice a week, you'll need much more. Even if you have a washer and dryer in your home, you won't cheerfully do laundry in the first few weeks. You'll have a lot to do, getting your strength back, changing, feeding, and bathing your newborn, so you may not want to waste those precious moments doing laundry. Finances permitting, more is better in the case of layette for the first-time parent. Some new mothers I know say that 4–6 items per size is still too low for their needs. Be honest with yourself, and avoid trying to be superparent by saving a couple of dollars. First-time parents should take steps to reduce stress, and have enough clothes on hand. Extremely inexpensive basics are available at discount stores if you need to fill in.

Gifts of clothing from the shower and in honor of the actual event will not always be the right size, or the right style or color. But unless it's easy to return them, keep them close at hand. You'll find them very useful at some future point. The snowsuit that threatened to swallow your newborn whole will be filled out a lot sooner than you think; and that huge hand-knit sweater will become an old favorite in no time. Even that pea green stretchy you swore you'd never put on your kid begins to look pretty good when you hit the bottom of the bureau and the top of the laundry basket at two in the morning!

Stages of Baby Clothing

Age	Activity	Emphasis on . . .	Types of Clothing
Birth– 3 months	Lies on back or tummy, or reclines in seats; bowel movements are very loose. Develops relationship with other people as they dress her.	Gentle maneuvering over head; many, many changes of clothing. Easy access for diapering. Durable fabric for lots of machine washing. Milk stain removal. Attention to temperature and comfort. Soft knitted fabrics.	Nightgown with drawstring bottom; stretchies, caps and hats, booties (if clothing is not footed), drool bibs, side-snap undershirts with no tight neck openings.
3–6 months	Lies on back or tummy, or reclines in seats: kicks and punches air vigorously. Rolls over. Bowel movements less runny. Develops a sense of order from the predictability of diaper and clothing changes and can anticipate familiar routines.	Fewer diaper changes than first 3 months. Easy access for diapering. Durable fabric for lots of machine washing. Milk stain removal. Attention to temperature and comfort. Soft knitted fabrics.	Stretchies, coveralls, gowns, underwear such as bodysuits (onesies), side-snap shirts, drool bibs.
5 or 6 months– 10 months	Sits up. Eats solid food. Starts to teeth and may grab anything, including socks, to chew on.	Clothing more varied. Easy access for diapering: snap legs. Full-length front zippers. Food stain removal. Soft knitted fabrics.	Clothing starts looking less like sleepwear and more like outerwear for more active baby, fewer stretchies and more coveralls; feeding bibs for meals. Caps or hats. Bodysuits still important. Avoid dangling doodads on clothing. T-shirts and leggings. Avoid dangling doodads on clothing.
8 or 9 months– 15 months (1¼ years)	Crawls, creeps, pulls up to stand. Can help participate in the dressing process by moving his legs, arms, etc., as they're named, and learns about his own body as he helps. Resents being still to get dressed: distract him with toys, teethers, cardboard baby books.	Durable, flexible "panted" clothing. Easy access to diapers. Food stain removal and ground-in dirt removal from crawling. Buy fewer pastel infant colors—they show dirt. Soft knitted fabrics, some woven fabrics. Footless clothes so baby can feel his feet and start to learn his gait.	Footless clothing like coveralls, ribbed pants. Clothing that is attached from the shoulders such as overall is important for crawling. Grippy socks. Clothing should cover knee on hard surfaces. Stretchies used mostly for nighttime sleepwear.
1 year– 2 years	Crawls, toddles, walks. Often refuses to be dressed—she is too busy moving. Or may want to join in because she's learning new skills, e.g., fastening Velcro or putting away clothes in hamper. Starts to be able to take off clothes—socks, pants.	Durable clothing, *quick* and easy off and on. Smooth, comfortable coverage of bulky diapers; quick access to diapers. Hold up pants to prevent tummy exposure. Knitted fabrics and sturdy woven fabrics.	Now baby needs mobile clothing to contain diapers, e.g., woven and knit overalls, elastic-waisted pants (with suspenders); 2-piece sweat outfits; knit jumpsuits. Continue to use footless clothing when possible so baby can develop a natural gait.
2–3 years	Toilet trains, runs, may attend preschool. Starts to have clothing preferences. Dressing time takes longer because he insists on dressing himself. Knows all names of pieces of clothing. Offer choices to foster autonomy and speed process along. May want to remove all his clothes in his search to discover himself.	Self-dressing. Clothing that pulls up and down easily for trips to potty. Dresses and skirts that easily flip up. Sweat separates, backup changes to accommodate accidents. Autonomy: Velcro, easy buttons, pockets for possessions. Comfort and simplicity. More woven fabrics. When safe (and socially appropriate), let her go without clothes if she wants.	No more overalls or complicated clothing. Time for toilet-training clothes: elastics-waisted pants and skirts. T-shirts, dresses, and tights. (See Toddler chapter for tips on dressing a toddler.)

SHOWER GIFTS

Judy: pink sweater and pink doll
Nina: booties, sleeper (pink pandas)
Kathy: sweater & hat set & booties
David, Suzanne & Willie: baby picture frame,
   2 baby bottles
   baby head support, blanket
Randy: music box, dancing bear
Piper, Marilise & Alan; Skye: suspenders
Piper & Skye: dress & pants set
Anna-Marie: skirt & pants set (green)
   short sleeve - pastel figures
Debbie: sleeper (white)
Lauren: A kangarockaroo
   & receiving blanket
Ethel: bunting - 2 pieces
Bernice: pink footless sleeper w/ triangles,
   & white teddy bear

Jean: snuggly & sleeper
David, Suzanne & Willie: music mobile
Rita: kangarockaroo
Antoinette: travel baby bag (pink),
   with diapers
Marilise: layette instructions
Betsy: book - Baby & life, stuffed dog,
   sleeper, receiving blanket
Jonelle: Rag doll, changing pad
Linda: pantaloon & blouse outfit
Retianna & Jaime: pink & white striped sleeper
Melanie: all pink sleeper & white booties
Nina: down comforter & sheet
April - red knit outfit & pajamas
   (2-piece) pink with white polka dots
Laura - white shorts

SIZE	HAVE	STILL NEED
0-3 MOS	1 PINK PANDA COVERALL (NO FEET)	3-6 SIDE-SNAP UNDERSHIRTS
	1 CREAM SWEATER, HAT, BOOTIES	5-8 STRETCHIES
	1 2-PC CUTE DRESSY BLOOMER OUTFIT	4 DRAWSTRING GOWNS
	1 PINK SWEATER	BOOTIES
	1 PINK STRETCHIE (FEET)	DROOL BIBS
		4 RECEIVING BLANKETS
		2 BATH TOWELS & WASHCLOTHS
		BLANKET
6 MOS	1 PINK & WHITE STRETCHIE (W/FEET)	2-3 BLANKET SLEEPERS
	1 STRETCHIE (COTTON) W/ FEET	6-18 STRETCHIES
	(LONG-SLEEVED)	1 COVERALL
	1 WHITE & PASTEL COTTON COVERALL	6 ONESIES, LONG SLEEVES
	(NO FEET)	4-6 OVER-THE-HEAD UNDERSHIRTS
	1 PINK & WHITE STRIPED OVERALL	SLIPPER SOCKS
	(NO FEET)	
	1 PINK COVERALL - COTTON (NO FEET)	
12 MOS	1 WHITE WOOLY COLD WEATHER	3 COVERALLS
	SUIT WITH FEET & HOOD	6 ONESIES
	1 2-PC PINK BUNTING SLEEVELESS	3 OVER-THE-HEAD UNDERSHIRTS
	OVERALL & JACKET	8-10 STRETCHIES
18 MOS-2YRS	1 WHITE COTTON LONG-SLEEVE SHIRT	SLIPPER SOCKS & EVERYTHING!

The Stages of Baby Clothing. The items you need when you need them.

Jenny Matthau's layette system. Jenny analyzed what she received at her shower (list on top) and grouped the items by each size range in terms of footed and nonfooted clothing (list on bottom) according to the Stages of Baby Clothing chart. Now it's clear what she still needs.

Often, when a parent dresses his child, both of them are in a hurry to get the chore done and neither is in the mood to pay much attention to what is going on. But dressing a child can become a small opportunity for play and closeness: a few seconds to touch each other's faces, to touch a toe or tickle a tummy, to examine and discuss the pattern of green and red boats on a t-shirt, to enjoy the pert sound of a snap. Though dressing is something adults in large part do for children, even very small babies involve themselves mentally and physically in the process in active and important ways. Having their arms, legs, toes, and tummies touched by an adult's hands and by articles of clothing, feeling the differences in sensation when skin is covered and when it's bare, listening to their parents saying the names of different body parts as they pull on shirts and slip feet through pant holes, all help babies identify the boundaries of their bodies. Because they are dressed several times a day every day from the moment they are born, and because their parents tell them what they are doing and about to do when they change them, dressing also helps babies learn to anticipate. By 4 or 5 months, your baby will begin closing her eyes and squinching up her face when you pull a shirt over her head, preparing herself for the feel of the cloth on her cheeks and nose. These early experiences of expectation are her first steps toward an understanding of time and order. . . .

Infants think and feel physically, with their bodies. When your baby grabs your thumb or pulls at your shirt, she's learning to feel her own hand better, to distinguish the sensations of moving her fingers from the particular sensations she experiences when touching different materials. . . . Babies are also acutely sensitive to the tone and expression of their parents' voices, the temperature of their skin, the quality of their touch, the tension in their muscles. You are saying "I want you to be comfortable" when you smooth out a sleeve along your baby's arm. When you tell your child, to avoid startling him, that you are going to take off his shirt, you are showing tenderness and respect for his feelings. When you hold him securely and confidently while you pull on his pants, you are telling him, "You can trust me." These demonstrations of your love and reliability help your baby establish the safe base necessary to feel confident about exploring an unfamiliar world.

—Amy Laura Dombro and Leah Wallach, Ordinary Is Extraordinary

- - - - - - - - - -
"I bought long-sleeved undershirts big and rolled up the sleeves. They lasted a lot longer and looked really cute."
- - - - - - - - - -

DEFINITIONS OF BASIC LAYETTE

Side-Snap, Side-Tie, and Over-the-Head Undershirts

Side-snap undershirts are generally preferred to over-the-head undershirts in the first weeks. You do have to lift your baby to get the garment around and on, but you don't have to pull it over the head, which is so delicate and unsteady in the beginning. All you need to do is lay the shirt down open, then lay the baby on it. Carefully pull each arm through, and fasten closed. Another version of the side-snap undershirt is the side tie. It can be tied firmly to fit an infant and later more loosely to adjust to the growing baby. Some parents prefer this garment for its longevity. Others dislike the ties which they say act like a wick with a wet diaper. As the baby's neck muscles develop and the torso lengthens, you can switch to the lapover-neck undershirt. This undershirt has a t-shirt type neckline with criss-cross seams at each shoulder, so there is give when you pull it over baby's head. It is less bulky under clothes than the side closing type. To put on a shirt with an over-the-head neckline, widen the neck and pull it on gently from the back of the head forward, holding the neckline open wide with your fingers over the baby's face, then put the baby's arms, one at a time, through the sleeves.

Side-Snap Undershirt.

A common problem with inexpensive 100 percent cotton infant t-shirts is the inevitable shrinkage that occurs with frequent washings and dryings. T-shirts that fit perfectly at first often shorten and widen considerably after only a month or so of use. When baby grows a little older and has less frequent diaper and clothing changes, many parents opt for higher priced t-shirts or onesies.

Side-Tie Undershirt.

Drawstring Gown (or Sack)

This is a great sleepwear item that's rarely understood by modern parents, but is recommended by all layette professionals for the newborn. It comes in one-size-fits-all (birth to nine months) and is most often made of 100 percent flat-knit polyester. New babies can kick all they want in this gown since it allows maximum movement of the legs while providing warmth and coziness in any weather. It's easy for parents to change diapers because of the drawstring bottom: you don't have to disturb the child to remove an entire outfit. Many nighttime gowns have a mitten feature on the sleeve that you can turn over to cover the hand, protecting the new baby from scratching himself in his sleep. (But keep baby's hands free when awake so he can explore.) It can be considered a daytime outfit when it's made of 100 percent cotton and has other "outside" features such as a hood. Be sure to tie the drawstring when you wash the gown or you may lose the string. Often the drawstring can be removed from the hem later on and the gown becomes a dress or nightie. Once your baby starts becoming more mobile—rolling over, creeping on her tummy—the drawstring gown is usually put aside. A really useful sack gown, available at specialty stores, is designed with snaps up the back and front and with elastic at the bottom. When the baby gets bigger, the two sides of the gown can be snapped together to form legs for a playsuit. This type of gown can last up to an entire year.

Over-the-Head Undershirt.

A kimono gown is often part of a layette package. It closes partially in front and is used in warm weather for newborns. It allows for ventilation and opens easily for diaper changes. But it is useful only for when baby is immobile (newborn till two or three months). Because it only closes on top, it's not adequate coverage for when baby starts to turn and move—she'll wiggle out of it.

Drawstring Nightgown or Sack.

Onesie.

Onesie or Bodysuit

This is the most recent item designed to simplify layette and now a classic. Parents rave about this undershirt, both long and short sleeved, that extends down far enough over baby's tummy to snap shut at the crotch. It is called anything from a "onesie" to a "bodysuit" to a "tummy topper." Parents love these because they keep the baby pulled together neatly. Unlike regular undershirts that ride up, it stays down and keeps the baby's skin from being exposed and prevents bunching up under other clothes. Only problem: if a messy diaper leaks and the onesie gets soiled, you'll have to do a complete clothing change. Instead of just pulling everything down from the waist in one step, the entire thing must be removed and laundered. This is why some parents prefer the side-snap t-shirt in the early weeks of frequent diaper changes.

Creeper.

Creeper

This is a one-piece garment with no legs that snaps at the crotch. It looks much like the onesie, but the function is different. Whereas a onesie is completely smooth in front to serve as an undershirt, the creeper is snapped or buttoned down the front and is meant to be used as an outfit, for playwear. It can be worn indoors, or outdoors as a summer outfit. Because of the closure in front it does not easily double as an undershirt, although a onesie is often used by parents on a hot summer day as a makeshift creeper. (See Summer, photo on page 132.) Creepers are usually brightly colored and decorated with blocks of color or appliqués, and can be found in 100 percent cotton or blends. In contrast, onesies are usually plain or solid-colored, 100 percent cotton. If they are decorated, prints or hand-painting keeps the front part smooth to go under other clothes.

Long-Sleeved Onesie or Tummy Topper. The cold weather version of the onesie. A hard-to-find item that can be found in the chapter, Biobottoms catalogue. See catalogue.

Stretchies and Coveralls

These make up the bulk of layette. They are one-piece, long-sleeved items with legs. Snaps up the legs and around the crotch allow for easy access for diapering. Some also simply zip from toe to neck. Most babies live in stretchies which are footed and made from flame-retardant synthetic fibers (which makes them conform to federal safety regulations for infant sleepwear). The stretchie in cotton/synthetic terrycloth is more attractive and usually preferred over the flat polyester knit because terrycloth looks more like a natural fiber. But both tend to pill and stain. Coveralls look a lot like stretchies but are usually footless and made of 100 percent cotton. They are "play clothes" (i.e., don't meet federal regulations for sleepwear) for when baby is awake. Many parents prefer coveralls because there is an opening at the feet for ventilation. Others complain that the legs on a coverall are an encumbrance to the very young baby because they ride up the leg when he is kicking vigorously. Those parents like to keep baby as free as possible to feel his environment on his skin. They tend to clothe their baby with as little on legs and arms as possible, until he's older. Some parents like the zippered type of coverall which can be gotten into and out of quickly. Others prefer snaps or buttons—they take longer but won't catch on baby's skin or push up his chin. If you use the buttoned type, make sure the buttons are sewn on tightly. When it comes to durability, stretchies last the longest but 100 percent cotton coveralls tend to be better looking for

Stretchie. What young babies live and sleep in most of the time. A 100 percent synthetic sleepwear garment.

Coverall. A 100 percent cotton playwear garment.

"Coverall." Footless infant clothing that literally covers all and can adjust for growth: Buy them a little larger and roll up the knit cuffs. As baby grows, lengthen them.

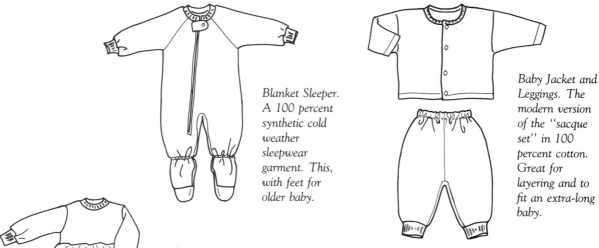

Blanket Sleeper. A 100 percent synthetic cold weather sleepwear garment. This, with feet for older baby.

Baby Jacket and Leggings. The modern version of the "sacque set" in 100 percent cotton. Great for layering and to fit an extra-long baby.

Bloomer Coverall. Many clothing designs that new parents see in the stores for their baby or toddler seem to resemble clown outfits. These bubble designs that look so overblown were first used in European kids' clothes. They are actually quite practical answers to the clothing needs of the young child, i.e., diaper coverage. Avoid bubble suits in which the material is as stiff as a man's dress shirt—those are too bulky for a new walker to maneuver in.

a longer amount of time because they don't pill. Footed coveralls are available for chilly homes in colder climates and are easiest to find in catalogues specializing in natural fibers. When coveralls come in heavier fabrics such as fleece or twill, they can be called anything from a "jumpsuit" or a "romper" to a "one-piece." You may even see the term "stretchy coverall" used in some catalogues which give the impression that they are made of natural fiber—these are probably still the regular synthetic "stretchies." Check the fabric content if you're still confused. For the price, stretchies in synthetic blends still win the budget race, and although they do pill, the new emphasis on contemporary designs and appliqués makes this practical item much more attractive than in the past.

Blanket Sleepers

Made of warm, flame retardant fabric and sometimes sporting a hood, the blanket sleeper will keep a baby warm as a womb would, even in the chilliest homes. The baby usually wears a stretchie underneath for additional warmth and an undershirt under that to protect her from the itchies. Since babies regularly kick off blankets, these sleeping garments are invaluable in cold climates. There are two types. The first is a sleeping bag with arms, a front zipper, and a horizontal seam sewn shut at the bottom. The seam at the bottom can often be removed (and in some cases, let out a few inches at a time) to accommodate growth. The second type has feet (shown above) with reinforced heels for traction for a crawling or standing baby.

Diaper and Sacque Sets

A diaper set is a matching outfit of over-the-head t-shirt and panties. They come in hundreds of colors and fabrics and are wonderful for the summer baby. For fall babies, you can find diaper sets with long-sleeved t-shirts and footed or footless leggings. Traditional sacque sets are short-sleeved, smocked, front-snap shirts with matching panties, almost identical to diaper sets. For a dressier look, they are often designed in a cotton/acrylic bubble stitch that makes them seem hand knitted.

Sweater Set

This is a matching cardigan sweater and cap. Cardigans are easier than pullovers to put on baby for the first year, and no matter what the climate, a baby will always need a sweater. For cold weather, a knit woolen or cotton cardigan and a hat that pulls over the ears and fastens under the chin works best.

Baby Booties. For indoor use when footless clothing is worn, and for cold weather use outdoors.

Booties and Socks

Babies' extremities get cold easily. No matter what the season, a very new baby should wear something on his feet. Warm flannel-lined corduroy booties and terry-lined cotton socks are the common choice if your baby is not dressed head-to-toe in a stretchie. The drawstring or elastic at the ankle of the bootie adjusts to the ankle. Some socks are now designed with an elasticized ribbing that keeps them on, almost like little booties. (Be careful the ribbing is not too tight.) Tuck socks in under the ribbing of a footless coverall so they stay put. If you can't resist some of the adorable baby socks with no elastic in the ribbing to keep them on, put a bootie on over, to anchor them. Or leave them free and resign yourself to the fact that baby's busily kicking legs will fling them off.

Comfortable Slipper-Sock Bootie. A hard-to-find item that is soft like a sock yet sturdy like a bedroom slipper. Available year-round at Shoofly, in New York City.

Keep in mind that as soon as babies begin to roll over, crawl and then toddle, socks make it difficult for them to gain mastery on a surface. "Keep socks off as much as you can during this time," says Jan Miller, founder of Basic Trust, an infant and toddler day-care center in New York City. "Parents aren't always aware that little babies love to discover their toes just the way they love to discover their fingers. If she wore mittens on her hands all the time, would she suck on her fingers, wave them, delight in them?"

Sometimes as early as five or six months, and usually at about nine months, babies start to grab for anything to put into their mouths. This includes pulling off their socks (and booties if possible) to chew on them as a teether. Katherine Karlsrud, M.D., a practicing pediatrician in New York City, says: "Regard anything that can be grabbed that is small enough to be put into the mouth as a toy and a safety issue: these can be aspirated. Avoid socks with dangling decorations or attached doodads when your baby gets to this stage and until he is over the age of two."

Cotton Knit Hats

Everyone knows that we lose the largest percentage of heat through our heads, which is why it's very important to keep a baby's head covered. Also, baby's ears are very sensitive to cold, so make sure that a hat will cover them. This is the one time when the rule of thumb—to dress baby for weather as you would yourself—does *not* apply. You may not need a hat; your new baby usually does. The cotton knit hats with the string under the chin that resemble a helmet are great for summer to ward off air-conditioning chills. They are also great liners for winter woolen or acrylic hats, which can be itchy. What do you

How one brother connects with his baby brother. Wearing the same clothes makes him feel close. The baggy pants for brother Chas are a practical roomy covering for his bulky diapers, and for older brother Kieven, baggy pants are cool.

do when your child refuses to wear hats and rips them off screaming? Stretchy sweater hoods (see illustration on page 126) that can be pulled easily over the head seem to be most acceptable to very little kids. The hood on a zipped-up sweatshirt jacket is also a good alternative.

Bibs

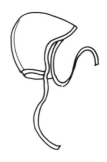

The main reason to use bibs is to protect your baby's clothing from stains and mess resulting from drool, spit-up, formula, and mother's milk. Parents are divided on the usefulness of bibs. Some parents swear by them and others think they're a total waste of time. It all comes down to whether your baby drools and spits up a lot (some don't, and may only need bibs when they are older and begin to eat solid foods), and how much it bothers you to deal with soiled clothing. Some babies who really do drool a lot may wear them all the time, and even have lacy dress bibs for special occasions. If you are breastfeeding, be prepared for breast milk stain, usually occurring around the neck, just under the chin. This is a stain for which there is no magic cure.

"Pilot" Cap. Made of 100 percent cotton and designed to cover all of baby's head. From Hanna Andersson. See catalogue chapter.

There are two basic types of bibs. (1) The ribbed neck type goes over the head easily. It's very good for active babies who won't sit still for a tie. (2) The type with snaps, Velcro, or a tie at the back of the neck works best on newborns who don't fuss as much as older babies when you put these on. Be careful of catching hair when you fasten it in back. Terrycloth is best for the first three to four months because it will lie flat on the baby, and you're not catching solid food with it. Lightweight plastic is good for when baby starts eating solids—just wash it along with your dishes. A heavier plastic bib, such as the molded plastic "pelican" type, fits around the neck and has a pouch at the bottom to catch food. This type is great for the child who's learning to use a cup, as it catches all the spills. However, a lot of kids don't like it because its cumbersome design and weight can make it difficult to belly up to the highchair table. For travel, avoid fabric and bring only the lightweight plastic ones that can be easily washed in restroom sinks.

Turn any towel, washcloth, or napkin into an instant bib with a napkin clip. Great for travel. From the Right Start catalogue.

Receiving Blanket

The receiving blanket is a printed or solid-colored 36" to 40" square of cloth—in flannel, cotton, or a blend—that's folded and wrapped closely around the newborn to keep him feeling warm and secure. They also help the nervous new parent feel confident about holding the baby—it turns the squirmy little baby with the wobbly head into a neat, manageable package. The nurse, or someone who knows, will usually teach you in the hospital to swaddle your baby properly in the receiving blanket. When my pediatrician, the late Virginia Pomeranz, came into the hospital room to visit our new arrival, the first thing she did was loosen the receiving blanket swaddled closely around the shoulders: "Let her hands go free—they're the only way for her to explore the universe right now." (For this, it's worth the extra effort to keep those little

Getting the Best Diaper Bag

Look for:

1. Adjustable straps that can be looped over your shoulders to keep hands free, or onto the stroller or carriage handles.
2. Lots of inside and outside pockets, including some plastic-lined ones for soiled diapers and clothing.
3. A built-in changing pad (can attach to the inside or outside of the bag).
4. A separate plastic compartment inside to hold several bottles so they don't roll around and spill on other items. An outside pocket for a bottle is often useful, as this is an item that is used and put back often.
5. Enough room for plenty of diapers, several bottles, food, bib, change of clothes, sweater, hat, toys, and maybe a change of shirt for the parent.
6. Easy-care fabric that wipes clean—inside and out. You may have to put aside an aesthetic approach in favor of practicality here. The bag should be *wider*, rather than *deeper*, so you don't have to fish around the bottom for things. The bag should also be lightweight and durable.

One parent's alternative to the diaper bag: "For a quick trip to the store with the baby I didn't schlepp the big diaper bag. I just buckled on one of those larger camping-type belt packs—loose, so it fit under the Snugli. The bottle fit in longways, with a diaper on top. And when she was two, I used it to hoist her up on it for a special little seat on the way to day-care. She loved that!"

A Classic Diaper Bag. This, and others, at Mothercare stores.

tiny nails clipped.) Of course some newborns may enjoy being tightly swaddled for the first few weeks. From the very start, your baby will assert his individuality.

Sturdy cotton receiving blankets are the best; the stretchy, waffley ones don't support the baby's body as well (but are fine for the baby who doesn't like being tightly wrapped). Buy one really nice one for going out, and cheap ones for home use. Baby will only need to be wrapped in them for a couple of months, but keep them around for later. They're useful to roll up as a mini bolster in a carseat, carriage, or infant swing, to use as a play rug when baby starts sitting, and as layering warmth in the crib.

Hooded Towel

After the bath, the hooded towel will wrap the baby's head comfortably while you dry her. It's thinner and softer than a grown-up's towel, and easier to manipulate on a baby. It can double as a beach cover-up or a summer bunting. There's even one that plays a lullaby as you use it: a fun gift to receive! The hooded towel often comes as part of a bath set which includes the truly useful baby washcloths. A thick, adult washcloth is no substitute for these thin, pliable baby washcloths that can get behind tiny ears and between little fingers.

Buying Tips for Layette

➤ If you're having the baby shower before your baby arrives, wait until after to complete your layette. And bear in mind you'll probably also get quite a few gifts of clothing in honor of the birth.

➤ Try to buy all your layette needs in one place. It's less confusing.

➤ Develop a relationship with a salesperson who'll be happy to answer ques-

"I thought the drawstring bottom sleepers were great. I was constantly worrying about the cold and with these I felt secure about my baby's kicking legs staying warm inside. I could change the baby's diapers easier than I could with the zippered sleeping bags. Also I liked the feeling that, after having bathed and changed the baby, I could give the string an efficient pull and kind of close up shop, at least for a while."

What to Pack in Your Diaper Bag

Getting out of the house with a new baby sometimes seems like it's taken the whole day to do only that! A packed diaper bag ready to go at all times is a gift a new parent can give herself every day. Most important: *pack the bag,* except for perishables, *the night before.* Don't bring a second "grown-up" purse for your own belongings as you did before the baby. For now, amalgamate everything in one place. If you're feeling especially frazzled, post a list of what should be in the bag near the front door. If you were never very organized before giving birth, start now!

1. Diapers. Pack more than you think you'll need, even though they're bulky.
2. Diaper wipes.
3. Petroleum jelly or diaper rash cream.
4. Burping cloths.
5. Bags for soiled diapers: reuse supermarket ones for plastic diapers, or use a nylon drawstring pouch for cloth diapers that get brought back home for diaper service pick-up.
6. Bottles of milk or juice in a small insulated container (if you're not nursing).
7. A change of clothes for baby. And maybe an extra top for yourself.
8. Lightweight baby sweater in case it gets cold.
9. A pacifier or two. If your child uses one, *this* may be the most important thing to pack, after the diapers.... Maybe *before!* Safety-pin an extra one to the inside of the bag.
10. Your wallet and keys in a small zippered bag.
11. Food and snack.

As your very young baby gets older, her necessities change. At six months or earlier, a teether, later a bottle of water or juice. At toilet-training time, a change of underwear and clothes.

tions. Some neighborhood stores may charge over the phone and send over additional layette items as you need them.

➤ In certain religions, it's against tradition to buy clothes for a new baby before birth. Many small stores will hold merchandise in their basements until they get the call from the hospital and then will process the order. (One New York baby furniture store has a motto, "We don't deliver until you deliver!")

➤ Don't unwrap or take off the price tags of any of your gifts in small sizes. Your baby may arrive already fitting the next size. Then, if necessary, you can exchange them for the right sizes.

. . . .

"You don't need five party dresses for a layette. One or two is plenty. In fact a bloomer or romper with a big collar or a nice print was the best party clothing for my daughter. She loves to grab her skirts and pull them up over her head. Often she'd end up wearing nothing at all!"

. . . .

Three styles for dressing boy babies. Left: a bright patterned hand-knit sweater was this mother's choice to use as the base to her son's wardrobe. She adds solid-patterned bright sweats around it, many from the discount store for plenty of changes. (See this same concept used for toddlers on page 222 in the Smart Shopping chapter.) Middle: this mother prefers quick, bright one-piece coveralls, to separates. Right: this mother prefers no-nonsense overalls (his older brother's), but she can't resist playful accessories!

➤ Bring a *measuring tape* in your purse when you're shopping without your baby to avoid mistakes. Mark his length with some masking tape on the measuring tape before you leave the house, for an accurate fit. The biggest problem in a stretchie that doesn't fit is that it's too short from crotch to neck. A good rule of thumb is: when in doubt, buy bigger.

➤ Research ahead of time. Don't be an earth mother, wing it, and have nothing ready! Around the sixth or seventh month of pregnancy send for all the high quality catalogues that are expert in layette (see the chapter on catalogues). Call the catalogue companies and discuss your clothing needs. You'll find that most catalogue phone salespeople are prepared for *any*

> *"I kept my two children in one-piece outfits, coveralls or stretchies, until they were able to walk. I had simple ones for home and dressy ones for going out. It was so much more comfortable and unrestricting. There was no need for booties or socks and their knees were always protected from dirt and bruises when they were crawling. All these outfits—the party dresses and the little pants—are really just for the parents."*

Three styles for dressing girl babies. Left: this mother uses basic t-shirts and leggings for easy pull-up-and-down diaper changes. She adds decorated t-shirts and socks for parties. Middle: this mother prefers bright-striped Wibbies cotton jumpsuits to support her daughter's high-contrast coloring and as an easy uniform. A hair elastic establishes she's a girl. Right: this mom "always wanted a girl" and dresses her baby in an unabashedly feminine and frilly way. Pastel pink and white are her usual color choices with a cute little hair bow always present. (Note: At about seven or eight months most babies start to pull any hairbows or socks off and put them to the mouth. Consider them as you would a small toy: Be careful. This may be the time to temporarily retire some of your own accessories: dangling earrings, delicate necklaces—all too irresistible not to be grabbed!)

questions, and they will not hurry you. Then talk with any experienced mothers you know and ask for their tips and recommendations. Then you can decide when and where to buy your layette. Ordering your layette over the phone is the best strategy for working expectant mothers, and those who won't have a shower.

➤ Trust the advice of any *experienced* salesperson who suggests high quantities of basics. You'll probably use every one.

➤ Don't buy everything in one size; plan ahead. For an average size (7–8-pound) baby, buy fewer items in three-month sizes and more items in six-month sizes. Your newborn is going to grow fast, and some parents say to bypass three months altogether in favor of six months. But, honestly, your newborn *does* have to wear something. You do really need *some* clothing in size three months.

➤ Buy lots of extra underwear and stretchies. You won't have to do the wash so often.

General Layette Tips

➤ Put cotton undershirts under polyester stretchies to protect baby's skin from scratchy synthetic fabric.

➤ To get tiny flailing fingers through long-sleeved sleepers, place a small ball—the size for playing jacks—in the infant's palm. The baby will reflexively grasp the ball and you can push the arm through easily. (Remove the ball afterwards immediately. You don't want him to put it in his mouth.)

➤ Face your child when you are helping her dress. Don't place her on your lap away from eye contact even though it may be quicker. This way you can encourage her with your expressions or distract her with songs or conversation.

➤ Once your baby stands, there's less need for footed clothes. Clothes without feet are flexible, adjusting to growth and heat factors. Look for knit ribbing at the ankles and cuffs. You can buy big and the clothes are still anchored. You can fold the ribbing back to shorten clothes and as baby grows, unfold! (See photograph, page 31) Bootie socks with puff printing on the sole for traction are good for the standing baby when the weather is cool or the surface he's standing on is rough.

➤ For sweaters, wool is not always useful. It's bulky and babies often get rashes from it. Cotton or easy-care acrylic is best.

➤ Put an infant in a rain poncho instead of a complete rain outfit. You can layer underneath when it's a cold rainy day, or use fewer, more lightweight layers when it's warmer. Also, a poncho will fit longer than a footed rain suit.

➤ Leggings of 100 percent cotton work wonderfully for long underwear and

The Detachable Lace Collar. No mistaking this bald baby for a boy. Her mother simply puts this pretty collar over all her unisex tops. Everyone's questions disappear. (The collar is also useful as a bib.) Another clothing "girl" message: lace socks layered under booties. However, on the question of gender in dressing your baby, Kathryn Karlsrud, M.D., says: "A child begins to perceive the difference between genders at about twenty-one months, and is only fully aware at about three years old. There's no reason to feel your new baby should be dressed 'girl' or 'boy.' Go ahead and use older brother's stretchies on your new baby girl or your daughter's pink lace-trimmed coverall on her new brother. As long as you don't care, the baby doesn't know and you'll save money."

under a snowsuit (instead of tights); under pajamas when it is cold, and of course, as leggings.

➤ If when the baby is six months old, you're tired of dressing her in stretchies, your first choice should be bibbed overalls—preferably with adjustable straps. These will take you into the stage when babies start crawling. Be sure there are snap legs for easy diapering. I recommend any garment that attaches at the shoulders, such as the sturdy OshKosh design or comfy cotton knit overalls for the efficient crawler.

➤ Collars that lie flat are best for infants who have no necks or who can't hold up their heads. Avoid thick, wide collars and bulky turtlenecks in the early months. Mock turtles are good, but hard to find: the Biobottoms and Bright's Creek catalogues always stock this item.

➤ Overalls look "together" in appearance—all the clothes are contained underneath. However, it does take time to tuck everything down in. Easy access sweat suits and coveralls are really the easiest after the crawling stage.

➤ Diaper pants, useful as underwear, are also acceptable as outerwear in summer. Novelty prints and appliqués are available for a dressier look.

➤ Don't put 100 percent cotton in the dryer. The shrinkage will seriously deplete your infant's wardrobe. Use cold water for everything in the washer. To dry 100 percent cotton invest in a wooden or plastic-coated lingerie rack. A popular choice is one that stretches over the bathtub. Bedding items, even those in 100 percent cotton, are, however, okay in the dryer—they are usually preshrunk. Check the labels. The Lillian Vernon catalogue offers many choices of space-saving drying racks.

➤ In the first weeks, baby's bowel movements are liquid, and *very* messy. Since new babies don't move around a lot, one way to save yourself a lot of laundering is to keep baby in a drawstring nightgown and lay an *extra* cloth diaper—flat—between the nightgown and the baby's own diaper, as an extra layer of protection. This way, if the diaper leaks, all you need to do is remove *it* and the *second* cloth diaper *under* it—*not* the entire gown (or sheets and blanket).

➤ Shoulder snaps in shirts for sizes six months through twenty-four months make getting clothes over the head much easier.

➤ Once baby starts crawling, stop buying white and pastel clothing: dirt *never* comes out at the knees. To help save a crawling baby's light-colored clothes, buy inexpensive four-year-old kids' tube socks. Cut off the toe part, keeping the ribbing. Pull these miniature leg warmers up over whatever baby's wearing. Baby gets more padding for crawling, and pants legs stay clean and wear longer. They also work for bare crawling summer knees. (Also, see illustration at left)

➤ Organize your infant's wardrobe so that the most used clothing is the easiest

The Clothes Extender. An antidote to shrinkage, this unusual item snaps onto any snap-crotch item to make it longer by one size. From the Right Start Catalogue.

"Kneekers." Elastic terrycloth bands to protect the knees of crawlers. Good for bare skin or over clothes to protect fabric.

to reach. For instance, with a three-shelf changing table, the kind that has a top drawer right under the immobile changing surface, you can use the less accessible top drawer or shelf to store extras of those basic items you don't use all the time, like extra undershirts, leggings and stretchies, next-size-up clothing, etc. The second shelf—the one that requires the least amount of bending over—holds the most often used "inside" clothes: onesies, stretchies, socks, and diapers. The third shelf on the bottom can hold the "outside" clothes, like sweaters, sweats, pants, and turtlenecks.

 Some very active older babies are adept at removing their clothing and diapers at night. Solve this problem by putting stretchies, coveralls, and

How to save time making up the crib: Layer several changes by starting with a quilted pad on the bottom. Then a felt rubber pad and a regular bottom sheet. Another felt pad and a second bottom sheet. A third felt pad and a last bottom sheet. (You can insert extra quilted pads also as you go along.) Add a top sheet and/or a lightweight blanket to cover baby. Just lift off each rubber pad and sheet pair as they get soiled—you have clean ones waiting underneath. No need to change the whole crib in the middle of the night!

On Making Up the Crib

Making up a crib, bassinet, or carriage requires the following items to be layered:

First, from the mattress up,
1. Waterproof felt rubber liner.
2. Quilted mattress pad with elasticized corners.
3. Fitted bottom sheet.

Then, to lay over baby,
4. Top sheet.
5. Lightweight crib blanket for layering. If the room is warm, use a few receiving blankets instead of a regular baby blanket to layer just the right amount of warmth.

6. Bumpers to line crib sides. Make sure the ties of the bumpers are firmly tied and knotted outside the slats of the crib.

Note: The "princess and the pea" issue! There is divided opinion about where to place the rubber protective liner. Many parents today place the stiff liner *under* all the bedding, closer to the mattress and away from baby. The quilted pad, which is softer and more comfortable, lies on *top* of the stiff liner, closer to baby. This means when a diaper leaks, the sheet gets soiled first, then the quilted pad, then the rubber liner: all *three* have to be taken off and laundered. In the past, the rubber liner was always placed on *top* of the quilted pad directly under the thin sheet, thus shielding the pad. Then, when a diaper leaked, only *two* pieces of bedding—the sheet and the stiff rubber liner—had to be changed. The quilted pad underneath could remain. Fewer soiled pieces meant less wash, but with the rubber liner just under the sheet, a harder bed for baby. These days, with time and convenience even more at a premium, parents are still more concerned with baby's comfort. They most often choose to place the soft, quilted pad on *top* of the stiff liner. There's more wash, but baby is more comfortable.

blanket sleepers on *back*wards—your baby can't reach the zipper or unbutton opening. The back-buttoned European coverall may be useful in this case. The opening is less convenient but the clothes will stay on.

TIPS: BEDDING FOR THE CRIB

➤ To save money on bassinet and carriage liners it's cheaper to buy the large-sized crib cotton-felt rubber pads from your baby store. Cut them up, and make your own. This way you can also size the felt rubber pad perfectly. Inexpensive plastic tablecloth liners can be cut up too and because they're layered underneath, baby won't be uncomfortable. Hold on to these: they will come in handy to protect your children's mattresses later during toilet training at home or traveling.

➤ Buy only lightweight comforters. Don't be swayed by the enticing appliquéd ones that are actually quite heavy and too stiff to lay over the baby. If you do receive one of these as a gift and don't want to return it, keep it for later. When the baby is sitting up, use it as a stimulating play rug.

➤ Have on hand at least one lightweight knitted blanket (make Grandma happy!). They'll cling to the baby when he moves around while sleeping. A crocheted blanket is not as useful because it's stiff and doesn't give with the baby's movements.

➤ Avoid sheets that have raised patterns, appliqués, or eyelet fabric. Although these styles are attractive, they're uncomfortable for baby to sleep on. Lay a soft diaper on top of it, under the baby's cheeks, if you have this type already.

➤ Make crib/bassinet sheets from old adult-size bed sheets. It saves money and the worn-in sheets are softer than new ones.

➤ *Never use a soft baby pillow.* Babies can smother themselves by working their way into it, not knowing how to back out of it. Don't even put that pretty embroidered gift pillow in the crib as decoration.

➤ A Snugglehead from the Right Start catalogue is an unusual and useful item designed for the baby who constantly pushes up into the corner of the crib or against the side slats looking for a cozy place. It is a hard, crescent-shaped bolster that curves around baby's head and is safe to push up against. It is weighted so you can place it anywhere in the crib and it will remain there.

➤ Bumpers can be 100 percent cotton or a cotton blend, and can come in a variety of prints. Recent research indicates the first colors to register with infants are black and white in contrast patterns, but keep in mind that bumpers are not just used for those early months. Many parents keep cribs till their kids are two and three years old, when they will be used mostly for sleep. If you want to promote a smoother bedtime transition, use a calmer print. Your baby can still be stimulated when he's awake with mobiles and other bright removable toys.

Use clothes to have fun with your baby! The hat protects, the bathing suit is a riot, and the glasses will be dropped any minute. Many mothers admit that one of the ways they distracted themselves from postpartum depression and their lack of sleep was to dress their baby up in some fun hat or cute outfit and go out for a walk. The compliments and attention were enough encouragement to go home for one more sleepless night. I recommend not dressing up your baby "perfectly." Take a humorous, lighthearted approach. Simply seeing an infant-sized baseball cap on a baby is cute enough to start up conversation and lift your spirits.

Great Shower Presents

Do give purely practical items:
- Any layette items (check the "Stages of Baby Clothing" chart, page 26).
- Diaper bag.
- Child-care books, such as Penelope Leach's *Your Baby, Your Child* and *What to Expect the First Year*. Or why not one of Dr. T. Berry Brazelton's books such as, *Infants and Mothers*, with the time schedule of his warm and informative TV show tucked between the pages? Or, videotape several episodes of the show and give the tape with the book as a present.
- Cloth diaper service for a month with diaper covers, or boxes of disposables.
- Carriage blanket.
- Novelty bibs.
- Brush and comb set.
- Basket of small, practical things: nail clippers, powder, diaper rash ointment, baby oil, thermometer, infant bottle, shampoo and baby soap, rubber duckie, medicine dropper, etc.
- A carrier such as Sara's Ride or Dr. Sear's Baby Sling (great for a nursing mom).
- An infant car seat (with instructions) that meets safety regulations. You need one to bring baby home from the hospital (mark maximum height and weight in ink on the seat in case instructions are lost).
- The classic Fischer Price musical mobile.

And some great unexpected shower gifts:
- Audio tapes: nursery lullabies such as the classic *Lullaby Magic* from Discovery Music, any of Margaret Miller's tapes, natural sound effects. Any songs by Raffi!
- *Pat the Bunny* by Dorothy Kunhart or other classic first books for baby.
- Silver picture frame for engraving.
- Baby's first year keepsake book.
- A really great stuffed animal.
- Presents for siblings. Find out *exactly* what they want.
- Costume such as a bunny or dinosaur outfit in size twelve or twenty-four months for baby's first Halloween. A great conversation piece at the shower!
- Lambskin or sheepskin mattress pad for the crib, or for use as a baby play rug.
- Novelty feeding plates (airplanes and cartoon character shapes).
- Complete set of the Gesell Institute of Child Development's books, from birth to age seven: *Your One-Year-Old, Your Two-Year-Old*, etc. Before you know it, your baby will be a

"If you think of a diaper as a piece of clothing instead of something to be thrown away, if you think about your baby's comfort, I think the argument [in favor of cloth] is won . . . If parents really want to know what it's like, they should spend a day in adult disposable diapers."—Caroline Spinrad, founder, Parents Promoting Cloth Diapers, Marin County, California

toddler, then a kindergartner, then school-aged. The inevitable *"What's* going on?!" asked by a first-time parent trying to keep up with their child's rapid development is answered clearly and quickly for each year in this heralded series of handbooks. It is usually impossible to find the correct year when you want it as these little books always seem to be sold out. Orderthem *all* way ahead of time for the new parent. What a gift having them right in the house for reference at the time of need!

- A mirror to put in baby's crib.
- A rocking chair or a check to buy one! A gentle rocking motion has a calming effect while feeding or just holding baby. A comfortable rocker often becomes the parenting center for the first year of baby's life. It's soothing not only for baby but also for a cranky parent. Be sure that the arms of the chair are low enough to comfortably nurse and that there are removable, washable pillows. Each chair has its own "rock" and should be "right" for the new mother. The glider rocker invented by Canadian manufacturer, Dutailier, is an unusual version of the old-fashioned platform rocker. Because it sits on a base, it takes up less room than the traditional rocker. Though extremely expensive, nothing can compare to its unusual and relaxed movement—some parents describe it to be as comfortable as sitting on a waterbed! Later, for toddlers, rocking is a panacea for hurt feelings as well as scraped knees. Researchers feel the rocking mimics the protected atmosphere of the womb. Consider giving the rocker as an early present to use during pregnancy—baby will sense the motion.

- Automatic 35mm camera and/or cache of film.
- A personal "gift certificate" coupon. Give, for example, a fully prepared dinner with enough for leftovers, delivered to the new parents' home three or four days after the baby's birth. Or, maid service (you or a professional!) for the first month. Find fun blank certificates in card shops or make your own. Also, gifts of your personal time cost nothing but are greatly appreciated: Give babysitting time for the new baby and/or siblings so the new parents can take a nap or go out in the evening. Or, give errand-running time for checkbook balancing, grocery shopping, or birth-announcement addressing. Only hitch: Keep your promise!
- A gift certificate from one of your favorite baby catalogues (or see catalogue section for suggestions) wrapped with an issue of the current season and marked with your "best bets."

   DON'T give things like crib sets (sheets, quilts, and bumpers), wall hangings, or infant furniture unless you know what the parents want.

"You do have to monitor changes a little more often than with plastic but I figure I save between $400 and $600 a year."

"I made the transition from plastic to cloth slowly. I started using disposables all the time, then only at night, and then just for travel. Now I'm pretty much into cloth totally."

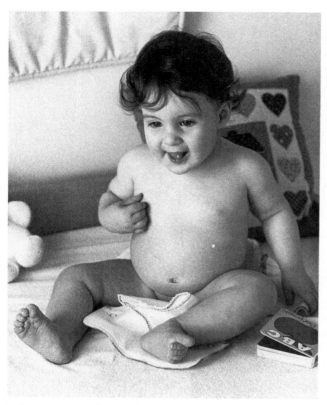

Baby sits on top of cloth diaper and diaper cover, waiting
to be diapered.

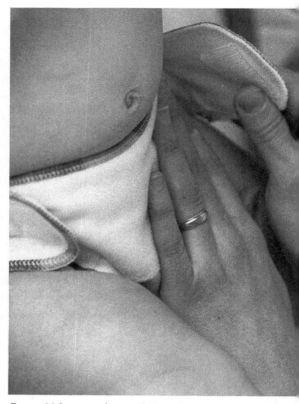

Parent Velcroes and snaps baby's diaper
cover shut.

CLOTH DIAPERS

Changing diapers is one aspect of infant care that may not invite sentimentality. But
slowing down is worth the effort from time to time. If a child has his diaper changed
six times a day until he's thirty months old, he will have had more than 5,400 changes
in his first two-and-a-half years. Anything a child experiences 5,400 times is important.

During the first few months, a baby doesn't understand the need to be changed
or why he feels more comfortable afterward, but he still learns from it. He enjoys being
shifted to a new place—the changing table or bathroom—that gives him another view
of the world. He enjoys the special feelings and smells. He enjoys the physical intimacy
and emotional interaction. Being changed is one of the special events of the day when
adults regularly touch him in predictable ways, talk to him, and focus all their
attention on him.

—Amy Laura Dombro and Leah Wallach, Ordinary Is Extraordinary

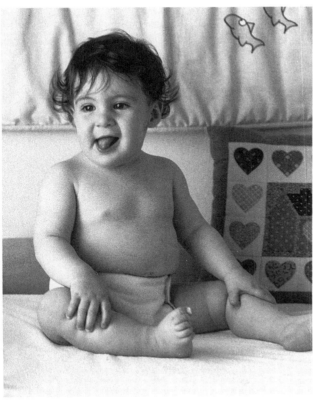

Baby is diapered.

The Pinless Cloth Diaper System of the Nineties. The Biobottoms wool or cotton diaper cover uses an expanse of Velcro-like fabric to easily enclose cotton cloth diapers. It's environmentally sound, breathes more than conventional plastic diapers, and is easier to use than you think.

An important issue facing new parents today is that of cloth versus plastic disposable diapers. It isn't just the fact that disposables end up costing more, or that many children get rashes from the chemicals in the synthetic lining and the plastic casing. The larger hidden cost lies in the real threat to the environment: plastic disposable diapers do not biodegrade no matter what the manufacturers advertise, and landfills will be holding them long after your grandchildren are gone.

I know how convenient disposable diapers are, because I used them with my first child. And I know that the idea of using cloth can definitely be intimidating to a new parent. Many of the moms and dads who now use cloth admit they only had the wherewithal to switch from plastic after their first child. But I can confirm that cloth diapers are anything but the hassle they're perceived to be. In fact, when I started using them with my second child, I was amazed at how easy they actually were.

· · · · · · · · · ·

"The moment of truth: grabbing the diaper out of the toilet and throwing it into the pail! Stainless steel kitchen tongs from the supermarket were great. Then, I found a plastic gripper just for this purpose, a 'diaper duck.' It has a hook so you can hang it on the back of the toilet to dry out."

· · · · · · · · · ·

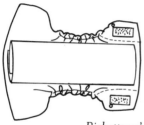

*Biobottoms'
Velcro-like closure on
their diaper cover is
pinless and quick. Just
fold the diaper into
three, and place it on
the cover with the
smooth side toward
baby. Make sure the
cloth diaper is
completely inside the
diaper cover. If
necessary, fold excess
length back inside the
diaper cover, away
from baby.*

Cloth diapers have really evolved with every other child-care convenience. The new Velcro closure diapers (see photos on pages 48–49) have made safety pins obsolete; the plastic gripper for the toilet allows you to rinse dirty diapers without a big mess, and diaper services make life as simple as possible—easier, in fact, than lugging huge cartons of plastic disposables around. If you *are* going to use plastic diapers, one major contribution would be to make sure the human waste is separated from the plastic and always emptied into the toilet, so it goes where it's supposed to go, and not untreated into landfills. And if you live in one of the pioneering states in the U.S., like Washington, Minnesota, and parts of California and Florida, that have recycling centers for these diapers, use them and encourage others to do so. If consumers start to mandate these facilities, more will appear.

Joan Cooper is president of Biobottoms, a natural fiber cloth diapering catalogue company that has a cloth diapering handbook and hotline. She and partner Anita Dimondstein, both mothers, founded Biobottoms in 1981 because they wanted natural fiber diapering for their children. Joan talks about cloth diapers:

There're three things operating in choosing a diapering system: the health and comfort of the baby, the convenience factor (and the pin-less system makes cloth more convenient than ever), and the environment. In 1983, mothers in the thirty-five and over

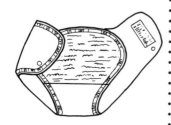

*Plenty of Velcro on
the front of the cover
adjusts daily to baby's
growing girth.*

Various Uses for Cloth Diapers

Even if you opt to use disposable diapers you'll want to have a dozen cloth diapers on hand:

- Place on shoulder for protection from burping and spitting up, and for general cleanup.
- Use as bib and protective cloth when nursing.
- Tuck over sheet in crib or carriage under baby's face to absorb drool. Change it twice a day without having to change the whole sheet.
- Roll up two and use on each side of the head as small bolsters to keep newborn head steady in carriage or car seat.
- Use to line plastic disposable diapers on hot summer days to avoid diaper rash.
- Cut in half to use as a soft washcloth and reusable baby wipes; use as baby towel.

You'll come to see these handy cloths as utterly indispensable until the need for them disappears around or before the baby turns two. Some mothers have even told me that they started a lifelong attachment to these cheap, absorbent wipers and have kept them around for household use long after using them for baby.

The Advantages and Disadvantages of Cloth vs. Plastic Diapers

When You Use Cloth Diapers from a Service

Prices are competitive if not slightly better than plastic. Free diaper pails with deodorant are often provided to store dirty diapers for pickup. If diapers are not used up for that week or you're away, there are refunds. Will adjust weekly allotment and sizes. Will adjust detergents if rashes develop. You will need Velcro the diaper covers, and a diaper gripper for the toilet. Plastic pants are optional. Positive for environment.

When You Buy and Use Cloth Diapers at Home

You will need about eight dozen diapers if you do laundry ever other day or so (about ten diapers a day, more for newborn). Prefolded diapers cost slightly more, but use slightly less labor. You will have to buy more as size changes. You have more control over altering the detergent if baby's skin becomes irritated. You need to buy a pail or plastic tub to soak the diapers yourself, plus diaper covers, plastic pants, detergent, softener, bleach, and a diaper gripper for the toilet. Positive for environment.

When You Buy Disposable Plastic Diapers

Buy as you go. Be aware they get much more expensive as baby grows. Don't overstock: baby may outgrow a size before it's used up. Most brands are in the same price range, except for the "biodegradable" (arguable claim—this is *rarely* true) type. Baby's skin may become irritated by chemicals and synthetic material. You need no other equipment, except the toilet to empty feces. Negative for environment, unless you can recycle.

range really seemed attuned to the environment. They'd been through Earth Day in 1971 and they were always planning to use cloth diapers. With our newly invented Velcro covers, we made it easy for them to make and stick with that decision. Now, most moms who are twenty-five through thirty-five don't even know what cloth diapers look like. They only know what they've seen on TV—plastic disposables. It's very hard for them to convert to cloth, except if their baby has a horrible rash. We're trying to help parents decide to go with cloth diapers before the baby is born. When the decision is made in time to buy diapers or order diaper service, and before habits get set, then it is much easier for the parents.

"I use both types: plastic for night and cloth for day."

Soon-to-be parents can check out the local diaper services and ask their pediatrician about the health factors. Network with friends who use cloth diapers (La Leche League is a good start) and research the ecological impact of using cloth diapers instead of disposable diapers. Even with the aggressive marketing programs used by disposable diaper companies (new parents will quickly find their mailbox stuffed with brochures, coupons, and trial diapers), I believe that as parents, our instincts to preserve and protect life will naturally extend from our family to the planet as we become more educated about the cloth versus disposable diaper question.

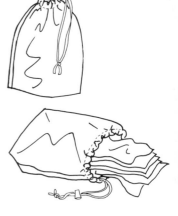

· · · · · · · · · · ·

*"Terrycloth diapers
are so absorbent! I
only need to use one
at night, instead of
double-diapering as I
used to."*

· · · · · · · · · ·

Tips on Cloth Diapering

➤ Call the Biobottoms catalogue (1-800-766-1254) immediately for their invaluable free cloth diapering booklet, and to ask any questions you might have. Biobottoms makes a point of hiring phone operators who are parents with experience in cloth diapering.

➤ Be prepared for a confusing onslaught of publicity for "official surveys" and "research projects" about how cloth diapering is "not any better" than plastic for the environment. These surveys are usually funded by companies producing disposable plastic diapers. If you want to know more about the environmental and health impact of cloth versus disposable plastic diapers, see the in-depth article on this subject: "The Diaper War: Not about to Bottom Out" by *Time* magazine reporter, Robert W. Hollis, in *Mothering* (#60, Summer 1991), and "Are Single-Use Diapers Compostable?" by Ellen Becker, Health Editor of *Mothering* in the same issue. Keeping yourself informed will give you courage to follow your convictions.

➤ Organize the diaper service ahead of time. Don't wait until the baby comes.

➤ If you're away from home all day, take two nylon drawstring bags, each in a different color. Put all the clean diapers in one at the beginning of the day. As the day progresses, shift the dirty ones into the other colored bag. When you get home you can just dump any contents of the dirties into the toilet and then throw all diapers into the diaper pail. Wash out the drawstring bags.

· · · · · · · · · ·

*"I like cloth during
the day because
they're softer and
there's no problem
with diaper rash. I
like the fact that
they're not
absorbent. I like to
change my baby a
lot to let her air
out."*

· · · · · · · · · ·

➤ Get preformed diapers that you don't have to fold yourself. They're thicker in the middle.

➤ Nighttime tricks: Make sure that the whole cloth diaper is inside the outer cover. If there's even a little bit of cloth sticking out, it acts as a wick and carries the liquid to the clothes and sheets. Don't forget to double-diaper if you need to. Use the new terrycloth diapers. They're ultra-absorbent for nighttime. For toddlers at night, use toilet-training underpants *with* a diaper.

➤ Travel tips: Reuse plastic grocery bags for dirty diapers. *Always* pack more diapers than you think you will need.

➤ Never wash wool and cotton diaper covers on the hot cycle of the washing machine. They'll shrink. Follow laundering instructions exactly.

*An easy Velcro
closure to let a toddler
build confidence by
dressing himself. By
OshKosh B'gosh, for
summer only.*

TODDLER

C hildren learn by doing things, and their activities integrate all kinds of learning at once. . . . When a child learns to dress herself, she is learning how to put her body together, developing fine motor coordination, improving her ability to perceive and match shapes, and developing a notion of planning (putting shoes on before socks doesn't work; putting socks on first does). The child is also learning social conventions (you can't go naked even when it's hot, there are occasions when you dress up), about the weather, and about the difference between indoors and outdoors. Whenever a child practices any new skill and perfects it, she is learning persistence, developing confidence, and confirming her sense of independence—that is, she is growing emotionally. Ordinary, everyday activities teach the whole child.

—Amy Laura Dombro and Leah Wallach, Ordinary Is Extraordinary

You've finally mastered the mysteries of layette, and all of a sudden (or so it seems) your child needs "standing up" clothes. Maybe, more appropriately, "marathon" clothes!

Your active toddler will now have new wardrobe needs. In addition to the need for clothing that still works for diapering, toddler clothing must also comfortably accommodate the child's rapidly changing body, and lots of running and falling down. Not to mention joyful stomping in puddles and mud piles. You might think "Great! Finally he's wearing grownup clothes just like us." However, a toddler's body isn't built like a miniature adult's—the diapers turn the torso into a pear, and those cute tummies ensure that the shirt will ride up or the pants ride down.

The clothing sizes are still as inconsistent as they were in layette. Many U.S. manufacturers in this size range (2–6x) are still using the pattern forms for babies born thirty years ago. In those days, an eighteen-month size fit the average eighteen-month-old child. These days, babies are much larger at birth. But some manufacturers just haven't kept up with these birth-weight changes. An eighteen-month-sized outfit could fit a toddler perfectly at eighteen months, but a bigger eighteen-month-old child could already be into size four. Also, surprisingly, many U.S. manufacturers don't seem to allow for the extra room that diapers take up in pants. European companies solve the sizing issue by using a height and poundage standard (not age) that accurately measures any size child at whatever age.

Toddlerhood is a very exciting time, as your previously dependent baby makes attempts at autonomy. But I've found that many first-time parents don't enjoy this time as much as they could. They're amazed, and often frustrated, by the force of their toddler's feelings about getting dressed. But toddlers are concerned about knowing and being themselves. They are far more interested in experimenting and discovering than standing still. They are motivated by action! Often, a child will try a busy parent's patience demanding long, involved dressing games. Or he'll announce "Me do it" and then take his own "child time" to accomplish it. Often a child will simply refuse to put on any clothes at all. Every item from undershirt to shoes may require, if not a battle, at least some creative persuasion. The answer "No!" seems to be their anthem!

Besides getting dressed, your child may also start to have some very definite opinions about certain items of clothing you want to put on her. Most of them aren't just arbitrary—if you understand the choices, you will probably find legitimate reasons behind them. But this may be frustrating because her language skills aren't yet fully developed to express herself, and you as the parent are still getting to know her. Aside from the inexplicable prejudices that come with the child's emerging personality, there are usually underlying reasons for a child's aversion to a piece of clothing: itchiness, tightness, unhappiness with the color or he may form an intense attachment to a certain baseball shirt, which he'll want to wear over and over, much to your distress. But to your toddler-into-twos, that shirt could be like a security blanket, and he'll cling to it through all the new challenges of standing up on his own two feet. A toddler girl may want to wear the same easy-to-pull-on skirt every day. She feels grown up getting it on herself and, practically speaking, it's comfortable when she's rolling on the floor. Who cares that her underpants show?

Dealing with the seemingly mundane issue of dressing your stubborn toddler is probably one of the first situations in which you really start to dig in and develop your parenting style. This is the time to develop patience by practicing strategies of simple give and take. It's also a time to watch your child's dressing behavior for fascinating clues to his personality and development. When your normally sunny child adamantly refuses to put his shoes on when it is time to leave his cousin's house, he probably is just letting you know how much fun he is having. However, if your child consistently refuses to put his shoes on when leaving places, it could be a temperamental pattern that needs to be addressed. He may be a child who has a hard time making transitions from one situation to another. You can use your observations of your child's dressing patterns to give you a fuller picture of your child's personality and temperament, and it will give you confidence in the future because you'll know through experience when to negotiate and when it's important to stand your ground.

One of the mysterious aspects of toddlerhood for a new parent is the fact of tantrums. Some children may never have one, some may have them a lot. And they usually seem to come out of nowhere. Once you've begun to recog-

. . . .

"Offering my two-year-old choices works on all levels. Asking which arm she'd like to put through the sleeve of her coat first speeds getting out the door. The same goes for safety. She used to refuse flatly to take my hand to cross the street. Then she'd refuse to walk forward or have a tantrum. Now she happily chooses 'which of daddy's hands' she prefers to take, and happily crosses the street."

. . . .

nize your child's emerging temperamental patterns in daily activities you'll be able to distinguish between different behaviors and act accordingly. (See the School Days chapter for further explanations of temperament.) For instance, if a tantrum does occur, it may be one of two types: a child is clamoring for a t-shirt of a sibling that doesn't belong to her and you won't give it to her—that's a manipulative one. Or a child with a "low sensory threshold" is being dressed in a scratchy, long-sleeved woolen sweater—that's a temperamental one. In the first case, your child may just be trying to get his way through his behavior. In the second, your child may not be able to help his behavior because it relates to an underlying temperamental issue. Once you figure out what kind of tantrum is occurring, the way you deal with each will be quite different. Dr. Stanley Turecki says in *The Difficult Child*: "When the outburst begins, stand back and look for five to ten seconds to figure out what's going on. What kind of tantrum is occurring? Once you have decided, take one of two tacks: With the manipulative tantrum, don't give in unless your original denial is unreasonable. If you've decided it is unreasonable, you're allowed to change your mind. But in all other instances, you must send a message to the child that tantrums don't work. If you give in repeatedly, you're telling your kid that the way to get his own way is by being a pest. Parents who give in to such tantrums will soon find that their whole attitude to the child becomes tentative and indecisive. The primary issue in any dispute becomes to avoid the tantrum. Instead, tell your child, in a planned quiet discussion, that he will never get his way through tantrums and start to enforce this new rule. Don't be too sympathetic. Do not say, "I'm sorry you're upset and crying, perhaps you can have the t-shirt later," but rather, "You cannot have this the t-shirt; that's all there is to it, and I want you to control your behavior."

On the other hand, the tantrum that results from a challenge to her temperament is something else and will probably be more intense. "There is a less conscious, planned quality, and more of a feeling that the child is out of control." When you realize that "she cannot help it," your attitude should be kinder and more sympathetic. The message you should send is "I know this is tough for you, I'll help you to bring it to an end." Try to correct what's troubling the child if you can. "If you allow her to take the sweater off, the tantrum may not end immediately, for the child might be locked in, but the tantrum will not go on as long as it would have if you had not allowed her to take the sweater off. This is not giving in; rather, you, as an enlightened parent, understand the real reason for the tantrum and are attempting to correct it.

"With either tantrum, when it occurs in a public place, *get the child out*. You'll achieve nothing by embarrassing the child or yourself. There's no point trying to stick it out, especially if you recognize a temperamental tantrum and you don't want people criticizing you for being so 'nice' to your child during a tantrum."

"My three-year-old daughter and her best friend in the building have this clothes changing game. They go through all the neatly folded clothes in no time flat, negotiating who's going to wear what, and pretending to go different places. It's a real friendship-in-progress. We moms end up spending a lot of time reorganizing or returning clothes to each other, which isn't one of our favorite activities. But let's face it, anything that keeps them interested that isn't a television show is worth any amount of refolding!"

Besides managing tantrums, current child studies cite the positive effect of day-to-day listening to your toddlers' opinions, especially boys. It will have a strong impact on social behavior later. Research done at the University of Rochester by Judith G. Smetana found that mothers were more likely to explain to their toddler girls why biting and snatching other children's toys were unacceptable.* If their boys did the same thing, they were just punished with little or no explanation. And they were usually punished more often. This may explain why girls, by elementary school in general, show more empathy and care-giving qualities than boys who (inadvertently) have not enjoyed as much dialogue on what constitutes acceptable social behavior. And it may explain why, though misbehaving peaks at age two, boys are the ones to go on to misbehave more than girls.

The implications of lessening punishment and increasing dialogue with toddler boys are exciting. When your little boy constantly runs away when you are trying to dress him, and you're in a hurry or tired, instead of snapping at him, easy as that is to do, realize that controlling your reaction and explaining why you need him to stand still is more than just "being nice." It's invaluable to his later social development. Talking about feelings and emotions, or taking the time to explain the social workings of behavior, is not something frequently done with boys in our society. Many parents may unconsciously equate toughness and strictness with "maleness." Not so, according to this research. Your child will not experience confusion about his gender with increased dialogue. Rather he will experience thoughtfulness and consideration toward himself as a person. In this simple and direct way he will be helped to become a thoughtful and sensitive person himself. Use this challenging time of toddlerhood to develop or expand your parenting skills. The patience and flexibility you train yourself to use now with your child will set the tone for a great relationship in the future.

Jan Miller, founder of Basic Trust, a renowned day-care center for infants and toddlers, and director of the Calhoun Lower School, both in New York City, says: "You have to have a freshness about it. Don't lose hope. If for the past three weeks you've had a hard time dressing your child, always have the attitude that today might be the day she dresses herself. I try to encourage the children. As I'm dressing them, I'll say things like 'Soon you'll be able to dress yourself,' or 'I know that you are going to be able to do this soon.' I try to have hopefulness and confidence come from my heart. In reality, it doesn't take very long to learn how to dress or go to the potty, it just seems long." Jan recommends giving choices about *how* to get dressed, not *whether* to get dressed. "I'll say 'It's time to go now; we have to leave. Would you like to dress yourself this morning or would you like me to help you get dressed?' If your child is still not able to get dressed, dress him yourself and say 'Next time, maybe you'll be able

Pockets, pockets everywhere! Pockets on his jacket, on the side of his pants, in the front of her corduroy jumper. Pockets are the first time most toddlers discover they can transport things themselves. Make sure they are deep enough so things don't fall out. Pockets as decoration in nonfunctional places (such as the side of the knee, or on the back of a jacket) are a disappointment to toddlers once they get used to this feature. Store owners tell me pockets are the main detail they look for from manufacturers of toddler clothing.

*Shapiro, Laura. "Guns and Dolls," *Newsweek,* May 28, 1990, p. 61

*Self-dressing can
encourage autonomy
in toddlers. Here are
some clothing details
that will start them off
with an early sense of
accomplishment:*

*Elasticized waists
make it simple to pull
her clothes on and off
herself.*

*Velcro closures let her
get her shoes on and
off by herself.*

Dressing a Toddler

For a child beginning to walk, getting dressed is equivalent to being restrained. At twelve to sixteen months, she's rejoicing in the new-found sense of independence that comes from being able to move herself. When you change her shirt or pants, you not only stop her from climbing on the couch, banging on pots in the kitchen, or crawling under the bed, you actually move her legs into an overall. It's understandable, then, if your toddler gears up for battle when you tell her "Let's change that wet shirt." She has an important cause—her selfhood—to defend.

—Amy Laura Dombro and Leah Wallach, Ordinary Is Extraordinary

Why is it such a big deal to get your toddler dressed? We all know how to put clothes on our child because we're the grownups. Right? Well, we all do know about the clothes, but it's another thing to manage an independent toddler who's just starting to assert himself. Often first-time parents, used to the first year with a less mobile baby, find themselves at a loss to effect the same calm results with their active toddler. Not to worry! Here are some tips on the toddler-aged to foster independence, help avoid confrontation, and set limits so you both can enjoy this short, but especially exuberant time in your child's life. Once most of these tips stop working, your child is probably too old for them.

1. Present two outfits (only) and offer a choice between them. Decisions that seem insignificant to you can be very satisfying to a young child. Your child will feel independent because he'll feel responsible for deciding what to wear. On the other hand, an open-ended question such as: "Shall we get dressed now?" will probably elicit a predictable "no." Don't try to change his mind once he's chosen—he'll feel you don't respect his choice, or that you're being phony.
2. Routine is important. Lay out clothing ahead of time so the child can get used to what she'll be wearing. Use a particular song or game that signals dressing and is short enough to maintain in different time constraints.
3. Distraction still works at this age. Start talking about what fun activity is coming up, and dress him while you've got his attention. He'll be looking forward to the future while you're taking care of the present.

to do this.' " Jan's advice to parents for getting dressed in the morning is this: "If you're used to dressing your child right before leaving the house, change that routine. Start the dressing process before breakfast. This way, getting dressed doesn't signal to your child the end of your good time together and the start of the day without you. Sandwich it in between rising and eating. Say something like 'As soon as you're dressed, we'll have breakfast together.' That way, dressing signals the beginning of something, not the end of it."

4. Use a mirror when dressing your child. This helps him see clearly the best way to put on clothes, as well as to have the fun of witnessing his transformation from pajama-clad sleepy head to ready-for-the-world toddler.

5. Use the colors and prints on clothing to teach children about shapes and colors. Make a game out of naming the colors and identifying the shapes—squares, circles, etc. Also, hold up separate actual garments naming *their* shapes.

6. If your toddler is exceptionally active, diaper her while she's standing up. (It *is* possible!) Laying her down to change her is often enraging for a growing child who's impatient to shed babyhood. If the change is particularly messy and you need her to lie down to properly deal with it, explain why, and offer a toy for her to hold she has not played with lately (which you have on hand for just such occasions!).

7. Dress in two stages if your child is a messy eater—the lower half before breakfast, and the top half afterwards.

8. Give your child the choice to dress by the time you count to three, out loud. This is a fun game that often works: as he anticipates each number, he'll feel autonomous because *he* is the one choosing which number to get dressed by. Don't get caught in the routine, though, of "two and a quarter, two and three-eighths, two and a half, two and five-eighths," etc., trying to be patient by giving him the extra chance (and thinking that you're teaching him math!) By now this game has lost its appeal and you're being manipulated. Find a new one.

9. Humor. Silliness! "Max, what do you think?! Do these socks go on my ears? What do you think? No? How about my nose? No? How about *your feet?* Oh, they fit perfectly!"

10. Last resort: If you're on the verge of losing it, hand over the task to anyone—husband, friend. Maybe they're not as experienced but they're fresh. Avoid constantly asking older siblings close in age to help at the last minute. It's confusing to your younger child who won't sense a "plan" to the morning, and may foster bossiness in the older child. If your child is over-tired or over-stimulated by a crowded, noisy environment, remove her from it. Calm her down, then begin again.

A stationary zipper (one that doesn't have to be joined before it can be zipped) on his belt pack can be easily zipped. His own waist belt pack that lets him carry his own treasures encourages an early sense of responsibility.

Toddlerhood can be divided into three stages of dressing: diaper wearing, for the child who's still too young to be toilet trained; diapers on and off, when the child is toilet training; and post-diapers, featuring new, autonomous self-dressing. The clothes that work best during the diaper-changing stage (when you're doing the changing) aren't the same as the ones that are most practical when your child starts trying to pull her clothes down and use the potty by herself.

FIRST STAGE: DIAPER WEARING

. . . .

"I found that the best things to wear at home till he was about twenty months were the pre-washed leggings and t-shirts that came in great bright colors."

. . . .

. . . .

"One of my friends who had a boy five years older than my infant made a casual remark one day. 'You'd better like everything you buy in size three. You'll be seeing it a long time.' I didn't understand what she meant then, but later I realized she was right. You buy to fit diapers, and then diapers come off, and the clothes will fit again for a whole season."

. . . .

➤ Look for snaps that line the crotch and pant leg. This goes for *all* overalls, jumpsuits, and pants. You'd be surprised how much clothing for toddlers doesn't include this essential feature of easy-open bottoms for diapering. And this is the time you need to be able to speed-diaper. An active toddler won't stay still for long. Sweatpants are the quick changing answer if you can't find leg-snapped clothing. If your toddler is into size four and still wearing diapers, it will be hard to find leg snaps in stores in this size. Check catalogues—they have them.

➤ The OshKosh bib overall is a popular transition item of choice when your child is moving out of stretchies and into more grown-up clothes. It smoothly covers your little "pear" who is still encumbered with bulky diapers. The fuller cut from the waist down negotiates easily over the diapers, and the bib-front with adjustable shoulder straps fits the narrower shape up top just right. Although they seem at first glance hard to get on and off, they really aren't—they're easy to get used to. These clothes work well for the diapered period before toilet training. Parents love the look of layered overalls because it has a "real clothes" look, and is a flexible uniform that is nearly indestructible. They can add or subtract t-shirts, turtlenecks, flannel shirts, blouses, or a jacket to adjust to any kind of

➤ weather. *Retire these overalls during the toilet-training phase* as they are too complicated for a toddler to get in and out of quickly by himself. Afterwards, when your child is finally trained, he'll enjoy fastening them up himself. If you buy overalls from other brands, *make sure* they have snaps or zippers to allow easy access to diapers.

➤ Two-piece sweat jogging suits are the choice of no-nonsense parents. They are fastest to undo—just pull down pants. Some parents swear by this combo because it works for both diapered kids and toilet-training kids. It also eliminates coordinating other pieces of clothing. The down side is, you do have the bunchy, droopy-drawers look as when the child was still diapered. A cotton knit jumpsuit from Hanna Andersson and others is another toddler time saver (see photos on pages 61). Instead of just pulling down pants, zip down the length of the jumpsuit, and pull down.

➤ Dress sets (with matching panties) are convenient toddler girl items that can give coverage without having to use pants (see photo on page 63). If you can't find them, add a pair of complementary-colored leggings or panties to any dress on hand.

➤ Some jumpsuits are designed with a very wide bubble shape. On the hanger in the store, it may look strange, but the extra fabric has a purpose—it accommodates diapers for a roomy, comfy fit. The full cut enables the child to move without the leg riding up and exposing skin between the pant and sock.

➤ Snap-crotch undershirts become less important as you move towards toilet

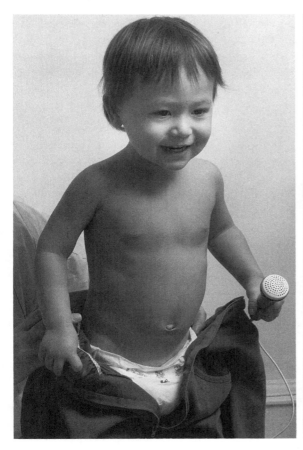

training, at which point you'll abandon them for good. It takes too much time to first pull down pants and then undo the snaps on a second undergarment when you're changing the diaper on an active toddler.

➤ Suspenders that were adorable in layette are *always* unbuckled by curious toddlers.

➤ Regular socks worn indoors without shoes are dangerous to a new toddler, walker, or dasher because floors are so slippery. Let her go barefoot inside or use socks with the no-skid bottoms. And don't overwax your floors.

Toilet training is the first context in which a child is expected to take responsibility for how she expresses internal sensations. . . . It's a scary step for many children because children sensibly feel some ambivalence about becoming "big." Taking a step forward means leaving something behind. There are definite advantages to running faster, climbing higher, wearing comfortable underpants with fire trucks on them, and doing

The one-zip, one-step jumpsuit makes quick work of diapering an active pre-toilet-trained toddler. No shirts to pop out or to coordinate. This one, a Hanna Andersson classic. Just pull down and pull up. An easy waist and roomy fit lets Max, a budding baseball player, practice his swings.

it yourself. On the other hand, you have to give up the bottle, follow more rules, and deal with the fact that you are a separate, fragile person, and your parents aren't always there to help you out. Most two-year-olds, if they had the words, would probably say they wanted to be big, but only when they felt like it. They have to decide they feel like it before they will use the toilet consistently.

—Amy Laura Dombro and Leah Wallach, Ordinary Is Extraordinary

SECOND STAGE: DIAPERS ON AND OFF, TOILET TRAINING

➤ *Speed* is the key criterion for successful toilet-training clothes! Pull-on pants with elasticized waists are quick for toilet training *both* boys and girls—only one step to get to the potty: pulling them down. However, many little girls simply refuse to wear pants. Skirts with leggings can substitute for pants—either pants or leggings can be pulled down in one action. Dresses do require two actions but are still easier than other complicated clothing—they need only flip up the skirt and pull down their tights or leggings and underpants.

➤ Time-consuming fastenings such as snaps, zippers, buttons, and metal overall closures should all take a back seat to the job at hand. Retire jumpsuits, overalls, and bubble suits until the training period is over.

➤ Have extra outfits. You'll need lots: toddlers can go through four outfits a day during this stage.

➤ For nighttime toilet training, consider investing in a few cotton "stay dry pants" from the Biobottoms or Right Start catalogues. This hard-to-find item is more absorbent than conventional training pants, holding up to one cup of urine. What a morale booster for your child who's had success training during the day not to have to switch back to diapers at night.

THIRD STAGE: NO MORE DIAPERS, SELF-DRESSING

➤ Surprise! The clothes you have temporarily retired, which were bought to fit over diapers, will return to fit a slimmer child once he's potty trained and has shed bulk.

➤ Continue using pants and skirts with elasticized waists. They can pull them on and off easily.

➤ Choose closures the toddler can manipulate himself. Buttons are the first and easiest choice. Unbuttoning is usually the first action learned. Avoid snaps, which often require grownup strength.

➤ Velcro closures on sneakers foster independence in the very young child. However, don't become so enamored of the convenience of Velcro that you forget to give her a chance to learn how to tie laces as she gets older.

➤ Pockets! Nothing makes an older toddler feel so self-sufficient as a place to tote his own stuff.

➤ Encourage her own ability. Consider using a timer to help your child get dressed in a certain amount of time. Avoid nagging by setting the timer

The matching cotton knit dress and panties is a modest solution to a party dress for a somersaulting toddler girl. Useful all through toilet training. By Hanna Andersson.

and making a game out of it. Help your child understand that she must be dressed by the time the bell goes off. This kind of competition with an inanimate clock is preferable to competitive games with siblings. You can also start to introduce the concept of time in this way—use a real clock with an alarm as the child gets older.

➤ Find a place to hang a few clothing items within his reach. Each morning he can choose some of the items you've provided.

➤ Label bureau drawers with homemade drawings of the clothing in that drawer. Most toddlers love to go fetch and are very proud to be able to perform simple tasks. Diapers are usually the first successful "go get" job. Then, a photo or drawing of socks on the sock drawer makes it possible for your child to "please go get some socks," etc.

➤ Start your child learning left and right by using those "feet" stickers that glue on the insides of the heels of shoes to show the difference (see photo on page 178). Toddlers can really tell the difference by seeing the direction of each big toe.

• • • • • • • • • •

"It's simple: you have to plan the clothes and you have to plan where you're going. Where are the bathrooms?"

• • • • • • • • • •

Nature's Timetable for Self-Dressing

Do not expect your twenty-two-month-old to dress himself or herself—even if the youngster has an astonishingly large vocabulary, is walking competently, and seems capable of all kinds of abstract thought. Self-dressing typically does not even begin—"begin" means some kind of gingerly attempt—until the age of two years, and the child who can accomplish it under the age of four years is rare. As a matter of fact, some of the intricacies are unlikely to be mastered before the age of six. Each child is different, and when it comes to putting on clothes, a number of different skills are involved. There are no hard-and-fast guidelines. Undressing and unbuttoning (e.g., pulling off a sock) are the very first dressing skills to appear, and the last dressing skill children generally learn is shoelace tying, about the age of six.

—Virginia Pomeranz, M.D., The First Five Years

"There was a period when Lucia had to change her clothes the minute she got home from nursery school at four o'clock. In fact she did a lot of changing of her clothes for quite some time, which I didn't mind, but then her younger brother David started clamoring for new clothes too. So what we did was to have a bath ready for them right after school with the pajamas all laid out for them to get into. This way we only had to go through two changes of clothes before bedtime."

Tips from Day-care and Preschool Teachers for Effective School Clothes

Preschool teachers spend a lot more time dealing with toddlers' clothing—five days a week, ten hours a day, year in, year out—than the working parents themselves. Getting outerwear on and off efficiently and trying to encourage successful toilet training is always on their agendas. Here is a list of the most common do's and don'ts from their point of view:

Clothing should not only be comfortable, it should allow a child to become independent.

—Jane Bailey, owner and director of five Montessori schools in New Jersey

Do's:

➤ Layer a child for indoor and outdoor comfort. If you put a sweater on your child, make sure she has a regular shirt on underneath so that the sweater can be removed when she gets hot. An undershirt isn't enough.

➤ Look for tops that have roomy, flexible necks. Necklines that are squared or have buttons at the shoulder let the kids pull their shirts over their heads easily without getting stuck in the neckline and screaming for help.

➤ Check with your school director and teacher about what kinds of outerwear are needed for school. Many preschools *do* expect to be able to take children out every day in all kinds of weather, others only on certain days.

➤ Foster the same dressing competence for both girls and boys. Preschool directors say parents (especially mothers) have a tendency to coddle boys by holding their jackets or putting them on for them, while expecting girls to dress themselves.

Don'ts:

➤ Jeans have no warmth or flexibility. A nice pair of soft corduroy pants or sweatpants for cold weather are preferable. Avoid expensive jeans with a working zipper, a snap fastener, and a belt for two-year-olds. They are of no

A Classic Jeans Jacket for Kids. Built for wear, it's functional inside and out. Hidden inner pocket transports three-year-old Olivia's "friends." By GapKids.

use to the toilet-training toddler (see photos on page 67). By the time a teacher helps him undo all three fasteners, he has wet his pants. Besides, the belt and waistline dig into his tummy when he sits.

➤ Don't send your child to school in high-tops, designer sneakers, or heavy work boots. They are cumbersome, difficult to get in and out of, and do not encourage independence. The slip-on Oriental-style canvas shoe is a good choice for indoor toddler play.

➤ Avoid a one-piece sweatshirt turtleneck dress for warm classrooms—there's no opportunity to layer. Though it's a dress, it's better for outdoors.

➤ Pinafores and over-the-shoulder straps often don't fit and fall off the shoulder. This is a constant irritation to the children. Unless you are willing to correct them by sewing or adjusting the straps properly, don't send your child to school in them.

When a child's hair is washed and combed, and clothing decent and comfortable, he or she tends to act more confidently. Teachers react more positively to clean children, and children seem to be aware of their own appearance. When parents bring their children in the morning, I often hear them compliment their kids about how "cute" they look. What you're telling your child is because they look attractive, they're pleasing you. I think that's a very superficial support. I would prefer to hear parents talk about how neat and clean they are. Of course at the end of an active school day, I expect them to look a little crumpled or messy.

—*Jane Bailey, owner and director of five Montessori schools in New Jersey*

Shopping Tips for Toddlerwear

➤ Buy knit turtlenecks and t-shirts for everyday use. Save stiffer, woven cotton, button-down shirts for special—they take so long to get buttoned that the child will have squirmed away before you're half done. Also, as your child starts dressing himself, turtlenecks and t-shirts will be easier for him to negotiate. Check turtlenecks to make sure the neck opening is wide and loose enough. Buy a size larger if necessary (see photo on page 79). Cotton/poly blends, especially in inexpensive turtlenecks, may be softer and more stretchable than 100 percent cotton.

➤ Buy boys' cotton or flannel shirts one size larger. The shirts will be longer so when you tuck them in they won't come out as the children run and play. The slightly longer sleeve length is not long enough to be a problem and you can get more use out of it as your child grows into it.

➤ To make an easy cold weather pull-on garment, buy button-down flannel shirts in the larger size and sew them closed up in front, except for the top three buttons. Layer them over turtlenecks.

➤ Select jackets, pants, dresses and skirts with pockets deep enough to hold all the little knickknacks toddlers love to collect. This way, you won't

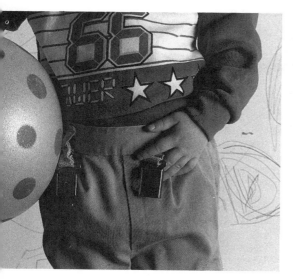
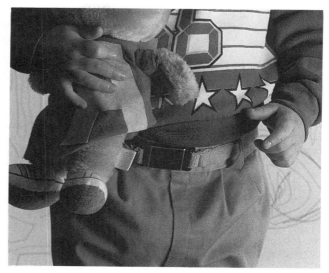

How to look like dad but still be in diapers. With false details of tailored pants, this design combines a grown-up look with pants that are easy to get on and off. If you can't resist the "real" version where everything works—the top button unbuttons, the fly opens, etc.—make sure the waist is elasticized or roomy enough to be pulled on or off without having to go through all those actions. Buckled up and ready to go. Pants can be pulled down for a fast diaper change without zipping, unbuttoning, unbelting. Fake belt buckle is unhooked to show this clever design.

always end up keeping track of them and they won't be disappointed because their treasures have fallen out of shallow pockets. Avoid clothes with pockets that are only decorative or that are hard to reach—this is very frustrating to the curious toddler.

➤ Buy pants with rib-knit cuffs: the antidote to carrying home portions of the playground and sandbox.

➤ Mid-calf-length socks are better than the ankle socks for a toddler. They don't seem to shrink as much as the anklet, and you can put them under or over the pants to save your child from the bare leg syndrome. As he grows and his pants get shorter long socks help fill up the gaps. In summer, they'll protect little legs from scratches and scrapes.

➤ This is the time to layer those cotton leggings under dresses, pants, or snow suits. They're great under nightgowns or pajamas as an extra layer on chilly nights; use them alone as a bright color accent, too. (See the accessories photo on page 154.)

➤ Iron-on patches or sew-on reinforcers are a solution to the problem of worn-out knees on toddler pants. Use contrasting colored ones on the outside to pep up a pair of ordinary pants. Or use softer, knit ones on the inside to line the pants.

. . . .

"Denim overalls worked until my son was just over two and he realized how heavy and constricting they were. He used to try and rip them off but since he couldn't, he'd end up screaming. We switched to sweats."

. . . .

➤ Don't buy V-neck sweaters and baseball jackets for the fall and winter—a V-neck doesn't protect the neck and chest enough. Use them in spring-time.

➤ Heavy wool sweaters can itch and can overheat a child as well as restrict movement. Cotton knit or acrylic sweaters are much more pliable and are fine for layering.

➤ Toddlers are very sensitive to discomfort. Even the reverse side of a cheaper puffy-printed t-shirt or the odd label may feel scratchy. If you remove a scratchy label leave in the size (or ink it in) to identify for future siblings.

➤ Don't toss out a beloved, worn-out piece of clothing without considering your child's feelings. A slow phaseout is preferable to "disappearing" a favorite but unwearable piece of clothing.

➤ Socks of 100 percent cotton are often too stiff and the heel is hard to get in right for toddlers. A blend is much easier on tender young feet. And save nonskid socks, a great invention, for running safely through the house. However, they are tough to get into shoes.

➤ The less complicated the shoes, the better. Buckles and zippers are too cumbersome. Stick to the easy on and off type.

➤ Reinforce any decorative details such as buttons or bows that hang off the clothes. Cheaper garments are sewn with less thread and need to be rein-forced.

➤ Keep those two-piece sweat outfits together in the drawer so you don't have to go hunting to find both pieces. You might set aside a special space for multiple piece and matching outfits.

➤ When your toddler starts sleeping through the night without diapers, get rid of the one-piece pajamas. Two-piece "big kid" pajamas are best for when your child needs to go to the potty at night and has to pull down the pants in a hurry. One hundred percent cotton long underwear is perfect for toilet-trained toddlers to wear as an added warm inner layer to keep the itches and chills away.

Dressing for socialization. For primary school girls, the current look is often large t-shirts, with narrow bottoms. Big tops loosely cover growing up bodies, and come in all lengths, short and wide, long and full. Girls this age often align themselves with their peers with a similar t-shirt or hairdo. The look isn't as free-form as it was earlier. The connection to their friends is what counts.

SCHOOL DAYS

ow that your child is going to school, there's more of a need for you to be organized with clothing. You need to have clean clothes handy on a regular basis; your child must be dressed by a certain time; and the clothing must conform to at least minimal standards of neatness and attractiveness. (Off the record, teachers have admitted to me—ruefully!—that they're not drawn to work with children who arrive looking unkempt.) Day care or school is the first step beyond the family circle. Your baby's out in the world now!

PRESCHOOL: SYMBOLIC DRESSING FOR IDENTITY

A child's school days may start as early as age one with a local play group or day-care center. These children are going to begin the socialization process earlier than kids who stay at home. That means they're going to have some early ideas about clothing that don't all come from you. However, it isn't usually until the toddler years are over (about two and a half to three) and certain developmental tasks of learning are mastered (running, talking, toilet-training, etc.) that most children then turn their attention to what they're wearing on their backs. My friend's daughter never seemed to take much notice of dresses until she started nursery school at age three. In just a few short weeks of preschool she decided all she wanted to wear was a dress—just like all the other girls in the class. She went from being a sweatsuit-wearing tomboy to joining what my friend called "the pink brigade."

Of course there are always exceptions, but children in preschool through kindergarten generally use clothing to experiment with their emerging identity. It's their first exposure to other children, but they are still influenced mostly by their own fantasies and ideas. Given the choice, they are more free-spirited now than in their later school years. New looks, varying styles and colors, some quite idiosyncratic, may be inspired by an older sibling, mom or dad, some character in a favorite book, movie, or TV show, or just by what's in the closet. Peeking into a class of four- or five-year-olds could be a lesson in creative expression for any fashion student or social psychologist!

Many first-time parents of preschool boys I've known are really surprised at some of the get-ups their sons put together. Again and again, I've seen boys link their identity experiments with those hats and t-shirts that advertise the child's current interest—very often some kind of male hero. Often parents, especially mothers, don't understand this, especially when the hero chosen is some marketed character who's rather violent. One mother told me that her five-year-old son lived for an adventure movie she'd rented once. It was about a ten-year-old boy in the Middle Ages who slew dragons and saved a princess (also ten years old). The little boy hero, however, was the only character in the movie in modern day dress—jeans and a scruffy t-shirt—creating a hero image that was accessible. "All Timmy wants to wear is this t-shirt. I'm really afraid he won't come out of it!" This obsession continued as Timmy assigned his playmates roles from the movie and acted them out on every play date. His parents got so frustrated they ended up buying five versions of the shirt, but setting up rules when he could wear it—not to school, but he could change into it when he got home. Then, one day it was over. "Now, he's a ghostbuster!" Another mother told me her four-year-old son loved to go to school each day as a different hero. He would insist on wearing the complete gear of a fireman one day—hat, boots, and all. The next day he was a baseball player, and the following day a king. His mother couldn't talk him out of it and was embarrassed every day by the stares he received until she was advised by his preschool director not to worry. "He's just trying to find out who he is. He'll pass through this stage." And he did.

Modern psychology says that it is natural for a young child to imagine he has superhuman powers. It's a logical way of dealing with a world much larger and more powerful than he is. Our challenge as parents is to help our kids grow up not needing superheroes while still encouraging them to enjoy their imaginations. One way to do that is to help them understand the difference between fantasy and reality. Timmy's parents did just that by defining the limits: he could wear the t-shirt and be in his fantasy during playtime and on the weekends; he couldn't wear the t-shirt when he was "in the reality" of everyday school. Timmy's mom says: "Now that he's six, we've relaxed a lot. We've had great conversations with him about what it means to be an actor and we look forward to every new character."

Of course, there are some schools that impose these clothing rules themselves. Some of the schools are now requiring all superhero gear, including t-shirts, be left home. They claim some young children can't pull out of it enough to concentrate. I tend to take a more relaxed approach when it comes to a three- or four-year-old. It's one thing if the child is disrupting the class. It's another if the rule exists just to control an imaginative child and hurry him into learning. Instead of banning the fantasy which is so much a part of this age, why not have special playtimes planned into the schedule when it's allowed? Then school can be perceived as a place to be yourself—have fun *and* learn.

Recent research at Yale University points to a future in which gender plays a less rigid role. Dr. Kyle Pruett, a psychiatrist at Yale's Child Study Center, has been doing a longitudinal study focusing on families over several years where the father is the full-time caretaker and the mother works full-time outside the home. Dr. Pruett notes that "traditionally, fathers have enforced sex stereotypes more strongly than mothers, engaging the boys in active play and complimenting the girls on their pretty dresses. But not these fathers," says Pruett. "That went by the boards. They weren't interested in bringing home little footballs for their sons or little tutus for the girls. They dealt with the kids according to the individual. As a result of this loosening up of stereotypes, the children are more relaxed about gender roles. I saw the boys really enjoy their nurturing skills. They knew what to do with a baby, they didn't see that as a girl's job, they saw it as a human job. I saw the girls have very active images of the outside world and what their mothers were doing in the workplace—things that become interesting to most girls when they're eight or ten, but these girls

were interested when they were four or five." Pruett is not saying that fathers are better at mothering than mothers, but simply that two individual parents are better than "one and a lump."[*]

Little girls experiment with their identity in other ways. Wearing a t-shirt with the current male popular hero is usually as far as a little girl gets unless there is an older or younger brother or neighbor to play that fantasy with. Because girls have started out as infants identifying with their mothers, and usually continue to do so, they grow up naturally defining themselves in relation to other people. Their human connections are continuous. There is no

[*]Shapiro, Laura. "Guns and Dolls," *Newsweek*, May 28, 1990, p. 65.

Dressing for identity. It is a common sight to see young boys, some as little as two years old, advertise their interests on t-shirts. They seem to be proclaiming: "This is who I am" or "This is who I want to be." Young boys about two to three years old are drawn to animals, dinosaurs, Mickey Mouse, and the Muppets. These are benign images they have learned to value in their protected home environment through books read to them, or cartoons they're allowed to watch. Later, in preschool, kindergarten, and first grade, periods when they are finding out who they are and learning to deal with their aggression, superheroes take hold, and they fantasize mastering their world through all-powerful superheroes. Later on, in elementary school, heroes take on a social aspect, reflecting developmental tasks at hand. Interests evolve toward sports figures, heroes who are part of a team, or even antiheroes. (See text for a discussion of symbolic dressing in more depth.) Dr. Thomas Armstrong, author of In Their Own Way: Discovering and Encouraging Your Child's Personal Learning Style, *(Los Angeles, Ca: Jeremy P. Tarcher, 1986.), says that there are many ways of knowing and learning and that intelligence takes many forms, not only linguistic and verbal. Children express their learning styles constantly in everyday activities, and this includes dressing. As yet, there is no research done on children's dressing patterns. However, based on Howard Gardner's model of the seven basic intelligences operating in children, Dr. Armstrong suggests: "For instance, the persistent wearing of a Ninja Turtle shirt might indicate several different intelligences at work. If he's a spatial child, he's drawn to the visuals of the graphics; if he's a bodily kinesthetic child, he could be drawn to the action portrayed in the image; he might also like to wear his jacket open with only the top button fastened around his shoulders so that his jacket serves as a cape and he can feel the action; if he's a linguistic child, he could be attracted mainly to the long and interesting names of each Turtle and other words in the design. Or, the choice of his shirt may simply be a reflection of a stage of social development—he's trying to connect with his peers. No one judgment is possible, but parents can put together a general schema of impressions to give themselves a framework of reference about their child." Costume Pajamas Shopping Tip: Superman and Batman t-shirts, shown here, are part of inexpensive pajama sets from the Brights Creek catalogue. They come with capes that attach with Velcro to be removed at bedtime. Safety note: If your child is the type who lives his fantasies and really believes he is a superhero, monitor his use of capes or other costumes that let him feel he can really fly. For some preschoolers the link between fantasy and reality is indistinct. Children have been known to have accidents, thinking they can fly.*

• • • • • • • • • •
"I never can tell whose underwear belongs to who even though my two girls are four years apart. For quick sorting after washing, I put an identifying 'X' for my oldest, two 'X's for my second. Then I got inspired and organized even more. One night I sat down and read the small print on every tag of clothing. I inked in a larger 'W' or 'C' for 'warm' or 'cold' washing on each tag. Now that really speeds it along."
• • • • • • • • • •

• • • • • • • • • •
"I started sewing knit patches on the inside of the knees of their pants, to protect their clothes from wear and tear. Now at six and seven when the issue for them is to be 'cool,' I have no problem continuing this because they don't even notice them.
• • • • • • • • • •

. . . .

"Most of our clothing fights center around the girls wanting to wear summer clothes in winter. Say a sleeveless culotte dress, or shorts! They'll wear them inside for play, then want to go out in them. Even suggesting adding layers underneath doesn't seem to work—they just don't get it! So, now I make sure to weed out those clothes from the closet before the problem starts."

. . . .

need for them to make a concerted effort—to rebel, in a sense—to "be a girl"—as boys do when they take the leap away from mom, toward dad. Girls may have less of a need to don superhero gear to master their world—they have nothing to prove because they've enjoyed gender continuity from the start. This is the real reason, I feel, that no female superheroes have gained the prominence of male figures.

Little girls easily find their fantasy inspiration in real life because their gender continuity lets them discover everyday heroines. Their moms, who must fulfill many different roles, are reality heroines if there ever were any. In any given week, the preschool girl may wear wildly varying images of clothes from her own "heroes" in real life. Don't be surprised if one day she wants to wear a party dress and sneakers, and sweats and party shoes, the next. She'll put together a gaudy top from the mall with her hot pink gym tights for a "cool" look she's seen on her baby-sitter. Not to mention an all-white outfit of t-shirt and skirt to be a "bride" or even "vanilla ice cream" (as one five-year-old told me with a gleam in her eye).

The world of superheroes is a very male world that doesn't offer much in the way of heroine images and many parents of girls complain about the lack of exciting female heroines. Wonder Woman was a character created by psychologist Charles Moulton in the thirties to fill that very void. Back then, she was quite an exotic creature, a female of Olympian strength equal to any male hero. Many grownups now in their fifties and sixties, *both* male and female, were inspired by this strong female heroine, as evidenced by a large attendance by both at a Smithsonian retrospective held in Washington, DC, in 1990. But as the years have passed, with the comic book industry attracting mostly male writers and editors, and with the readership composed of young men who are mostly over twenty-one, there is little impetus to create an independent female heroine with all the attendant merchandising opportunities of toys, clothes, and equipment. Most female heroes in superhero movies are adjuncts to the male heroes and rather uninteresting. Because of the early emphasis of explaining rules of conduct to little girls, mastery of their environment is ranked equally with "niceness." Perhaps because of this, identifying with any of the current male superheroes (whose victories are usually based on physical violence) does not easily appeal to their value system. One popular female that *does* appeal to both little girls and boys is Pippi Longstocking. Because she lives alone and takes care of herself (her father lives as king on a faraway island) she functions as a grown-up within all her stories. She masters her environment with magic, cleverness, humor, and independence. Rarely is any violence used. Superheroes who live by their wits, not the sword, are hard to find and rarely seriously merchandised.

And whether we like it or not, or whether we understand it or not, these years are the years of "pink and purple are my favorite colors." Whether a

Symbolic dressing for identity. Piper, from age five-and-a-half to six, experiments with lots of appearances, identifying herself with different important people in her life: For that important first day of first grade: The glasses—fake ones—mean she's smart, the braids she saw worn in the schoolhouse on Little House on the Prairie, and the knit "suit" is like a grown-up's. The whole ensemble has not reappeared since that first scary week of "real" school. Looking cool like her older sister, Skye, in the t-shirt of the moment and shared homemade surf bracelets.

preschool girl is "gifted," a "tomboy," "out there," or "normal" (ha! ha!), and even if parents are committed to raising a "liberated female," pink is the number one choice in clothes, followed soon after by lavender. Mothers like to claim it's because "it's all that's in the stores," and retailers trip all over themselves offering the latest trendy fashion colors. But pink is still number one. Psychologists say it has a lot to do with the symbolic thinking, typical of the three- to six-year-old child. It's part of trying to find out what it is to be a "girl." There is no obvious uniform to "be a girl" as there has been for boys (fireman, policeman, etc.) and pink is one color our culture still codes as "female." There are also many theories offered by color experts, but the fact remains, you can't go wrong with pink!

By the time preschool girls reach kindergarten it is often possible to pick out their individual clothing styles, visual cues to their friends who they are ("That's not Caroline—she'd never wear a dress!"). Some girls may only want to wear dresses, and a certain kind of dress. Others—often in imitation of an adored brother—eschew the pinks and purples and prefer a sloppy jeans look right down to the untied shoelaces of their sneakers. I often feel the little girls who favor a "boy look" have discovered sooner than their (first-born girl?) peers about the ultimate comfort of a t-shirt that doesn't have to be tucked in, or a sweatpant that can be pulled on or off—no problem—and that also takes care of the worry about undies showing. Any talk about "gender identification" problems I find premature and mused about mostly by inexperienced first-time parents.

Selma Fraiberg discusses this in her book *The Magic Years*: "There are many compromises within the personality between feminine and masculine goals . . . which need not create conflict. The little girl who leaves her dolls to go out

> *"Eddie hated wool sweaters. I tried t-shirts underneath, but when it got hot in school, the sleeves would still itch. I changed the sweaters for a plain sweater vest over a long-sleeved shirt for indoors. His chest was warm, and he didn't itch. I kept the wool sweaters for outdoor play."*

Dealing with the Batman in Your Life

Socialization is the major task for preschoolers. Why not use each child's creativity as a learning tool for everyone?

Atticus is Batman. I couldn't imagine him without his fantasy. It's his creativity. But I worried that it might isolate him from his friends who weren't into it as much as he was. One day he asked me to help him make a cape. I made a real project out of it—measuring the length and the width, deciding what color to paint it (black of course!), how it would tie and still be comfortable, etc. When we finished, everyone else in the class wanted one too. There we were, the whole class, including me, sitting at the table with brown paper capes painted black—each attached to a pair of shoulders with wooden clothesline clips.

—*Marigrace Gaughan Walker, preschool director for three- and four-year-olds, Armonk, New York*

with the boys to chase Indians [nowadays it'd be the Shredder] is not necessarily in danger of abandoning her femininity. The most casual appraisal of our childhood friends will remind us how many tomboys grew up to be excellent wives and mothers,"—and bread-winners! It is only when a little girl actively *rejects* "femininity" (and this will be evident *beyond* her clothing choices) that a parent should look a little further.

In primary school kids start to work in earnest on acquiring real-life skills of reading, writing, and math. Besides mastering school skills, they're interested in finding their place in that real-world context of the structured school day. This is also reflected in how they start to dress themselves. Kids are no longer just using clothing for creatively discovering themselves, they are using it to discover others. They are learning who they are in juxtaposition with their friends.

PRIMARY SCHOOL: DRESSING FOR SOCIALIZATION

Communication and socialization are so important now that first graders on up start to align themselves with a particular best friend or a certain group, and often may dress in such a way as to fit in. Even children who are not interested in what they wear will probably fall in pretty much with the do's and don'ts of school-yard fashion. Brand-name consciousness is not the issue in these younger grades that people think. That comes later on. Their primary concern is not to stick out too much and chance looking "dorky," and to look "cool." Fads catch on fast now, since they spend all day, every day, and often after school, around each other. Some of these are the despair of their parents: a few years back in one school it was considered hopelessly square to zip up a jacket, no matter how cold it was. If you can keep your sense of humor, some of these fads are downright hilarious! In another school, little girls would start off for school in a normal pair of matched socks. When they arrived, they'd exchange one sock for another from their best friend. They'd wear them that way—identically mismatched—all day and exchange them back at the end of the day.

Parents may resist the less individualistic, pack mentality that seems to become so important now. They may miss their preschooler's "creative" style or dislike the trends that captivate their child. Interestingly, early elementary school art teachers have told me they often notice a drop in experimentation in their classes during this time. However, most child psychologists and psychiatrists underline the importance of these early friendships and group relationships. They believe it prepares kids for the intimacy of long-term relationships in later life and gives them a context within which to understand the larger workings of society.[*] If dressing like their friends can make children

* * * * * * * * * *

"I have three girls under six, and my first and third are fashion free-spirits. I've always wanted to have a sweatshirt printed for each of them that says 'I dressed myself this morning.' Or one for me that says 'They dressed themselves this morning!'"

* * * * * * * * * *

---

[*] Flaste, Richard. "Sidelined by Loneliness," *New York Times Health Magazine*, April 28, 1991, pp. 14–15.

. . . .

"Michi has an accelerated sense of style and I think it's from day care. Since she was two, all day, all week, the other kids have been her extended family. We've been through every look: 'Little-House-on-the Prairie' dresses; sweats over leggings; the hair bow on top of the ponytail, just so; shoes that don't match, even a sneaker with a cowboy boot! The advice I've always been given is 'What harm?' and 'It'll pass' as these crazes do come and go. I've actually gotten used to it and now even look forward to what's coming next. Safety, like sneakers for gym—those were issues that were not negotiable!"

. . . .

feel accepted by their peers, then parents would be wise—within reason and the family budget—not to discourage it.

This concern may even extend to how their own parents dress in front of their friends at school. Parents' reactions to these requests range from brushing it off with a laugh to actually being insulted and taking it personally. This may be one of the first times they've heard objective criticism from their "baby" (other than "But *why* can't I have another ice cream? You're *so* mean!"). If the requests persist, plan a time for sincere discussion and use dialogue to find out about other issues that are probably involved. Did friends make cracks about you to your child in front of others and embarrass him? The reasons could be myriad. I recommend relaxed compromise. Changing a pair of shoes or earrings will let your child know you understand and care about how he's feeling. But changing the whole way you look (I've known some parents who've considered this) will not. Doing that will send the wrong message—a scary one—to your child, i.e., he has too much power over the person who's supposed to be protecting him. This stage will pass when your child gains more confidence and understanding of his own place socially.

Then there are the mavericks who start their own trends and march to their own drummers. Your child may be one of these clothing individualists. In some families, parents who are considered fashionable themselves may encourage dressing as a creative outlet. And yet I know many other parents who are completely oblivious to fashion, who have ended up with a primary school trend-setter. From my observations, there is often little causal relationship

The two C's for primary school boys: comfortable and cool. This gang of first graders' uniform is laces and hightops. No matter what they end up wearing to school, they'll mix in their bright surfer accessories and clothes. Left: Cole prefers traditional sportswear. His different-colored laces are his nod to the group. Second left: Ben wanted to wear his whole sweat outfit—black with neon writing on it—but his mom toned it down with a bright yellow turtleneck. She bought it huge so it was loose around his neck because he hates tight clothes. Added bonus: it looks cool hanging below his sweatshirt. Substituting jeans helped to reduce the drama of all-black for school. Second right: Sam lives in sweats; this tie-dyed shirt is his pride and joy—just like his cool older brother. With his dark hair and fairer skin, he naturally supports all this vibrant color. Far right: Steven has the cool surfer haircut left over from summer. It looks great on him and he loves it, but when Steven's mother started readying his clothes for school, she found that when she dressed him in any of last year's trendier clothes he had that still fit him, he was overpowered—all you saw was the haircut and the clothes. Hair is not specifically "clothing," but it has impact much as accessories do. Originally the haircut was meant to give him a little pep, but now the haircut didn't look right: it had too much pep! To keep the haircut he loved, she figured out ways to tone down the clothes: Remove the matching pants on the bottom and substitute simple sweatpants. Go totally against the trendiness by emphasizing classic preppiness: Add simple suspenders. Now Steven reappears. And the laces stay, of course.

between the parents' particular taste and a child who dresses "creatively." In fact, talent in the clothing area often appears to many parents' bewilderment ("Peter has such a sense of style. It must have skipped a generation!"). How primary-school-age children choose to dress always provides fascinating insights into what kind of personality, interests, and other talents they possess. Children, even in second or third grade, can't always verbalize how they feel and may not even want to. Just stepping back and observing them in ordinary everyday activities such as dressing can provide you with as valuable information as any of the best parenting books. This is why I always try to look and listen carefully to what my kids' clothing preferences are: they often tell me more about their emotional state or what's going on at school than they themselves could ever verbalize.

Uniforms

Uniforms appear to be going through a resurgence of popularity. There is a definite reason for this conservative swing: With the disappearance of many of the clothing standards that gave structure to our society in the past (the

· · · · · · · · · ·

"I went to parochial school and always wore uniforms. Now, it's hard for me to see the kids in public school wearing sweats or play clothes. I dress my three boys in khakis or if it's jeans, with a tuck-in knit collar-shirt, not a t-shirt. I like to add a little formality so they take school seriously."

· · · · · · · · · ·

Preschool girls use clothes to experiment with their emerging identities. They go through any one of a million looks if allowed until they usually settle on something by second, third, or fourth grade. These four-, five-, and six-year-olds each have their own style, from "pink and purple are my favorite colors," to "what my mom laid out for me to wear" (not often!), to "whatever my mom wants me to wear plus what I want to wear," to "the more appliqués and wild combinations the better." Not pictured are: "what my brother wears," "what my doll would wear," "what a teenager would wear," and "this is the only thing that's clean" and "this is the only thing I want to wear." The password here, in the early school years, is experimentation. Left: Haley likes the simple tradition of a kilt and a shetland sweater but adds cotton leggings under to take away the scratchiness. She always adds a little extra "something"—today, a tulle sparkley birthday headband and polka dot socks in the grown-up color, black, and a little plaid bow tie pin. Children this age don't match clothes. Each item is viewed separately. Second from left: Stephanie, "Pink is my favorite color. Now look at my go-go boots." Second right: Jenna, in a creative mix that makes total sense to her—her favorite doodadded top over pants (they're not scratchy like her wool tights) and party shoes: perfect. Her easy-care hairdo, devised by her mother's friend for her fine flyaway hair when she was two, is now her trademark. With a haircut like this, who needs jewelry? (Note: A classic geometric haircut can work wonders for a little girl tends to look disheveled or who favors unusual combinations of clothing. If the hair is neat, and finished-looking, no matter how free-form her clothing choices are [from the neck down] she'll still look "together.") Right, Katie wears anything her parents put on her as long as it's not too tight and has a lot of colors. She really likes the socks she has on—they match the flag in her classroom. Look and listen for all kinds of hints about your children's temperaments and talents in the most basic way they may have to express themselves: by dressing.

• • • • • • • • •

"Ben had gone shopping with me two weeks before starting first grade, and loved the baggy corduroy pants we bought. But a week after we started, he came home only wanting to wear straight leg Levis like his friends—none of the rather expensive baggies we'd bought. As he gets older, he doesn't want to be different and I understand that, but I also want him to learn to follow through. So we made a deal—those baggy pants for dressy and weekends, and Levis for school."

• • • • • • • • •

casual dressing mores of the nineties call more for what's "appropriate," not for what's clearly "right" or "wrong"), choosing what to wear is based on almost totally subjective criteria. This puts more responsibility on the family for daily clothing decisions.

Some parents I know, who are uncomfortable with what they feel is too casual or lax in the clothing rules of their nonuniformed school, have instituted their own family clothing rules. For instance, some parents of boys won't allow t-shirts for school, only knit shirts with collars, or turtlenecks. Or they won't allow sweats, only pressed jeans or khakis. Some little girls are dressed in "proper" plaid school dresses and buckled leather sandals to go to the school yard. Never mind their best friend is in bike pants and sneakers. Parents who adapt their own clothing standards usually have to depend on their own persistence to keep them going—and they'll incur their own stress going against the more casual trend.

Other parents are able to avoid the daily issue of what to put on for school when their kids attend a school that requires a certain uniform. With no choices, there is certainly less morning stress, and there *are* many positive points about uniforms: Besides the budgetary advantages, uniforms can add a note of seriousness that may help a student focus more on study than play. Uniforms can create an exterior unity among the students that may even help a shy child feel more comfortable socially. Not to mention safer. Recently, many inner-city public schools have had great success introducing uniforms to combat the thefts committed both to buy coveted fashionable items and to protect pupils from being robbed of their own expensive clothing. The uniform policy has often ended up with the added benefit of encouraging the kids to have pride in their schools. And as children get older, any possible clothing or fashion prejudices on the part of friends or teachers are reduced if everyone wears the same thing. Depending on the family budget and school, parents can save much money. Frankly, for a lot of parents—*and* some kids—uniforms during the school hours are easier.

However, the jury is still out regarding the advantages of a long-term approach of imposing standardized dress. Certainly the opportunity to use dressing as a creative problem-solving area has to be put aside. Whether this has any effect, positive or negative, on children's developing creativity is still to be determined. I do know that when a child is put into a uniformed school because of continual dressing problems in the mornings (and I've heard several parents who admit to this as a last desperate move!) the problem is not alleviated—it is just put off. One parent told me that the trauma every Friday morning, the one day her uniformed girl is allowed to wear "real clothes," makes up for all the tranquillity of the other four days. In this case the temperament of her little girl went right with her to the new school and still had to be dealt with.

I'm of two minds about uniforms. On the plus side, for parents, there's the unmistakable convenience and budgetary factor. And for teachers, uniforms create a visual sameness which may cut down on distraction in the classroom and may help students to focus on work. On the minus side, I wonder whether a teacher looking out into a sea of identically dressed children is really able to "see," and work with the individual personalities and learning styles of each child? Our educational system focuses on verbal and mathematical skills, but not every child is equally competent in language or math. Do uniforms foster the same scholastic expectations for every child, whether or not they have the competency? Dr. Howard Gardner of Harvard University (and other psychologists) posits that there are at least *seven* basic types of intelligences operating in children, if not more. He says that education should address all these capabilities of learning and should be as interesting and engaging as play. Do uniforms dull educators to the myriad of possible creative expressions in their students? And lastly, but most importantly, from the point of view of the children, I have questions about putting off the normal "real life" task of choosing and dealing with clothing. Aside from the temperamental aspect (as mentioned above), do uniforms send a message to kids that they have to "be someone else" to be able to be successful in school? And do uniforms signify that play is now over and it is time for (boring) work? There is no hard or fast answer to this issue. Ultimately the decision is up to each family. If a family opts for uniforms, I tend to favor using the best of both worlds: regular clothes with a dress code. Kids can still express themselves subjectively, be more easily "seen," and feel like individuals. And the objective restraints of a code teach them to understand how clothing can be used as a tool for self-respect and social interaction in life.

- - - - - - - - - -

"Ellie is six and goes to a school where there's no school uniform, but there is a dress code. She's a total free spirit—she'd wear sequins and silk if she could—but we compensate with uniform skirts to her liking (they have to twirl) and exciting headbands which no one seems to mention."

- - - - - - - - - -

Dealing with your children's clothing preferences and morning moods are the major obstacles to getting out of the house on time. Even assuming there is enough clean clothing in the house, parents often find the morning an ordeal. Having problems getting dressed is probably one of the most common reasons for day-care or school lateness. Being late for school makes it difficult for kids to get into sync with their classmates and with what's being taught that day. Teachers tell me that sometimes it will take a child till early afternoon to overcome a late start, and all that morning tension. And most teachers feel that continual lateness definitely affects learning and social development for that school year.

GETTING DRESSED AND OUT OF THE HOUSE IN THE MORNING

If you end up always hurrying in the morning at the start of the day, it's stressful for everyone, particularly children, according to child psychologist David Elkind, author of *The Hurried Child*. He has a lot to say about the impact of a hurried morning schedule on younger children:

Hurrying, like any stressor, has a subjective dimension. We know, for example, that children of about eight years and younger tend to engage in "magical thinking"—they often believe that their wishes, feelings, or acts bear a causal relationship to parental acts. Young children tend to perceive hurrying as a rejection, as evidence that their parents do not really care about them. Children are very emotionally astute in this regard and tune in to what is a partial truth. To a certain extent, hurrying children from one caretaker to another each day, or into academic achievement, or into making decisions they are not really able to make is a rejection. It is a rejection of the children as they see themselves, of what they are capable of coping with and doing.

Children at this stage take the part for the whole. They sense a little rejection in the parent and take it for the whole of the parental attitude. Young children are not relativistic but, rather, think in absolute terms. So, when we engage in some necessary hurrying, our young children may misperceive a part of our attitude for the whole and miss our very real love and concern for them in their global and undifferentiated perception of a bit of rejection.

. . . .

"Rasheeda used to be such a tomboy. She has three older brothers and she used to be one of them. Now that she's in second grade, she's gone completely the other way. She'd dress like a tart if I let her. Anything to be different from her brothers, whom right now she hates."

. . . .

He further explains how we adults tend to assume that children think rationally like we do, and that kids will understand why they have to hurry if they're given an explanation. In reality kids don't think at all like adults. Modern-day parents may resist this idea, citing the incredible accomplishments of their three-year-old reader or five-year-old violinist. But these early accomplishments, though terrific, are not the same as an emotionally mature perception of the world. Even if a child can read or play beautifully, he's still egocentric—still in the symbolic phase of "magical thinking." And this is light years away from adult logic. How children *are* similar to adults is in their feelings and emotions. And often adults have no idea of the depth of their child's feelings. No matter how virtuous the reason (you let your child sleep later so *he* could have some extra sleep) or how *patiently* you explain the reason for hurrying (you have to hurry him so he doesn't miss the bus for school), your child will *always* balk at hurrying. He'll dig in his heels—by whining, continuing to play, or just plain slowing down his pace and looking upset. It's not just to annoy you. What you are trying so hard to convey in a rational manner, your child will process in his head as rejection. He can't analyze like an adult and be able to separate your tense reaction to your problem from himself. He picks up on your *emotional* state—probably impatience and irritability at the time. It's the tone of your voice he'll pick up on, not the rational explanation. As Elkind says,

When we have to hurry young children, when they have to be at a day-care center or with a baby-sitter, we need to appreciate children's feelings about the matter. Giving children a rational explanation, "I have to work so we can eat, buy clothes, and so on," helps, but it isn't enough to deal with the child's implicit thought [or feeling]—"If they really love me, they wouldn't go off and leave me." We need to respond to a child's feeling more than to his or her intellect. One might say, for instance: "I'm really going to miss you today and wish you could be with me." The exact words are less important than the message that the separation is painful but necessary for you too. And it is equally important, when you pick your child up at the end of the day, to say something about how happy you are to see him or her. By responding to the young child's feelings, we lessen some of the stress of hurrying.

One very important way David Elkind suggests to offset the stress of hurrying is the very simple, old-fashioned practice of politeness.

Sometimes our tendency to think of children as not sharing our feelings leads us to compound the stress of hurrying in a different way. When we are in a hurry we are sometimes impolite and thoughtless to young children because we assume they are not as concerned about such things as we are. But children are very sensitive to signs of parental caring. If we need to break a promise about taking a child to a movie, the park, or the zoo, it is very important that we apologize and make it clear that we really are sorry. In the same way, when we ask children to do something for us, to save us time, or to help us out, it is really important to say "please" and "thank you." Being polite to children speaks to their feelings of self-worth (as it does to adults), which are always threatened when we hurry them. When we are polite to children we show in the most simple and direct way possible that we value them as people and care about their feelings. Thus politeness is one of the most simple and effective ways of easing stress in children and of helping them to become thoughtful and sensitive people themselves.

If thinking and speaking in an emotional way is a new approach for you, don't hesitate to read *How to Talk So Your Kids Will Listen and Listen So Your Kids Will Talk* by Adele Faber and Elaine Mazlish. Written by two mothers who spent years in a parent group with Dr. Haim Ginott (author of *Between Parent and Child*) this is the widely acknowledged textbook of how to successfully communicate verbally with your child. *Loving Your Child Is Not Enough* by Nancy Samalin also describes a plethora of situations, many about clothing, to teach communication skills with kids.

Besides acknowledging your child's feelings about hurrying, most parents say *the key to a calm morning is having a routine they hang on to for dear life.* It's not what events are included in the routine that are the secret to success. Nor is it how early you start. What makes the routine work is that the *sequence* of events in the routine never varies. Whether morning dressing starts before or after 7:00 or 7:30 is not the issue. Whether dressing always comes before or after teeth-brushing, or breakfast, is.

Favorite Parent Tips for Getting Preschoolers Out of the House

➤ "Getting her out of the house on time? It's all up to the night before. If she gets to bed on time, she's fine. If not, forget it!"

➤ "Chris gets distracted in the mornings. He'll spy his toys and want to play.

How to get out of the house on time in the morning: Always start the night before! Get your child to bed on time. Use creative strategies to speed the bath along: With goggles, you'll get his hair washed without the sting of soapsuds.

With some drops of blue food coloring, you can transform the bathtub into a Florida pool! On special occasions (nothing else has worked!), let him get into the bath with his clothes on and undress in the water. The clothes have to be laundered anyway.

I have a five-minute warning, then a two-minute. Works like a charm."

➤ "Max is three and a half and obsessed with animals, and his favorite t-shirt is one we ordered from a nature catalogue. I couldn't believe it when I found myself blow drying this t-shirt one morning just to get him out of the house! I decided to spend the money and order three more copies of it. Thank God we still had the catalogue and they still had some left."

➤ "In kindergarten, Samantha only wanted to wear her cheap stuff we bought on the weekends from the mall. I wanted her to wear my fantasy of a well-brought up little girl: a smock dress with a proper grosgrain ribbon in her hair. (Of course I'd never worn that—I grew up in the country!) So we struck up a deal. She could wear what she wanted on the weekend, Tuesdays, and Thursdays and my choices on Mondays, Wednesdays, Fridays, and holidays. It worked and we stopped arguing. Now at nine years old, she puts herself together in a creative way I never could, mixing trendy things with 'my' classics."

➤ "My four-year-old used to drive me crazy dawdling in the morning. One morning after I screamed at him again, he looked up at me *so* sincerely and said: 'Mommy, I'm only little. I don't know *how* to hurry up.' I melted. That's when I decided it was really up to me to start earlier.'

➤ "We lay out the clothes on the floor for the whole outfit for the next day. Flat like a paper doll. But the first thing she has to put on, the underwear, is laid next to her bed. Laura wakes up slowly in the morning and seeing the underwear first, gets her moving."

➤ "We play follow-the-leader. First I'll put something on, then he will. All the way, till we're both dressed. Other times, I'll follow his lead. This works even faster."

Favorite Parent Tips for Getting Primary Schoolers Out of the House

➤ "Breakfast is served when the clothes are on."

➤ "Part of our bedtime routine is laying out the next day's clothes. When I can't get them focused, we turn on the weather channel, and it helps them decide."

➤ "I try to have some of their favorite clothes clean at all times. Sometimes this means trips downstairs after dinner. But my kids are faddish now—there's always a new 'favorite' even if they've had it in their closet for months. This way, whatever they want to wear is available with no last-minute crazies and I don't spend money on duplicates."

➤ "We need one whole hour—at least!—from waking up to dressing to leaving the house. Until I realized this—I'm the type who can get up and out in ten or fifteen minutes—my first grader and toddler had lots of late days on their reports and I yelled a lot. Now, their faces are a lot happier in the

Gorillas in the Morning!

Does your child wake up grumpy every morning in spite of any and all of your clever getting-out-of-the-house routines? Dr. Lendon Smith, author of *Feed Your Kids Right*, explains in his book: "If your child is depressed and non-communicative upon arising in the morning and seems alert and cheerful two hours after breakfast, the previous evening's meal may have been at fault. Usually it turns out that a sugary dessert or a bowl of ice cream at bed-time has excited the body to over-produce insulin, thus forcing the blood sugar down. Daily or hourly fluctuations are almost always due to food." Dr. Smith believes that all humans are basically cheerful and gracious, and when they are not it is because something is preventing this attitude from surfacing. "If your child is the up-and-down type during the day—for no good reason, he's okay, then he's not okay—it's time to think of food allergies." Dr. Smith described it to me this way: "You're giving him choices (would you like to wear this or this?) and all he can do is growl back! You're trying to reason with the brain, but you're talking to the spinal cord. She's not a human being right now—she's a gorilla! Stop talking, and go get some protein food or a good snack. Wait twenty minutes—it takes that long after food is ingested to raise the blood sugar. Now you can go back to reason. You can prevent this behavior by making it a habit to give a little protein snack before bed-time. For the sensitive child it will help keep the blood sugar level up during the night."

morning on the way to school, especially my first grader, who has enough time for the hairdo of the day."

➤ "We went through a time when Alicia and I continually locked horns in the morning. I tried every parent tip I could, short of writing Mrs. Piggle Wiggle. One day, my husband—he's more laid back—hid behind his newspaper and said 'Surprise me today.' Alicia ran right into her room to think up an outfit—it really appealed to her dramatic side. Right now he's in charge of dressing most mornings, and she'll usually come out with some flourish to accompany her outfit, like a ballet or rap dance step she picked up at school."

➤ "I have one easy rule: if they don't pick their clothes out the night before, I make the decisions for them in the morning. It took only a few days till they realized they'd have to put up with my 'yucky' choices!"

THE FUSSY DRESSER

If you still end up arguing or negotiating about clothing ad infinitum, even after setting up reasonable routines, you can do several things to remedy the situation. First, from a temperamental point of view, you may benefit greatly by reading *The Difficult Child*, by Dr. Stanley Turecki, a practicing child- and family psychiatrist in New York City. He has a surprising amount of compassionate and practical parenting strategies to explain how these seemingly mundane clothing struggles can teach you a lot about your child. In his revised 1989 edition, he makes no less than twenty references to temperament and its relationship to clothing. Dr. Turecki says that inborn temperamental traits make the child who he or she is. Once we understand how those traits work in each of our kids, it's a lot easier to stand back and parent in a positive way. Difficult behavior about clothes, he says, "can often be linked to a difficult trait, and parents need to look for the underlying temperamental causes. It helps to know there are reasons for this behavior."

For instance, if you have a finicky dresser to whom clothing "feels funny," or whose clothing combinations are often called "wild" or "interesting" because of her strong and unusual preferences, besides being creative, your child may have a *low sensory threshold*. This means the child is "sensitive"—physically, not emotionally—to color, light, appearance, temperature, or how fabrics feel on the skin. A child with a low sensory threshold may actually need fewer pieces of clothing in cold weather because the child truly feels hot. Dr. Turecki also describes "I don't like it" behavior—the common theme heard in a child with the temperamental trait of *initial withdrawal*. Such children have a hard time with new things. Says Turecki, "In this area, labeling (not the negative type) is extremely important, part of your recognition that the child is not simply being contrary but is definitely bothered. Don't challenge his threshold (by criticizing him). Instead of reacting to what you think your child is doing to you (e.g., 'Why do you always give me a hard time over your sneakers?' or

'Why don't you ever like anything I buy you? You're so spoiled.'), put a name to it with a declarative description: 'I know it doesn't feel right when your sneakers are tied too tightly . . .' or 'You're very sensitive to the tags on clothes,' and 'I know it takes you time to like new things.' " Dr. Turecki suggests Velcro for the child who feels his or her laces are too tight and dialogue for other problems: "With children over the age of three years, simple, planned discussions about their reactions to change or sensitivity to clothes can be very helpful. And once the child is able to recognize some of his temperamental patterns, he will gain more self-control. Well-managed children can say to their parents 'I'm not used to it yet. Give me a little more time.' " The less judgmental you are and the more warmly you encourage, the more likely you are to get your child's attention. Dr. Turecki's solutions show how those temperamental traits that are tough to parents now can be used to advantage when their child is older.

The following chart describes the many ways children can interact difficultly with clothing. If your child has a strong temper and no amount of discipline or bribery seems to help get him dressed, here are some tips. I've taken Dr. Turecki's descriptions of difficult temperamental traits that apply to clothes and listed them on the left. The second, third, and fourth columns comprise my fashion shopping tips to minimize clothing struggles, plus parenting approaches inspired by Adele Faber and Elaine Mazlish, authors of *Liberated Parents, Liberated Children* and *How To Talk So Your Child Will Listen and How To Listen So Your Child Will Talk*, and Nancy Sauralin, author of *Loving Your Child Is Not Enough*. Don't think: "I'm giving in to a demanding child." Think: "I'm making a choice to respect his individuality and temperament."

Dr. Lendon Smith on How to Calm Fussy Dressers:

"Ruling out that it's a matter of winning over the parent or just too many choices, children who are especially rigid about their clothes usually have a magnesium deficiency. It goes along with being ticklish, sensitive, goosey and craving chocolate. They may have trouble relaxing or sleeping at night. These children are unable to disregard unimportant stimuli—that's why clothes bother them. They may have trouble in school too. It's not always easy to spot a magnesium deficiency. It often doesn't show up in testing or the child may just have a genetic need of more magnesium than normal. Often it's a matter of working backwards from symptoms. Magnesium has a regulating effect and I've found that 500 mg given daily is a great help. After two or three weeks, parents should see calmer behavior from their child."

If you are interested in more information on how to raise healthy kids and deal with behavior problems through diet, refer to Dr. Smith's comprehensive book on childhood nutrition *Feed Your Kids Right*.

"My oldest child used to constantly complain about her clothes. Whatever she had, it wasn't right. It was scratchy, itchy, or too tight. When I started taking her shopping with me, the arguments ended. So when my next child dawdled about dressing in the morning I figured it was the same thing. But even when I bought her comfortable clothes she had chosen herself, we'd still end up in a lot of fights. Finally I realized I had one problem but two different kids. My oldest tends to be literal. For her the problem was about the clothes themselves. But with my second child, it wasn't the clothes at all. She just didn't want to go to school. Two different kids, two different solutions!"

Clothing and Temperament—The Fussy Dresser

Difficult Temperamental Trait:	How It Shows Up in Dressing	What to Say	Solutions
Low Sensory Threshold "Sensitive"—physically not emotionally; highly aware of color, light, appearance, texture, sound, smell, taste, or temperature (not necessarily all of these); "creative," but with strong and unusual preferences that can be embarrassing; clothes have to feel and look right, making dressing a problem; doesn't like the way many foods look, smell, or taste; picky eater; bothered and overstimulated by bright lights and noisy settings; refuses to dress warmly when the weather is cold.	• Clothes have to feel right. Very sensitive to how clothes feel on the skin. The tags "hurt"; the seams are "too scratchy"; the jacket is too fat (quilting in a parka is too bulky). May go through several changes trying to get dressed or end up tying shoelaces over and over to get them "tight enough." May prefer clothing to be worn oversized (loose enough), or tight to the body (loose clothes "don't fit"). • Clothes have to look right: very sensitive to colors. Picks clothing with strong unusual preferences that are often totally mismatched, e.g., stripes with stripes, or orange with red, or only purple. Often wants to wear only his color preference which may mean he ends up wearing the same clothing items all the time. • Needs less clothing to feel comfortable: "I'm hot" he'll claim. Refuses to dress warmly when the weather is cold, but never seems to catch a cold. Wants to wear underwear, or bathing suits, (or nothing!) around the house. • When shopping, gets overwhelmed in crowded, noisy, bright settings. May run wild or have a tantrum in large department stores or small, overcrowded shoe stores. • An older child with strong preferences may be opinionated and comment on his parents' choices in clothing, or on friends who "don't look good to them."	• "I know this sweater doesn't feel right. Why don't we try something else?" Or, "Let's put a t-shirt under it." • "I know red looks funny to you. You really like pastels." • "I know you feel hot even though I don't. Since it's really cold outside, let's carry your jacket with us, in case you need it." • "I know you don't feel like shopping right now. Just hang in there for a few more minutes, we'll head on home." • "I know you'd rather I wore different shoes. They're certainly not your taste, but, boy, they feel comfortable to me."	• Don't judge your child as "spoiled" or "picky." He can't help it. Realize his reactions are real to him. As soon as he is able to understand, talk to him about this trait and explain it to him. • Focus on knits, not wovens. Knitted fabrics that drape on the body are more comfortable than, stiffer wovens, and the seams are smoother. • Avoid: over-the-head garments unless you buy them larger for a roomy neck opening. • Use lightweight layers. Avoid: anything bulky or heavy. (Jackets are the main culprits.) Check that the armholes are not too high and the chest is not too tight. • Avoid: anything stiff or scratchy. Check the fabric and the seams. • A child with an "inborn color sense" about his clothing, may actually physically be more comfortable in his choice. • If he's safely dressed for the weather, relax about what you want him to wear. But this doesn't mean he can run around naked in front of visitors at home. Post rules of cleanliness and weather safety even for the very young. • Shop in smaller stores. Go when they are least crowded. • Teach your child to appreciate differences in others. Casually point out unusual (to him) combinations on other people. Mention why you like them. Don't take your child's criticism of your own choices personally. Be flexible, but don't change your style completely—that sends a weak parent message.

. . . .

Clothing Problems of the Fussy Dresser and What to Do about Them. (Definitions in column one courtesy Dr. Stanley Turecki)

. . . .

Difficult Temperamental Trait:	How It Shows Up in Dressing	What to Say	Solutions
Poor Adaptability Has trouble with transition and change of activity or routine; inflexible, very particular, notices minor changes; gets used to things and won't give them up; has trouble adapting to anything unfamiliar; can want the same clothes or foods over and over.	• Wants to wear the same thing over and over until it's way past outgrown and is too tight, tattered, or too short. (This may also be a sensory threshold issue.) • A favorite piece of clothing (a blanket or jacket) is washed or mended and he complains. • Has difficulty using an old favorite for a different activity, e.g., "That's my school sweatshirt. I don't wear that in the woods." Or, "That's mine!" when clothing that's outgrown is to be given away or to a sibling. • Has difficulty with clothing that signifies change. Refuses to put on shoes or jackets to leave. Or refuses to put on cool weather clothing (jackets, sweats) after he got used to summer ones (shorts, sandals, t-shirts). • May resist party clothes, or wearing anything he's not used to. • An older child may refuse to borrow clothes from a friend for a last-minute overnight situation—and even demand his own familiar ones be brought over.	• Prepare him ahead of time. Explain about clothing purchases ahead, e.g., "This parka is for you now, and your brother, next year" or "We're going to such and such store to buy XYZ for a planned shopping trip. First, we're buying shorts and t-shirts, then we're having a snack. Then some new socks. Then we'll be home in time for your favorite cartoon before dinner." Stick to it. Give him time to get used to change: "We have to go soon. I'll be back in five minutes." A few minutes later (don't get distracted and have it turn into half an hour): "Now we have to go. Ready?" • Use statements of fact to indicate change is necessary: "It's time to go" rather than "You're not ready yet? You haven't even found your shoes?" • Acknowledge his difficulty: "I know it's hard to leave when you're having such a good time." Bring an end to a frustrating activity: explain why it's hard to leave in a quiet moment at home, e.g., teach him what "You're getting locked in" means. Tell him what's good about it too. Excite him with what's ahead: "Let's get your pajamas on so we can finish last night's story." Don't bribe. He'll catch on and you'll be stuck. • Use wish fulfillment for a very young child as a creative distraction: "Oh, I wish I had twenty t-shirts all with dinosaurs on them. Each would be a different color and wear a different kind of hat!" He'll get involved with the fantasy and start moving.	• Advance notice is the key to help this child prepare for change. Make routine and advance explanations into never-fail habits in your house. Delineate the sequence of events but don't overexplain. Use charts for schedules. Take a few minutes to explain the rules or schedule of every shopping trip or clothing purchase. • Discuss outgrown clothing alone with your child if he's having trouble giving it up. Be patient with your child's inability to let go of a piece of clothing. He's not necessarily selfish—more likely he's "locked in" for one reason or another. • If it's convenient and possible, get duplicates of the favorite sweatpants or t-shirt. You're not spoiling your child, you're smoothing logistic problems ahead of time. Your very young child won't be aware he has four bird shirts—he'll just know one is always clean. • Place party clothes in the closet and let them sit there a few days till he gets used to them. Or, include him in the purchase. This goes for any new clothes.

Difficult Temperamental Trait:	How It Shows Up in Dressing	What to Say	Solutions
Initial Withdrawal Shy and reserved with new people; doesn't like new situations; holds back or protests by crying or clinging; may tantrum if forced to go forward. (Initial withdrawal is the first stage of poor adaptability.)	• Rejects any new articles of clothing. What you perceive as a great outfit, just what he'd love, he perceives as new and scary. (Ironically, they can often then become old favorites.) • Doesn't like dressing up for special occasions. The party clothes are strange (they haven't been worn before or lately) and he hates to stand out in his clothes and be called "cute." (He already feels uncomfortable in social situations wearing his regular clothes.) • May be afraid or embarrassed to wear Halloween costumes. • Sudden changes in a parent's or familiar caretaker's appearance (change of dress or new haircut) may upset her.	• Objectify: "I know you have a hard time wearing something new, but let's give this sweater a try." Or, shorter, "I know this is new for you." • "When you're ready. I'd love to see how this looks on you. For now, I'll just put it in your drawer/shelf/closet."	• Don't take it personally! Don't get frustrated and give in to your child's withdrawal with an ultimatum or bribe. Talk about his feelings with him and develop strategies to deal with his shyness: just communicating what he is going through can help. • Present new things when your child is rested. Keep *your* enthusiasm at a minimum. An offhanded manner puts less pressure on him. Take him shopping and let him help choose. • Put new clothing in her closet or drawer, and let her get used to it. • Don't let grandparents or relatives give clothing as a present; they won't get an enthusiastic response, and might be hurt. You are not dictating their choice of gift; you are trying to assure a happy, natural response to them. • For Halloween, use face paint and call it a night. Or, let her carry her crown in her hand while wearing her regular clothing. She'll likely enjoy costumes when she's older and can join in with peers.
Distractibility Has trouble concentrating and paying attention, especially if not really interested; doesn't "listen"; tunes you out; daydreams; forgets instructions.	• Has trouble getting dressed and following the morning schedule, gets distracted by sibling's toys. • Loses clothing. Has difficulty bringing clothes home from school and friends' houses. • May "forget where she put her shoes" and then "can't find them" even with directions. • Can throw a tantrum if clothes take too long to put on.	• "It's hard to get focused when you just got up. Need help getting dressed?" "Oh, you left your jacket? I know it's really hard to remember when you're having such a good time. Let's call XYZ and track it down." • "Boy, this clothing is hard to put on. Let me help you." Or "Let's put something else on."	• Establish eye contact when asking something, or checking on him. *Keep it short and simple.* Avoid irritability or sarcasm. Routinize. Lay clothes out the night before. Buy duplicates of problem basics like sweat jackets. • Avoid complicated clothing. Avoid multiple closures, double laces. • Avoid closets and drawers crammed full of clothing. It's too confusing. • Check lost-and-founds and friends' homes frequently.

Difficult Temperamental Trait:	How It Shows Up in Dressing	What to Say	Solutions
Irregularity Unpredictable. Can't tell when he'll be hungry or tired; conflict over meals and bedtime; wakes up at night; moods are changeable; has good or bad days for no obvious reason.	• Clothing preferences change daily. Says "I have nothing to wear" with a full closet. • Goes shopping with you and buys something she loves one day. Hates it and won't wear it the next. • Goes through phases of different preferences frequently. (Likes clothing short, likes it long. Likes it tight, like it loose. Likes it classic, likes it "cool.")	• "Gee, you loved this yesterday. I guess you're in a different mood today. Let's put it away for now. • "Oh, you're having a hard time picking out an outfit today. Let's go in and find something really weird/great/cool. What about your …"	• (Routines and schedules are very important with both irregularity and distractibility) • Categorize and clean out the closet. This really works. New clothes appear. • Shop locally. Keep tags on new clothing till they've been finally "accepted." Avoid catalogue clothing for this child. • Don't react immediately to clothing requests. If requests continue, take them seriously. • Round up hand-me-downs from other families for a wide possibility of choice. But keep the closet organized. Hand-me-downs are not as homogeneous as those bought for a first-born and too many can be overwhelming. • Keep favorites of the moment clean, if possible. Put clothing that is out of favor out of sight. Bring it out at a later date. By then it will be new again. • Use humor if they are locked in. • Consider your child may be overtired.

I believe that many difficult children have a vivid and unusual creative imagination. In part this is because they seem to be more in touch with how they feel. It's as if their more intense temperament has made them more aware of their responses. The circuits are open and the result is that the children seem freer, more open, empathetic, creative, and exuberant.

. . . They can be more individualistic, more in touch with themselves and less conformist than their nondifficult peers. In short, the chance for a wonderful mix of specialness and intensity often results with these kids.

—Stanley Turecki, M.D., The Difficult Child

LEARNING PROBLEMS AND THE DRESSING PROCESS

Another tack to take not only with the fussy dresser but with every child is to watch not only *what* your child wears, but also *how* he uses clothing in the dressing process. It may help to alert you early on to any learning or organizational problems. According to Judith Schneider, Assistant Director of the Stephen Gaynor School in New York City, and an educational therapist in private practice for sixteen years, many skills required for dressing reflect a child's learning style. And every child's learning style is different. The advantage to observing your child's dressing habits is that many of the skills involved in getting dressed are the same ones your child is trying to master in school. The four main learning skills necessary to successfully manage the dressing process are:

1. *Sequencing.* This is the ability to go from A to B to C to Z, to be able to see the proper placement of things in *space* and to be able to understand the proper order of events in *time*. A child with *temporal* sequencing problems would have problems understanding the timing of events, such as what comes first, what comes in the middle, what comes last. She'd have trouble with the order of putting on clothes or managing the morning schedule to get out of the house. In dressing, *spatial* sequencing relates mostly to recognizing right and left in putting on shoes, or, with clothing, knowing front and back and inside or out. In school, sequencing is a skill that can most dramatically affect learning how to read: You need spatial sequencing to go from left to right on the page, and temporal sequencing to remember the words you read at the beginning of the sentence by the time you get to the end of the sentence. You need these not only to decode the meaning of each word, but to be able to string them together for the full meaning of the whole sentence. A child with difficulty sequencing might not easily be able to tell what day it is or when the weekend is coming.

2. *Fine motor skills.* The ability to use the fingers, as opposed to the hands or arms, in an agile way is necessary to put on and take off all clothing. For a

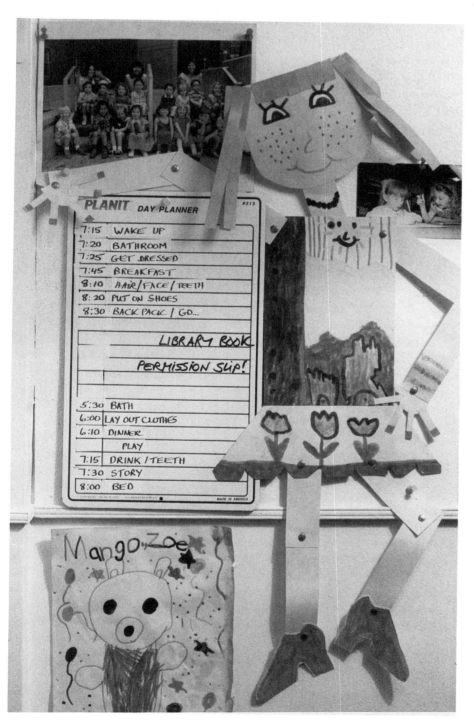

PLANIT DAY PLANNER #313

7:15	WAKE UP
7:20	BATHROOM
7:25	GET DRESSED
7:45	BREAKFAST
8:10	HAIR / FACE / TEETH
8:20	PUT ON SHOES
8:30	BACK PACK / GO...

LIBRARY BOOK

PERMISSION SLIP!

5:30	BATH
6:00	LAY OUT CLOTHES
6:10	DINNER
	PLAY
7:15	DRINK / TEETH
7:30	STORY
8:00	BED

Mango Zoe

A memory jogger for an overnight visit. Make a game out of a reminder list. Insert it into the overnight bag of your child who tends to lose his clothes.

child with problems in this area, buttoning and unbuttoning and shoelace tying and untying will be a continual challenge, taking him far longer than is usually necessary and maybe causing him tantrums of frustration when he's tired. Some children may take until eight, nine, or ten years old to feel comfortable with these tasks.

3. *Organizational ability.* This skill is often lacking in kids with learning problems. While children without these problems develop morning dressing routines themselves, kids with inner confusion can't do this autonomously. They have to be helped to create their own system unique to them. If parents are unaware of this kind of disability, the morning can be a very unhappy time—for their child, who's trying as hard as she can to get it together, and for an irritable parent in a hurry, who may see her as dawdling, not paying attention, or even lazy.

4. *Memory.* Most people may joke about their memory if they forget something, but when it comes to a child with a learning problem, it's no laughing matter. Memory problems, especially if undiagnosed, can lead to a lot of tension in the morning when everyone is trying to get out ("You *just* had your backpack a minute ago—*now* where is it?"). For kids with memory problems keeping track of items like sweatshirts which come on and off according to the weather, or remembering where in the house they put their shoes is a constant struggle. Such children are very aware of their problem, because nothing is immune, not even a favorite new baseball hat. It's easy for them to feel life is out of control and they must be doing something wrong if they can't even keep track of what they love.

JUDITH SCHNEIDER'S DRESSING STRATEGIES FOR THE CHILD WITH LEARNING PROBLEMS

If your child is having any kind of struggle in school, what you learn at home will help round out the picture and vice versa. And if there aren't any learning problems per se, the following information is invaluable for any parent who wants to reinforce the learning process going on at school with the child's clothes at home. Judith Schneider's number one rule is *routinize!*

1. Choose clothes that are easy to put on. "Just imagine how demoralizing it is to a child with fine motor problems to have to face his inadequacies first thing every morning before the day even starts," Schneider points out. Instead of "proper" buttoned shirts, use turtlenecks and be sure they are roomy enough at the neck. Or use knit collar-shirts that require only one button (or none): Button the lower one ahead—it will still fit over the head. Replace all laced shoes with ones that fasten with Velcro. Buy parkas

with zippers and Velcro plackets, and jeans or skirts with snaps, or elasticized-back waists, not buttons.

2. Help your child learn organization by categorizing clothing. Line clothes up according to category and subcategory. So pants can be sorted into pleated, sweat, and jeans, and skirts can be categorized as pull-on, cotton-knit, jean, printed, etc. Separate them with homemade cut out dividers and color-code them. This will reinforce categorizations your child is learning in school, such as the grouping of animals; as land, water, mountain, or desert; as grown-ups or babies; as farm or wild; etc. Mark drawers with pictures or drawings of what's inside. If it's winter, and one drawer has both short- and long-sleeved t-shirts (the first for indoor play), put a picture denoting not only the item, but the *season*—*summer* or *winter*. Keep the shirts in two piles. If it's 20 degrees outside and the child wants to wear a t-shirt, refer him to the pictures. ("Oh. That's an outside shirt for summer, not winter.") If your child tends to get spatially disorganized with too much visual clutter, consider putting doors over open shelves to reduce the visual stimulation.

3. **Lay out the clothes the night before—of course!** For many reasons, this is helpful. For any child with learning problems, all of the problems are frequently worse in the morning: there's the normal tension of getting out, plus it just takes this child longer to do things. Lay out the clothes in *early* evening or when your child is still fresh, *not* at the end of the evening, before bed when everyone is running out of steam. If you wait until bedtime when the child is already tired, you're just transferring the time of the argument. To reinforce sequencing skills, first, *talk over* with your child what comes first, etc. Then, *lay out* the clothes in the order of dressing, left to right on the floor, desk, or other surface, in the order that she's going to put them on. This will *visually* (and physically) support the *mental* order of getting dressed and reinforce the task of reading left to right.

4. Depersonalize early morning tension and set up an organizing center with a full-length mirror and a dry marker board. Near the kitchen is usually a good choice, or wherever everyone gathers. On the board, arrange columns for two checklists—one permanent and one changing. For instance, on the left, use permanent "reminder" sticker labels for the daily necessaries that never change in the schedule: wash face, brush teeth, comb hair, get dressed, check weather, backpack, lunch money, etc. Line them up in the sequence of the morning or evening schedule. The first thing to be done could be at the top, the second, underneath, and so on. On the right, use the unused part of the board to write in the daily changing needs: "permission slip signed for school trip," "athletic gear for after school," etc. The list depersonalizes everything. This means, for example, that they'll find it harder to be mad at *you* when, after checking the weather, they find they have to wear boots. (You might even have them check the weather the

"Jason could never keep track of his clothes. Even when we finally broke down and bought him the expensive school jacket he'd been dying for, he couldn't hold on to that—he actually lost it two days later! That's when I knew something was up. We had him tested at his school and it turned out he did have some learning disabilities, one of which, sequencing, plus poor memory, accounted for losing everything. It was a relief for me—and for him—to find out what was going on. Now I name-tag any important clothing. It was really that jacket that got me moving."

. . . .

"I really view my child's sense of style as a special talent. No one else looks like her—but somehow it works. She's not exceptional at math or reading, but when it comes to clothes, she's tops!"

. . . .

night before.) The full-length mirror is not just for vanity—it's also to depersonalize the morning rush. "Often learning disabled kids have no 'observant eye' and even after taking enough time may look disheveled. Instead of being negative by saying: 'You look sloppy—fix your shirt,' use the mirror to objectify: 'Take a look, honey,'" suggests Schneider.

5. Train your child's memory by making it easier to find her clothes. Figure out the problem items with her—the backpack, her shoes, the hairbrush, whatever. Then choose together accessible places where they are always kept. It makes it easy to keep those items locatable. Have a special hook where you always hang the backpack after coming home, or after homework. Definitely *don't* keep the shoes back in the closet somewhere—find a place right where the shoes get kicked off upon arrival. This could mean a space or little shelf near the front door or somewhere in the kitchen. Keep the hairbrush in a place that's logical in the sequence of the morning dressing routine. It may not be useful in the bathroom *before* the clothes are put on. It may be better in the child's room on a special shelf near her closet, for after dressing, in the kitchen, or even in the front hall on the way out.

Judith Schneider's final caveat: "Don't become so obsessive about your system that your child feels intimidated. Keep it light and warm. The point of the system is not to have a 'perfect' child or morning, but a happy one."

BIRTH ORDER

I can spot first-borns at forty yards. They look like they've stepped off the cover of Vogue *or* Esquire. *The second-borns look like they've stepped off the cover of* Field and Stream. *No matter what, the first two children in a family are always night-and-day different. The second will always be different from the first. First-borns have adults as their models. They're the buffers, shock absorbers for every other child on down. What the second-born child sees above is the model to be the opposite of. Especially if it's the same sex.*

—Kevin Leman, Ph.D., *author of* The Birth Order Book

. . . .

"I think the birth order in the family is significant. My first boy lives in jeans. My second prefers sweats. I think he wants to assert himself."

. . . .

Of course many children don't care one whit about their clothing. One mother told me that her second son would be happy "wearing a pillowcase with two holes cut out for his legs," and in the next breath talked about the "pillowcase" boy's older brother who happens to adore clothes. Is birth order coming into play here? Is younger brother asserting himself by being the opposite? Many parents feel that each of their children adopt specific styles in response to their siblings. I've noticed that often kids pick clothing in response to the person "in front" of them. One mother of six I know explained it this way: "My first is a jock in her choice of clothes, I guess like me—I live in sweats. The next girl is as girly as they come. My third is a boy—and he's just normal. Then my next two girls are just the reverse—the fourth child is frilly [is she asserting her femininity in reaction to the brother "in front" of her?], and the fifth child is a jock. Now the sixth—she's into her own thing—all different patterns of stripes and plaids with a connecting color, usually blue." Another interesting example is a first-born girl who is second in order to a first-born boy. She has not only her mother's wardrobe but a whole other set of different clothing references to react to—her brother's. She may feel equally comfortable with both "vocabularies"—ruffly dresses for a party as well as her older brother's coveted cast-off (and pilled!) Batman pajamas on a sleepover. Watching the clothing interaction between siblings can be fascinating and informative.

A child's clothing preferences can even have an effect on whether a child is more easily understood by a parent. One parent told me her little girl was "no problem—she's happy as long as she has her jewelry on." Even if a child is "easy" about clothing, it is often still interesting to see why and how they're "easy." For this little girl who's "no problem," her passion for accessories is something her fashion-conscious mom is proud of—she thinks it's fun and creative. In this instance an "easy" child is a matter of "good fit" between the child and her parents. However a problem fit may occur if another less fashion-conscious parent finds her preoccupation annoying, even very, very difficult to deal with. Such a family might view this little girl as "stubborn," not "creative," for her persistent noncomformity. For such a family, extra effort may be needed to appreciate and understand the daughter's preferences. Smart compromises may be necessary. Very real feelings of estrangement can build up on either side over the minor issues of clothing choices. Another example of how fit works would be a very active boy who adores army hats and the vigorous imaginative play that goes with them. He couldn't care less about his clothing. His style and behavior might be a real problem for first-time parents who live in a city apartment and who place high value on order, civility, and their antiques. But in a family of boys on a farm, his clothing style and high activity level would probably be fine, maybe even the norm of that more casual outdoors environment.

Clothing preferences and styles in preschool are as individual as the child and often as changeable as the choice of friends or favorite activities—and they may have nothing to do with the style of the parents! Keeping up with your child's changing tastes during this time of emerging identity is not always easy. My suggestion is: Keep the clothes they suddenly won't wear, as they may come back around in a month or two. Remove them from the closet temporarily (so choices remain simple) and return them at a later date when they may be "rediscovered." If not, what's the point of making an issue over it? There are other more important things to stand your ground on such as safety, manners, and bedtime.

FAMILY FIT

. . . .

"Andrea, my first, was obsessed with having skirts that twirl when she was three or four. She called them 'spin skirts.' It drove me crazy because they're so hard to find. She'd end up wearing the same one every day. I thought we'd never get through this phase, and I bought one whenever I spotted one in bigger sizes to be prepared. Of course, now there are lots sitting in hand-me-down boxes that she never wore when it was suddenly over.

. . . .

CLOTHES BASICS

Jeans

Most parents think of jeans as a basic, functional piece of clothing, and it is true that there is no fabric that can withstand wear and tear better than denim. However, nowadays, jeans have also become a fashion item that com-

A great-fitting pair of jeans lets Duncan show off his cartwheel. With an elastic waist and full leg, this design accommodates growth and assures a comfortable fit. Buy a size bigger and roll the cuffs. By Gap Kids.

bines the romance of the rugged cowboy image with the fashion savvy of European designers. In reality, jeans are also stiff, not that comfortable for kids who are used to knit fabrics, and they are not especially warm, unless lined in cotton or flannel. Every kid's dream is to get hold of a friend's hand-me-down jeans or jean jacket that is beat down by numerous washings. The trick is to find jeans that are designed with comfort in mind.

Tips: How to Fit Jeans

Look for jeans made in a lightweight denim with a full leg and elastic waist. Be sure to have your child bend and sit. Check the "rise," the distance from the waist to the crotch. Be sure it fits and is not too short. Also, check across the seat and around the leg, especially if your child prefers straight leg jeans. Check the fiber content of that type of jeans (have they been preshrunk?) so that the perfect fit—snug or loose—found at the store doesn't disappear with the first washing. For a child who needs or prefers a looser fit, or who is tall for his age, buy the next size up. For the tall child, who may not fill out the jeans in that next size, find a cool belt or roll up a bandana and use it as a scarf-belt. For the child with the preference for a looser fit, or who is built stockier in the middle and needs the next size for room only (not length), roll up the cuffs. You can add suspenders to both.

The Secret of the Gap's Success

Susan Fischer, one of the foremost children's clothing designers in the U.S., is the mother of a six-year-old boy. When she was Vice President of Design and Product Development for Baby Gap and Gap Kids here's how she described all the planning involved at the Gap to make a simple garment great. "We're all mothers here and we constantly talk about what we'd like to see. We consider our classic jacket and jeans to be the best fashion value for kids in our store. It's a utilitarian garment, but it's also fashion. We work on every detail to make it fit, and have the right attitude. We take pains to find the exact authentic copper or gunmetal for the rivets, or for the right look on the label. For durability, all the pressure points are triple-bar-tacked (stitched)—the corners of the pockets, insides of the pockets, and the end of the fly. The elasticized waist on our jean is practical but we made sure it was still something an older kid would wear, and while the fuller leg is more comfortable, it's European-looking at the same time. If we see a new, let's say, wider shape of leg at the bottom coming from Europe, it would have to work for both comfort and the look." Fischer is a stickler for American authenticity and has been known to travel to Boston to view Ivy League college rowing races or to New Mexico to track down authentically patterned and colored Indian blankets. Who knew so much went into designing such simple stuff?

"For the first two weeks of kindergarten, Jeremy refused to wear his new jeans. All he would put on were his summer bike pants and a big sweatshirt. I figured it was just because he wasn't really that cold. But actually he was too embarrassed to wear his jeans. He couldn't get the snap closed by himself after he went to the bathroom at school. I quickly taught him the old trick I'd learned growing up in Kentucky. Get your jeans shut by pressing your body against the wall and holding your thumb against the inside snap."

So what is the difference between the jeans you'll find at stores like the Gap and lower-priced stores? Lower-priced jeans that are not as durable make up for this in styling. You'll be amazed at the amount of "fashion" you can find—paint-splashed denim skirts, pockets that are lined in neon fabric, or bright motifs and playful mottos puff-printed on jackets. Often the details on this type of denim item, such as attached pockets, are not as sturdy as on the more expensive brands. If your child loves it so much that she wears it every day, you may see fraying pockets sooner than you want. If you don't need to hand it down, this may be no problem since kids do outgrow clothes quickly. If your child likes jackets roomy, as many primary school kids do, the jacket may last more seasons than you expect: it may be time now to spend a little more for better quality. For down-and-dirty outdoor play, or for handing down, a classic sturdy jean jacket without doodads, but in sturdy denim, and with reinforced stitching may be the answer. The appeal of denim is in its wide choice of price and look.

Gymnastics Wear

Gymnastics clothing is the new major influence in the clothing of primary school girls. The ethereal pull of the single romantic prima ballerina has been replaced by the more active, powerful image of team gymnastics. The Olympics and the accessibility of the sport (female gymnasts competing worldwide and seen on TV are at most fourteen or fifteen) have profoundly influenced the dreams and fantasies of little girls in the nineties. Savvy girls' bodywear designers understand this—it's all about feeling powerful, light, free, *and* part of a *team*.

Gymwear design has introduced body-conscious cuts and new, stronger color combinations to little girls. Pastels don't seem to click—brights have more impact for this dynamic sport, and they are often juxtaposed against black for even greater emphasis. As the surf look is cool for boys, gymwear is cool for girls. Away from the gym, favorite comfortable pieces often find their way into their everyday wardrobes: a skirt pulled on over a favorite leotard or capri leggings, whether it matches or not. In this case, the two C's apply: comfortable and "cool."

Shopping Tips on Buying Girls' Bodywear

➤ Best choice is found at mall stores such as K-Mart or Kids-R-Us. These stores specialize in this type of clothing because it's cheap (usually from $8 to $14 for a leotard) and fits in with the lower price range of their other clothing offerings. The advantage to the customer is that these items "turn" (sell) quickly and enable the store to bring in new looks frequently. This is one clothing category where the discount stores lead high-fashion stores. If you live in the city, specialty stores and department stores offer

Sweats: The Facts: Advantages and Disadvantages of Inexpensive and Quality Sweats

Inexpensive Sweats

Find these at mass merchandisers such as Sears and J. C. Penney for $11 and up, at discount and outlet stores, for as low as $7.

Advantages

- Best buy to clothe a child. You'll be able to afford several.
- Lighter in weight—better for warmer seasons.
- Thinner and lighter fabric. Good for kids who don't like bulk.
- Come with the latest popular logos and bright designs that kids love.

Disadvantages

- Pill after a few washings, stain easily, and hold static. (Wash them inside out.)
- Elastic cuffs, not a rib knit. You can't buy them a size bigger and roll them up for longer use; you'll have to buy them to fit now.
- More basic in color. Less choice of unusual colors, especially in solids.
- Often sold in sets when you may only need the top or bottom.

Quality Sweats

Find these at specialty stores like the Gap and department stores like Macy's, and in catalogues like Hanna Andersson, Biobottoms, and Franne's Kids for $18 to $24.

Advantages

- Roomy fit. Sweats that are cut wider can be worn for more than one season.
- 100 percent cotton or cotton/poly blends that last longer and are not likely to pill.
- Heavier-weight fabric, and sewn with double-needle stitching at the seams making for better durability.
- Available as separates, and with fashionable colors.
- High quality details such as hidden side-seam pockets, drawstrings, and triple-stitched waistbands. Can be handed down.
- Rib-knit cuffs on the pants let you buy larger sizes and roll them up for longer use.

Disadvantages

- More expensive. Watch for end-of-season sales and stock up on sizes if your budget is tight and you prefer this type.
- No motifs, few exciting appliqués.
- Heavier, more bulk. A very active child may feel inhibited or hot.

"My son used to insist that all he needed was a sweatshirt when it was below freezing outside. It was a daily fight all winter. So I decided to make it a family project. I put a thermometer outside his window. Then I made up a chart that listed every ten degrees outside. We cut out pictures of clothing that looked like his from catalogues and we made a game of figuring out what he needed to wear by trial and error. Every day when we came home, we'd tape pictures of the clothing he'd needed to wear for weather of that temperature onto the chart. He really got into charting the weather, and eventually only needed to look at the outside thermometer himself to get dressed."

The Shapes of Girls' Gymwear—Something for Everyone

Patricia Shea, one of the major designers of girls' bodywear in the U.S. and head designer at Jacques Moret Kids, says: "When shopping for girls' bodywear, don't worry about conventional rules. Buy it if it looks good on your child and she likes it. With such a body-conscious item, you should focus on positive remarks. 'Oh Sweetie, you look great in this one' is highly preferable to 'You shouldn't get this one because . . .' *Never* make your child feel she has any body problems! No one child's body is the same and they all develop at different rates, stretching out into different proportions at different times. They may have a thick waist at seven or eight and a wasp waist at twelve or thirteen. And a child who has stick legs could end up stocky at eighteen from participating in school sports." The following is Patricia's description of what each shape is best suited for:

1. Flutter sleeve leotard and matching skirt. One of the most available, attractive looks manufactured by the dance company Monacoe. This is a favorite often chosen by the preschooler who likes to wear skirts, and who is not yet old enough to take gymnastics seriously. The skirt is usually discarded after a few wearings—it's too cumbersome for gym. But it can be used for another sport such as ice skating. This is an expensive purchase, a best bet for a present from grandparents and especially worth it if there are younger girl siblings to hand it down to.
2. Skirted leotard. A feminine look. Chosen more often by younger preschool girls. The hip ruffle is flattering to the stocky child.
3. Sleeveless tank. Parents often feel this looks too much like a bathing suit, but it is the most comfortable and most practical for gymnastics.
4. Classic leotard. Practical with more upper-arm coverage for modesty. A real Olympic look when worn in striped patterns, long sleeved.
5. Unitard. For the more confident child who is not afraid to stand out, or for the active child for whom unencumbered comfort is everything. Useful as a base for costumes or as a winter layer for skating.
6. "Wrestler" leotard. A cute, harmless version of a teenage look, and a good value for all the detail. Most kids don't know this shape comes from wrestling. They're drawn to it because of the lively details.
7. Capri leggings (or bike pants) and cropped top. Practical, because with two pieces separate, it accommodates growth. Evaluate this look on your child's body. It may look too adult.

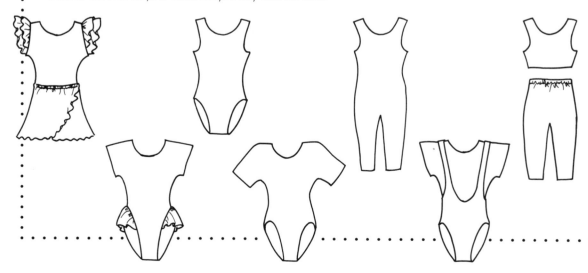

limited choices, if any. They tend to sell expensive versions of this look, usually three-piece outfits that aren't really as functional as a simple one-piece. Look in adult sports or gymwear stores that sell kids' sizes, and local kids' gyms that may have a corner where they sell a limited selection. This is one item you'd be hard-pressed to find in a catalogue.

➤ Look for a lined crotch. It's not so much for perspiration—kids don't sweat much at this age. It's because synthetic fabrics don't breathe. Often girls love gymwear so much that they want to wear it all day. Some children are susceptible to rashes if they haven't changed frequently enough. The normal time of a gym class is no problem. Gymwear made out of synthetics is cheapest, holds color the best, and wears longest. Pure cotton gymwear is harder to find and more expensive but breathes best.

➤ Avoid three-dimensional decorations on activewear. If your little girl doesn't want a plain look, look for puff-printing, stripes, or color inserts of fabric that lie flat and don't get in the way.

➤ Avoid footed tights. A child can slip. Footless tights or leggings and bare feet are preferable. If the weather is cold, buy her lightweight gymnastic slippers.

➤ A plain one-piece tank bathing suit is often a good pinch hitter for a gym class if it's in a solid or striped pattern. If it still fits from summer and she likes it, use it all winter.

A word about girls' gymwear worn as streetwear: This is the one area of girls' clothing where I feel parents have a special responsibility to monitor their child's freedom of expression. Because gymwear is made out of stretch fabric, it hugs the body. This second skin is necessary for gymnastics and other sports such as bike riding. And children love it because it's so comfortable. But when gymwear such as leggings, bike pants, and crop tops are worn outside the gym and on the street as many adults do, it's no longer only a matter of comfort. This clothing is often provocative. For children, the issue of appropriate clothing comes into play. Kids, on their own, do not have a discerning eye about this. Developmentally, they're not even aware of this issue at five or six years of age. What looks modest on one little girl can look inappropriately adult on another.

Young children have no idea about modesty. Their exuberant physical movements are not socialized yet. It's up to the parents to become sensitized to this issue and control it. The manufacturers won't. They contend their clothing is "fun" and "trendy" and any talk about modesty is called a "fifties mentality." I disagree. I have talked to many parents about this issue and most are aware of this problem: "I don't want my six-year-old walking around town like a little Lolita" or "Every bathing suit we tried on was cut up to her waist and she's only five years old."

Unfortunately, there are no hard-and-fast rules. It's not a case of the color black being too adult (although this color does often figure in). It's more a matter of parents using their visual instinct. What is the coloring of the child (is she plain or dramatic)? How does the clothing fit on the child (is she stick-like or curvy)? How does the child move physically in these particular clothes (is she reserved or very casual)?

Here are some of my tips on this subject:

1. Make a habit *as soon as* your child starts to wear stretchy leggings that a skirt *always* goes over them "for streetwear," any skirt. This will remedy most inappropriate looks.
2. Relegate certain gym outfits only to the gym. Be consistent and don't give in. Purchase other stretchy clothing that is more appropriate for the street.
3. Turn it into a learning experience. Show her the difference between how stretch fabrics work on the body versus stiffer woven fabrics. Explain as she gets older about why you care about her wearing gym clothes in a certain way.
4. Let her wear them however she wants to at home, on play dates.
5. If you're watching TV and some (probably most!) of the female characters are dressed in sexy stretch clothing, or your child sees someone on the street in a provocative outfit, talk about it with your child. Find out what she thinks it means. Discuss particular ways the outfit could be made more appropriate. Include sons in this discussion.
6. Remain positive and nonjudgmental.

Modern thinking on dressing twins states that dressing them differently fosters individual identities. Jamie and Erika's mother started out dressing her twins identically, then branched out into identical outfits, but different colors. She's deciding as she goes along. (Note: Large collars are flattering to babies and young children. They balance the size of the head, which is larger in proportion to the body.)

TWINS AND MULTIPLE BIRTHS

grew up as a twin at a time when it was unusual to dress twins differently. My mother had a progressive pediatrician who suggested my twin sister and I go to different schools. With different school uniforms and different friends during the week, for all practical purposes, we lived our lives as single-borns. So on the weekend and for parties I *liked* dressing the same: it emphasized the special connection we had that I couldn't express during the week. We had the freedom to make the choice ourselves, because in our carefully separated existence, we didn't have to face the daily frustration of being mistaken for one another.

Today, dressing twins and triplets identically flies in the face of conventional child-rearing wisdom. Today's thinking is that if you dress your multiple babies differently from the beginning, you'll be more likely to encourage each child's separate sense of identity. Practically speaking, it will make telling them apart easier. You may think you'll just have a little fun in the beginning dressing these two womb-mates identically, and then change over when they get a little older. However, many parents tell me that once the pattern of dressing alike is started, it is a hard habit to break. By allowing the multiples a choice of clothing, you can encourage them to assert their own likes, dislikes, and separate personalities in a very concrete way.

Clothing sends a message to the world about how we view ourselves; in the case of multiples it's transmitted in stereo. Your twins or triplets may get used to all the attention they attract when dressed alike, and they may even come to regard it as approval. They may also think that this attention pleases their parents. This is all very confusing to a twin who's trying to carve out his or her own identity. Most of us take it for granted that when we walk up to a friend, we'll be called by the correct name. Identical twins don't have that guarantee: they have to work for that automatic identification as they grow up. So if your twins are regularly dressed in their own clothing, family, teachers, and friends will learn to tell them apart.

In my discussions with child-care experts and mothers of twins over the years, I've learned that when you dress your twins alike, you're more likely to compare them, perhaps fostering competition. You may find yourself unconsciously assigning distinguishing personality traits that can be perceived by you and the children as good or bad. Other siblings in the family will often see the identically dressed twins as an impenetrable clique, and feel left out. By dress-

"In my twins' group, I noticed that the first-time parents were more likely to dress their kids identically. I was already aware of the distinct personality of my older first child, which made me look automatically for the differences, not the similarities, in the twins."

"With my twins, less is more. Less clothing, less laundry!"

ing your twins or triplets alike, you are sending a subtle message to yourself and others that these kids are actually alike and interchangeable.

The challenge when dressing multiple-birth children is to be organized, then to create an environment that allows for the development of each child's separate and distinct personality. One way many parents start is to color-code each twin's clothes when they're infants. By using two different color schemes, parents are able to remember which piece of clothing goes with each child. If you have multiple girls, try pink on one, purple on the second, and turquoise

"I always thought that Jessie looked better in red, and that's why I seemed to always dress him in it. Then I realized that Dylan looked just as great in red. It dawned on me that since Jessie was the smaller and quieter twin, my putting him in red was a way of making him look bigger and more outgoing—more equal to his brother. Even I had some subconscious urge to see them as the same, or at least as equally powerful, something I've tried hard to keep other people from doing!"

Identical twins as individuals. Dressing twins alike or differently is considered an identity issue. The current theory on dressing identical or fraternal twins emphasizes that twins should dress differently from the start to foster their own separate identities. Jesse and Jake's mother has done just that. Both are wearing the same shirts over turtlenecks, their cool weather uniform, but in different colors. Both have different jackets with the same coverage. The only thing the same: their shoes. You can't argue with the best fit. Because the boys were second-borns, she'd had the experience of parenting already and was able to see them as individuals from the start. Parents of first-born twins more often fall into the pattern of seeing (and dressing) their identical twins as the same, until their personalities emerge later.

Jacqueline and Tiffany are an exception to the "dressing twins differently" theory. They choose to celebrate their twinness, and dress alike for now. This is their choice and their parents are flexible and respect it. Jacqueline and Tiffany at school. Because they wear uniforms all day, every day, most of their life is spent not viewed as twins. Clotheswise they are just like all of their classmates.

> *"I offer my two boys a choice between the clothes I buy them. Once they decide, that shirt or pants then belongs to one or the other. If they want to swap, that's their business. I also keep a special bin of 'share clothes' that either child can take as they please."*

or yellow on the third. This way you'll always be able to grab the right piece of clothing when dressing your triplets and friends and family won't mistake who's who. Also, your toddlers can recognize their own clothing by the color. For example, one twin might always wear red and green and the other twin, royal blue and yellow. As they get older, say three or four, and their tastes start developing, you won't need the color-coding, and in fact it will be impossible to keep up.

As a twin, and as the mother of two girls close in age, I suggest a neutral approach about dressing alike or different. Some twins or triplets seem to thrive on staying separate from each other, while others develop very individual personalities sticking happily together. The key is to listen to your children—*you* and *they!* are the experts in this case.

Tips

➤ All parents of twins and triplets name the washer and dryer as their single most important investment. Explore all possible ways to get a washer and dryer into your home before the birth of multiples.

Jacqueline and Tiffany on the weekend. On their own time, they choose to "be twins," something they're not during the week. Their individual tastes come through with accessories or a change of hairdo.

➤ The mother of multiples needs to become an efficiency expert. And you need twice the patience of the single-birth parent. Talk to other parents of twins to learn time- and hassle-saving systems that work. It is the little things—the attention to detail and organization—that will make life easier for the mother of twins.

➤ Change gifts of matching outfits into different outfits simply by having the twins wear the matching outfits at different times. You can also sew on different appliqués, embroider the names, or dye them different colors.

➤ Multiple-birth babies tend to be smaller than the single-birth baby, and they get lost in the newborn sizes for average-birthweight babies. This is

. . . .

"I don't keep my triplets' clothing in their room upstairs. They spend all their time playing in the living room on the ground floor, so I had shelves installed in a section of the coat closet in the front hall for their daytime stuff. Since it takes so long to get three little kids ready to go out, this way two can play while the other is getting dressed. It cuts down on me having to keep running upstairs for missing items."

. . . .

one case when size "three months" in layette is truly useful. You can just wait for the twins to grow into these clothes, or, if the fit is important to you, Mother Care has a wide selection of clothing made specifically for tiny newborns.

➤ Use the Mothers of Twins clubs to get great used clothing at great prices. The clubs that are located in affluent areas will have superior quality clothing, so it's worth it to look for those clubs. Look in your local telephone book or ask your pediatrician.

➤ Put the socks on first! Your children's attention span is short, and socks are very difficult to get on the feet of two squirming children at the tail end of the dressing process.

➤ Find reversible garments (sweatshirts with popular characters and cotton jackets are usually available). You can buy two and dress twins alike or not, whatever you and they prefer that day.

➤ Buying clothes from a coordinated grouping is a way for twins to be differently dressed but still connected (if they want to be). Buying different styles in the same pattern is one way to do this. For example, you might choose a checked pair of pants for one and a skirt in the same check for the other, or any number of combinations.

➤ Separate drawers are a good idea for older twins, who need to know the boundaries between themselves. However, maintaining one drawer for basics has proven to be a good idea for those clothes that the twins use interchangeably, such as underwear, socks, and PJs.

➤ Before the birth of your multiples, read *Siblings Without Rivalry*, authored by Adele Faber and Elaine Mazlish. This will put you miles ahead by explaining—in words and actions—how to minimize competition and encourage the unique gifts of each child.

Things to Consider when Dressing Twins and Triplets

Dressing Alike

1. They'll stand out—people will look and comment more.
2. One of the identical outfits may be dirty or lost.
3. You may end up paying full price most of the time. It's difficult to find identical clothes on sale, and if you do, watch out: they may have been passed over for a good reason. Best source for secondhand identical twins' clothes is a Mothers of Twins club.
4. One twin may be larger or smaller than the other. You'll have to become an early-bird shopper to find the same outfits in different sizes.
5. Twins may feel like dressing in something different.

Dressing Differently

1. It's often hard to find outfits that are equally attractive. You'll need discipline and time to keep searching for comparable clothes that won't shortchange either of them.
2. If you assign a different, predominant color to each child's wardrobe, choose colors that enhance your children's colorings equally.
3. Both children may prefer the same color. If so buy totally separate outfits, not the same outfit in different colors.
4. Sometimes you'll have to just leave a great outfit on the rack because there isn't another that's equally appealing.

"My two-and-a-half-year-olds are fraternal. But I definitely take pains to dress them differently when they're around their own friends. Even though they're not identical, some of the little kids still get mixed up and call them by the wrong name."

Boots that encourage autonomy. This popular boot has rubber handles designed right in. Any age child from toddler on up can now pull on her own boots. Get it in the color combination that is light-colored at the sole. You or your child can mark her name in indelible ink to distinguish hers from others.

OUTERWEAR

Y

COLD WEATHER BABIES

our infant's clothing and outerwear needs vary according to season and climate. And layering is the key to cold weather dressing. The air between the layers provides extra insulation and a layer or two can be removed to accommodate a temperature rise during the day. The coming-home-from-the-hospital basics for a Northeastern baby born in late spring are diapers, short-sleeved undershirts, nightgowns, stretchies and/or creepers, receiving blankets, cotton socks or booties, and a cotton hat. A fall or winter baby in the same climate requires a slightly different wardrobe—*long*-sleeved undershirts and tights, stretchies (no creepers), a sweater and warm hat, socks or booties, and a waterproof snowsuit. It will cost more to clothe the fall or winter baby than a spring or summer newborn.

Bunting or Pram Bag

The most expensive article you need to buy is a snowsuit, pram bag, or bunting. For cool weather—spring, fall, and winter—keep baby comfortable in a bunting made of fleecy fabric like Polarplus. This is a plush polyester that looks just like wool but is nonallergenic and luxuriously soft. It stays warm when wet, dries quickly, and draws moisture away from wet skin. For really cold winter weather, protect baby with an insulated suit with a wind-resistant and water-repellant nylon outershell that is filled with either down or polyester material. It frequently has arms, a hood, and a bag-like bottom. A less popular version has no arms (less popular because trying to get a grip on a bagged infant

The three-in-one down snowsuit from the Company Store catalogue goes from infancy through toddlerhood and adjusts to weather changes. One size fits six to eighteen months. Buttoned closed with a separate piece inserted inside on the bottom as a bunting bag for a very young baby. (To fit carseats, snap into legs.)

Snapped into legs as a snowsuit for a mobile toddler. Arms and hat are removed for less frigid weather.

is like trying to hold a watermelon—you need the "arm handles"). If you *do* choose a bunting with arms, avoid lifting your baby under his arms—he's too little to support his body weight himself. Some buntings have two pieces: the under-bag, which is lightweight, and an outer bag layer for very cold weather. Most buntings feature a loop for the carseat, baby seat. Check to see if this conforms to your own carseat or stroller—often they don't. A bunting zips up the front or sides. It's easy to get baby in and out of, keeps the baby snug and secure, but usually only lasts for about three months (with the exception of the three-in-one snowsuit, shown at right from the Company Store) until your baby becomes more mobile. Then it's time to move on to a snowsuit with legs. Some parents bypass the bunting entirely and buy a snowsuit their infant can grow into.

Baby Bag^R

Baby Bag^R

This baby snowsuit was designed by Elizabeth Andrews for her extremely active five-month-old girl who "screamed whenever she saw the snowsuit coming—she *hated* having her arms put through the sleeves." To avoid the tantrums (as they lived in Maine, these happened frequently!), Elizabeth made her own design with no arms so her baby could be slipped in and out quickly without the struggle of the sleeves. The arms were free to move around together *inside* the suit and there were no more tantrums. The added bonus was that all the activity inside the suit generated more body heat than if the arms were separated in sleeves, on the same principle as happens in a mitten as opposed to a glove (see Gloves, page 126), causing extra heat to rise from the suit and warm baby's face. Chapped cheeks, common in the cold of Maine for babies, are happily prevented.

Now, Andrews markets these suits everywhere, most notably in the L.L. Bean catalogue. She explains the suit's unusual shape: "The suit is designed so that you lift the baby from the bottom—one arm lifts the baby, the other supports his back, so there's no stress on the baby's arms [thus avoiding the slippery watermelon problem of a regular armless bunting]. The legs are designed [in a high "W"] primarily to fit easily into any stroller, carseat, or front and back carrier. The bag just slips right in and any restraining straps can be safely secured. The top zips down and adjusts to drape open around the baby's shoulders so the arms are totally free when inside the car or home. There are three sizes. If your baby is born right at the start of the cold season, 'Small' (birth to five months) is best—newborns prefer the cozy, secure feeling. Because a newborn is so tiny, the middle size is too roomy—he will slide around too low in the bag. 'Medium' (three to twelve months) usually fits babies born earlier in the year who are larger by cold weather, and 'Large' (five months to two years) is designed specifically to last into toddlerhood. Some toddlers live in climates where the ground is too icy and slippery to walk, so the Baby Bag^R will still be useful."

HOW TO CHOOSE AN INFANT SNOWSUIT

The most important consideration in buying an infant snowsuit is your climate and lifestyle:

Carmen Nieves, a children's clothing retailer for twenty-five years at Morris Bros., N.Y.C., gave me this perspective about buying a snowsuit. Do you drive everywhere and will your infant go from house to car to store, so you'll be dressing and undressing her constantly? Or do you spend hours a day walking around outside with your infant just bundled up in a stroller by herself, or close to you in a front pack carrier? Can your finances support the purchase of a bunting for the first few months, before switching to a snowsuit that may or may not fit next season? Exactly how many weeks or months of very cold weather can you expect?

The snowsuit is made out of either down, poly-filled nylon, quilted material, or fleecy fabric like Polarplus. It has legs, arms, and a hood. The one-piece type has either one zipper down the front or double zippers running from the neck down the front, slightly past the hips to the legs. The two-piece snowsuit has bibbed snow pants that resemble overalls and a hooded jacket. There are also one-piece snowsuits that have removable booties and mittens that make it possible for the child to wear the snowsuit when she starts walking.

Plenty of parents zip their newborns into a one-piece snowsuit from the start and let them gradually fill out the casing. This is cost-efficient, at least, and certainly not harmful to the immobile baby (who doesn't know how funny he looks in the carriage lost in the folds of a toddler snowsuit) but it may not be as cozy as most newborns like. When the child starts walking, you need to be careful of buying too big: snowsuits can't just be rolled up in anticipation of next year's growth. I know it's tempting to buy big, because snowsuits are so expensive but a too-large snowsuit will make movement difficult and even dangerous for the child who's still a little unsteady on his feet. Try to locate a hand-me-down from a friend, or look in school and church bazaars for second-hand snowsuits. Snowsuits don't get worn out very easily because kids only wear them during the few months of cold weather and outgrow them so fast. If your baby is born in March and you expect only a few more weeks of average cold, you can layer like crazy and achieve the same effect as a snowsuit, without wasting money on an item that will only be worn a few times. "If your child is born in the fall, you'll have to use the snowsuit from November to March," said Ms. Nieves, "and it will only last that first year. However, if your child is born in January, February, or March, I suggest you buy one quite large with legs that would fit a toddler. You'll only need it for a few weeks' wear. Then put it away. It will be fine for next year, and best of all, because it's late in the season, you can get it on sale."

The best rule of thumb to follow in layette winterwear is the advice most pediatricians give:

The Double-Zippered Snowsuit. A popular choice for quick exits and entrances. For total protection, zip up all the way, slightly over baby's chin. In less cold weather, unzip partially, and tuck excess fabric back inside, under itself, to expose baby's chin. The winter snowsuit booties and mittens snap or side button to the snowsuit so they can be added or subtracted according to need.

1. Don't overdress your baby. This is sometimes hard to avoid for first-time parents and is the most common cold-weather misconception. The rule of thumb is: dress your baby as you would yourself with the Patagonia tip in mind (see below). Midwinter prickly heat is not uncommon for overdressed babies.

2. Always use a hat, especially if it's windy, even if *you* don't feel the need to wear one. Most babies are bald (or almost) and their scalps have many blood vessels through which body heat can be lost rapidly. Knitted pullovers (balaclavas) that cover the neck and tuck into the snowsuit are ideal.

Safe Winter Layering for Babies and Toddlers Depends on Their Activity Level, Not Yours

Older children catch on quickly to layering their clothes for changing temperatures and exertion. When they get hot, they peel off a layer. When they get cold, they put on a layer or zip their jackets up to their chins. When babies and toddlers get too hot or cold, they can't tell you about their discomfort except by body language—anything from quiet fusses and fidgets to scrunched up little red-faced screams.

Consider the difference between baby's activity as a passenger and your exertion as a means of transport. Jogging behind a stroller or cross-country skiing with a child on your back generates body heat and keeps you warm. Your child, however, with minimal activity, may be losing vital heat. Until children are old enough to express their specific needs, they depend entirely on you to monitor them and select the right clothing. The pay-off will be a comfortable and happy child who early on can discover the pleasures of the outdoors.

—Patagonia Catalogue, Fall–Winter, 1990–91

The Bibbed Snowsuit in Soft Polar Fleece with Jacket. The jacket can be removed or used separately for warmer temperatures. From Baby Bag^R

We're understandably concerned with protecting our children from being too cold and exposed, as well as from being too hot and uncomfortable. I've found a lot of first-time parents tend to overdress their children because they're nervous about their kids catching cold. You've probably seen children looking like little snowmen in their overstuffed snowsuits, hardly able to wave their arms.

When my first child turned four she seemed to think it was always summer, no matter how cold it was outside. After a lot of arguments and deals ("Okay, but the first time you get a cold, you're wearing this! *And* wearing what I want you to wear the rest of the winter!"), she never did catch cold, and I realized

TODDLERS AND SCHOOL-AGE CHILDREN

she was perfectly comfortable in her minimal layers. Some school-age kids don't seem to feel the cold in the same way adults do. However, toddlers' bodies *do* lose heat more quickly than adults' do. "Dressing kids for cold weather can be tricky," the Patagonia Fall 1990 catalogue points out. "The youngest can't tell you how they feel and must be monitored for chill or overheating. The older ones catch on quickly to layering but have strange little quirks only their intergalactic-plasma decoders can decipher. Throw in activity and weather conditions, and winter gear can indeed seem complex. You need to consider individual tolerances, levels of activity and prevailing weather conditions."

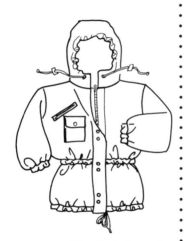

The ideal shape of jacket for a toddler: Maximum coverage over the rear end with the bulk of fabric controlled by a drawstring waist.

Here's how the Hermann family layers their primary school-aged kids for skiing in mid-winter Vermont:

1. thermal long underwear (or tights)
2. sweatpants
3. ski pants
4. turtleneck
5. flannel shirt
6. light sweater
7. down vest (optional under ski jacket)
8. ski jacket
9. cotton socks
10. thermal socks
11. cowl neck scarf (or "neck gaiter"—the warmth of a scarf, the comfort of a sweater)
12. pile mittens with nylon shell

Tips

➤ Know your climate. Speak to your pediatrician about children and cold weather if you need guidance as to what is appropriate dressing for your area. Individual tolerances vary (some kids don't get as cold as others), as do prevailing weather conditions. And the same temperature on a calm day can be experienced as colder on a windy day.

➤ Keep the jackets simple. Very young children only want to be comfortable and flexible. Fashion becomes an issue later in primary school.

➤ Evaluate how warm you need the items to be. Do you need fail-safe 100 percent down? Can you get away with 100 percent poly-filled nylon? Or do you need a combination of both? (See the "down" paragraph on page 123.)

➤ It's not necessary to spend a huge amount of money on a jacket for a child between toddler and age six—children grow through sizes so very quickly, that sometimes they'll go through two different size jackets in one season. You may want to spend more on a better make of coat if you plan to make it a hand-me-down.

Make up your own skating outfit. All little girls want to wear short skirts in 20-degree weather just like they see on TV. Here is how to do it without having your child freeze: Any skirt from a gym outfit or a knit full skirt that you already own can be used. (If it goes to the knees, prepare to shorten it!) Make it special with leg warmers (adult ones from the dime store), layered for warmth and color. Most little girls don't care if the top matches the skirt, or even if it's covered by a sweater, as long as they're wearing "that" skirt. Bundle her up on top, and layer her legs on the bottom. (Note: Spray-paint stripes on her skates to match her outfit. It's an easy way to find her skates among the many at the rink, and a special gift to the next recipient. The best place to find hand-me-down skates is at school fairs.)

➤ Pick the right jacket for the appropriate activity. Don't buy an expensive brown leather aviator jacket (or even a knock-off) and expect it to last like a nylon parka if your child wears it to play rough-and-tumble games outside.

Jackets mean more than just warmth to the primary school child. Arriving at first grade, boys like jackets that give them identity and connect them to their peers, or at least don't distance them from them, by being too high-style or by being too obviously the choice of a parent. Eddie's leather jacket is like his dad's, while Brian's school letterman jacket signifies he's now a big boy in elementary school. In outerwear, the yearly fashion trend is reflected in styling and color. The quality consideration is, however, always the same: How well is the garment made? How long will it last? The only real issues in the lengths of jackets, aside from fashion, are warmth and preference. Kids' jackets and coats come in the following lengths:

1. *Bomber—to waist. Not the warmest. But a look.*
2. *Hipster—below waist, to hip. Manageable for rigorous play in the field or park.*
3. *Stadium—popular especially for the toddler and preschooler because it has maximum coverage (over the rear end) and is still flexible enough to play in.*
4. *Knee length—also called car coat length. Not for play. Usually the length for a navy dress coat.*
5. *Boot length—cumbersome. Only for frigid weather.*

Jackets and coats start to become a fashion issue in the early primary school years, when six- and seven-year-olds become acutely aware of what their peers are wearing. For boys, especially, there seem to be prescribed, unspoken rules of jacket fashions. And boys aren't always guided by what we adults consider common sense. I've seen boys choose jackets in the bomber style that come only to the waist, providing no coverage to the rear end, and then wear them with a thin pair of jeans even in freezing temperatures. However, it's unlikely that kids are such slaves to fashion that they'd suffer, even to look cool. So you can be sure a child will come in to change if he gets uncomfortable.

Now, a word about down jackets. Down jackets *can* be washed in the washing machine. Down is lightweight yet very warm, and keeps the body temperature even because it allows moisture to escape. Polyester looks thinner than down but actually weighs more; since it doesn't allow moisture to escape, the child can get clammy and overheated. Because of its high price, down remains a matter of personal preference based on your winter outerwear needs. If you choose down, you may want to order through companies like the Company Store catalogue or local specialty stores that specialize in selling down goods directly from their factory to the customer (see catalogue list, page 232). Some children are thought to be allergic to down. They may be in fact just allergic to down that has not been cleaned thoroughly. Many parents laud Company Store down jackets for the lack of allergic reaction.

. . . .

"She was a December baby, so I'd stick her in a stretchie, then the Snugli, then zip her up under the sweatshirt jacket I'd used for maternity. That sweatshirt turned out to be my favorite piece of layette. Instead of doing battle with the squirming chicken in a snowsuit, I bundled her up under that oversized sweat jacket, then my winter coat.

. . . .

EVERYTHING YOU EVER WANTED TO KNOW ABOUT SNOWSUITS FOR THE TODDLER TO SEVEN-YEAR-OLD CHILD

➤ Still the most popular choices are two kinds of snowsuits: the two-piece with overalls and jacket, and the one-piece with a single or double lengthwise zipper. The only difference from the infant version is that, since the child is now walking, the feet are not enclosed. The two-piece is most versatile because the jacket can be worn by itself when it's not so cold, or can be removed indoors for comfort without having to remove the entire suit. The one-piece single zipper type assures total insulation, requires fewer steps to get on and up, but must be completely removed for indoor comfort.

➤ Buy snowsuits only one or two sizes larger or they'll completely overwhelm your child and make movement difficult.

➤ If you buy a two-piece snowsuit, make sure the chest bib is *high enough* to keep the child warm if the jacket becomes undone. Look for adjustable straps on the bib so you can lengthen it and add another season to the life of the snowpants.

➤ Elastic-waist pull-on pants are frequently part of a snowsuit set, but it's not as useful as a bibbed pant. The built-in suspendered shoulders with the bib, both front and back, prevent shirts from coming out. With nonbibbed regular style pants, it is not uncommon to see parts of a toddler's bare back

"It could be twenty degrees out and my boys would each have on a long-sleeved t-shirt, a sweatshirt, and an unzipped jacket and be happy as clams. And even though I knew they were fine, I'd still be embarrassed. I always felt like people were thinking, 'Look at that kid, he's going to freeze, what a terrible mother!' But honestly, I've learned. My kids just don't get cold."

completely exposed in frigid weather after *every* layer of clothing on top has pulled out of his pants. Often a parent is carrying him in his arms completely unaware. If you already own nonbibbed pants, you can remedy this with a pair of suspenders attached to the pants to keep the shirts in, or use a longer jacket.

➤ Zippers on kids' jackets often have a short lifespan. Look for the coats and jackets that have a zipper as well as additional snaps, buttons, or Velcro. This feature helps you get by if you're at the end of the season and the zipper goes.

➤ European snowsuits run larger than the American sizes. American snowsuits often don't seem to take into consideration the clothing underneath.

➤ Check all adorable, printed snowsuits for pliability. The printing process stiffens the fabric and you may be sacrificing softness for style. This applies to treated cotton chintzes, nylon prints, and even the very expensive European snowsuits.

Tips: How to Get Your Very Young Child to Put On a Cold Weather Jacket

1. Put his hand on a cold, closed window or out an open window and let him feel how cold it is outside.

2. Take the jacket with you and carry it outside. Even an older kid may have a hard time imagining how cold it is outside when she's still inside. When she feels the reality of the cold, she'll ask for her jacket without protest and you'll have avoided a fight.

3. Be mindful of reasons for the resistance, such as uncomfortable details your child is unable to tell you about. Is the sleeve too tight to accommodate a bulky sweater? Is it wide enough across the chest and loose enough under the arm? Does it push the child's neck up uncomfortably when it's zipped to the chin? The Patagonia catalogue for kids (see catalogue list on page 234) hilariously describes this last syndrome as tender young skin being "repeatedly stabbed with tiny ends of dry spaghetti."

4. Sometimes kids just don't want to put on their heavy jackets for the simple reason they're too tired and it takes too much effort. This can occur at *any* time of day! In this case, help them with it instead of pushing them to do it themselves.

"I put the Bert and Ernie key chains on my twins' jacket zippers. This keeps one entertained while I'm putting the jacket on the other one, and I think it's really encouraged them to want to learn to zipper their jackets themselves."

5. Find some feature on the garment that's special and relates to something they like. One mother doesn't even call the item a jacket; she calls it "camping gear," saying she wished she'd had this kind of coat when she was young, and tells why. A family story may do the trick.

6. The start of the fall season is a time when children may have the most difficulty putting on coats. Coats are unpleasant reminders that summer is really over and very young children can have seasonal transition problems. Have a talk with your child about the changes of seasons and the start of school. Acknowledging his loss may help. Teachers say it usually takes till

mid- to late October for children to feel acclimated to being in school again.

7. Consider using a heavy sweater with a quilted vest rather than a heavy, stiff jacket.

8. Check out what the other kids are wearing. A primary school child is starting to feel peer pressure now, and her jacket may be different from all her friends'. Try to make allowances for this.

9. If it's dangerously cold, explain firmly that you're not giving in this time, and why.

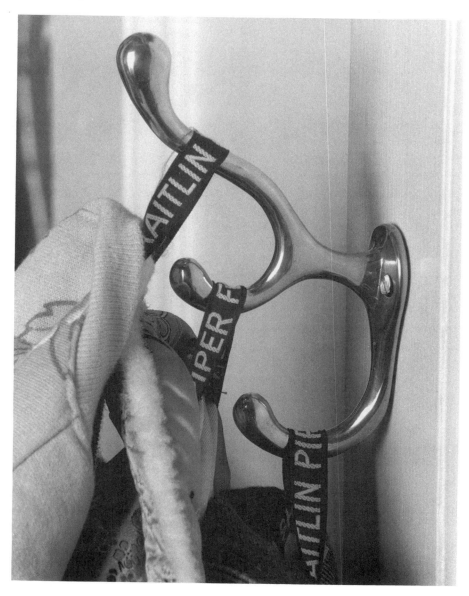

Double-Duty Clothing Organizer. Sturdy, extra large name tags with the name woven in, not just stamped, can be seen from a distance, and double as a hanger loop. Assign each child his or her own hook to encourage autonomy. Tape their names above them. By Cash's of Coventry, England. Order through the Brett Forer Greetings Co., 161 Avenue of the Americas, 13th floor, New York NY 10013. This hook and many other useful organizers are in the Hold Everything catalogue.

The Balaclava. A hooded hat that resists being pulled off by babies and toddlers. This one is by Hanna Andersson.

GLOVES

"Everyone recommended these suits with two zippers up the front. That was great till she started getting active. The twisting and screaming that went on was unbelievable while I tried to get her to stay still for both zippers. It wasn't worth it. I went out midseason and bought a single-zipper suit!"

Now, about winter gloves. The warmest gloves for a small child are the mitten type with a water- and wind-resistant nylon outer shell and a pile inner lining. The fingers moving together inside against each other generate more heat than in separate-fingered gloves where fingers move in isolation. Mittened gloves are appropriate for playing in the snow as well as sitting in a stroller. As kids get older and engage in more active sports—skiing, biking, hiking, etc., fingered gloves become more important: They can more easily grab a sled or manipulate a ski pole. And since the older child is creating more body heat with these active sports, he's not as cold as the younger child. Also, as kids grow up, the mitten shape is deemed "babyish" compared to "cool" fingered gloves. Most experts admit, however, that overall, the mitten shape is warmest; when kids realize this later on, they usually switch back.

Most gloves are designed as if the hand is flat. But if you take a piece of fabric, lay it flat, and design the glove flat, when the hand goes into the glove and curves into its natural shape, the shape when the hand is at rest, there is always extra bulk. One catalogue offers what it calls an "Alpine" glove. Patagonia's "Alpine" glove for a kid may seem extravagant at $35, but if she's playing every afternoon on the ski slope where you live, it may be worth it.

Now how do we keep track of those gloves, no matter what they cost? Look for D rings attached to the wrist area of the gloves. They can be hooked together or to a jacket. Consider sewing or gluing with fabric glue a large name tag on the *outside* of the mitten for quick identification. Pick a color of glove that's unusual. For the older child avoid the strings looped through coat sleeves—these are embarrassing. Most parents resign themselves to the loss and expense of gloves no matter what measures they take. And, frustratingly, gloves are rarely on sale, even at the end of the season. More likely, they're sold out!

Now about the "Freekie Freezies" your child may be wild for. These have been an immensely popular cold weather glove. Each has a particular design—rainbows, geometrics, etc.—that kids love. The designs pop up when it is cold, and disappear when your child is back inside and warm. They are designed to look like a ski glove and are usually cleverly merchandised on racks at your child's eye level—the plethora of choice can be irresistible. However, even though it looks the part, this glove is just a gimmick. You can't count on it in frigid temperatures—it's actually not warm enough.

Shopping Tips

➤ Specialty store sales last longer than department stores'. If you go into a specialty store in the middle of winter, you'll most likely find a jacket on sale. In department stores, warm outerwear will have been moved out to make way for next season's offerings.

➤ You can always find a lightweight nylon jacket with flannel lining for infants through 6x in the less expensive stores like Caldor's, Ames, K-Mart, etc. This is a harder-to-find item in department stores. If you do find them there, they're usually imported and expensive.

➤ Shop ski stores or sporting goods stores for good outerwear, gloves, hats, and those great cowl neck gaiter scarves that do away with dangling ends. If your child hates wearing hats, try a thick ski headband, ear muffs, or knit headband.

➤ If you want to buy a sturdy winter coat for your child, don't be seduced by the beautiful, European-designed long woolen coat, or the gold-buttoned pea coats for boys. Remember that these kinds of coats are good only for dressy occasions. They're not flexible and your kid really can't play in one.

➤ The warmest jacket for the young child is the one that goes over the rear end: the ski type with the drawstring at the waist is good and flexible. You can also buy the jacket a little larger and roll the sleeves. (See illustration on page 120.)

➤ The only jacket color you can't hand down to a boy is pink. It's best to go the primary color route.

➤ Stiff, unlined plastic raincoats are pretty uncomfortable, so it's worth it to spend a little more to get one with a flannel lining. If your child hates bulky outerwear, buy this coat bigger so it will have a larger armhole for layering. If she hates the bulk of coats, a raincoat with a removable flannel lining can be worn over a summer t-shirt, unlike an unlined one that needs a thick sweatshirt under it for enough warmth on a chilly day. The lining can be removed, but it does make the raincoat a heavier garment.

➤ Rain ponchos are great for any kind of climate. In the cold, you can layer clothing or even put a coat on underneath. They can be bought large enough to last a long time. Catalogues such as Childcraft and Biobottoms always have this hard-to-find item. But don't put a poncho on your child

. . . .

"At my shower for my twin girls a good friend bought two snowsuit overalls with matching jackets. It all looked like too much! Thinking I was being so smart, I returned them in favor of a cheaper, and what I thought was easier, all-in-one double-zippered style. Well, every time I go indoors I have to unzip four zippers and remove both their suits totally! With the first gifts, I'd just have had to remove their jackets. I wish I had it to do over again. I just didn't know how practical those first suits were."

. . . .

. . . .

"I used a quilted cotton jacket and pants as a snowsuit. The only problem was how often the jacket would ride up and expose bare skin. If I did it again, I would look for overalls."

. . . .

"I use humor a lot. With three kids under six, getting out of the house in the winter is really brutal! When I feel I'm on the verge of losing it, that's when I bring out the story I made up about how great it would be if I were an octopus mommy. Then I could do so many things at the same time. One arm could change the baby's diaper, one arm could zip your jacket, another arm could find a hat, another arm could read a story, and so on. Then the kids start adding what other arms could do. Our imaginations go wild and we end up giggling hysterically. If you're a parent, it really helps to be a stand-up comic, but, like a good comic, I only bring out the octopus mommy when I need to bring the house down!"

to play. It can catch on play apparatus. They are best used as "going somewhere" coats.

➤ The answer to wetness when your preschooler is learning to skate, ski, or is just playing in the snow: nylon sweatpants that slip up over everything.

➤ Make sure the crotch and leg are roomy enough—cheaper versions are cut narrow and you can't bend in them. By second or third grade they will be deemed babyish, but by that point your child isn't falling as much.

➤ Little kids love the raincoats that have animal mask hoods. They're available from Brights Creek (see catalogue list on page 232), for example, where they come in duck, lion, dog, shark, bunny, and dinosaur styles, in a variety of colors, along with matching boots and umbrellas. However, around age five or six these novelty raincoats may suddenly be judged too babyish.

➤ Buy coats and jackets a little on the large side to get two seasons out of them. But don't buy them too big: they won't be warm enough and your kid will be uncomfortable. Some children like outerwear to fit snugly and refuse to wear "bulgy" jackets: They would rather be cold! If so, buy cheaply to fit now. This preference means that you'll probably need to buy a new jacket every year (on the other hand, that preference also could change tomorrow!).

➤ Thermal underwear is warmest, cheapest, and most durable in a cotton/polyester blend (not 100 percent cotton or wool) and can be used as comfortable unisex leggings or tops in the house.

➤ If your child wants to wear summer clothes in the winter, try layering. Add underneath: long underwear, tights, turtlenecks, leg warmers, bike pants, and leggings to the cotton dress. Add on top: vests, sweatshirts, an extra t-shirt.

➤ Name-tag *every* piece of outerwear prominently. These are the items that tend to mysteriously disappear, forgotten at a friend's house after school when the weather changes. Put name tags on zip-out linings, too. Invest in the large woven tags. They're more expensive but the most visible and durable (see photo on page 125).

The Summer Pack. Two American summer traditions meet—surfing and the Ivy League. For the first, shirts hang long and outside, and pants are knee length, for the second, shirts tuck in, and pants are mid-thigh.

SUMMER

or kids, summer is the best combination of the best situations: no school, hot weather, pools, beaches, and lakes open for business, no alarm clock, and best of all, no dress code. If there *is* a uniform for summer it's wild colors in shorts, t-shirts, and bathing suits. Most of the kids I know would gladly do away with the shorts and shirts and wear just the bathing suit from June to September, twenty-four hours a day.

WHAT TO LOOK FOR IN A BATHING SUIT

For Girls

1. *Fabric.* The best fabrics are Antron/Lycra, nylon/Lycra, and polyester/Lycra blends. (Without Lycra, suits will stretch and lose their shape.) Color is most vibrant in Antron. When buying a suit in a printed fabric, check to see if the print appears on the inside of the suit—if so, it's a good fabric, patterned in what's known as a *wet print*, saturated with dye. If not, it means that the print has been transferred only onto the outside of the fabric and you may have problems with the color rubbing off. A *screen print* is slightly raised and may also rub off in time. When you pull the fabric and white appears, this is known as "grin through," and is an indication of a cheaper make of suit. As kids begin to reach age six, a suit may last more than one summer. Parents now may choose to invest in the pricier suits for durability. Rinse your child's suit thoroughly after she swims in a pool—chlorine is very damaging to the fabric. If the bathing suit has a ruffled edge, it should be a finished one, not raw, or the fabric will fray. A full, wide ruffle, as opposed to a skimpy one, is the sign of a quality suit.

2. *Comfort.* There is nothing more annoying for the parent, and frustrating to the child interested in dressing herself, than a little girl's bathing suit with mystifying parts that go on separately. They're too much for the under size 6x crowd to get in and out of. So keep it simple with two-piece suits, t-strap, or tank suits. It's hard to resist some of these cunning designs, and if you can't, make sure you have a backup that's easy. Make sure any white or light print bathing suits are lined. Also, if there are any studs or scratchy trim on the suit, make sure there is a comfortable lining or your child may not wear it.

3. *Style.* The best design for a little girl is the t-strap which will stay up no matter what. Avoid suits that are too skimpy in the crotch or are cut low in

What's a "Wedgie"?!

The backs of girls' bathing suits for the most part fit from the crotch to the hip in a V-shape. "Often they are cut in too narrow up the sides, mimicking adult styles, and there is not enough fabric to fit comfortably around the natural line of the buttocks of young children," says designer Nicole Stevenson. "This creates what kids commonly term a 'wedgie.' Instead of fitting correctly, the back of the suit is too skimpy and the fabric folds into the child's buttocks. This is very annoying to the child who ends up constantly tugging at the suit to pull out the fabric. No matter how much your child may love the suit, the discomfort will become intolerable, and the suit will end up staying in the drawer." This design mistake has nothing to do with the shape of your child and no alteration can correct it. To avoid this: have your child try on every bathing suit, pair of shorts, even underwear (buy one pack first). Be especially thorough with sale items. And don't assume because a suit is expensive, or comes from a known manufacturer, that it is immune to fit problems.

The best-fitting bathing suits for girls: the t-back and the cross back. Why? Both suits have straps that will not fall off the shoulders.

the back: With a U cut the straps often fall off the shoulders. Wide straps, crisscrossed, and adjustable straps stay put better than the thin strips that imitate mom's bathing suits. Diagonal lines, ballerina ruffles, or side inserts in a one-piece bathing suit are slimming. For skinny girls, avoid wide hip ruffles; they can make them look sticklike. The best swimwear for infant and toddler girls are bubble suits that allow for diapers.

Too many bathing suits for little girls these days are inappropriate to their age: prints in neon and black with cutouts, or skimpily cut leotards. This isn't a conspiracy to make your little girl look like a tart. It's a matter of dollars. Fabric manufacturers have to sell all of the fabric in a single print run to make money. Often, children's bathing suit manufacturers only have enough orders to use just part of a print run. It's just too expensive to order an entire print run with rubber duckies or sweet little hearts. So they end up using leftover pieces of grown-up print runs for children's suits. Even though that cute cutout is cost-effective for the manufacturer and an adorable duplication of mommy's, I find the end result unsettling. For older girls, pastel prints or bright primary colors can still be stylish but won't send the wrong message. Two-piece suits (not bikinis) and cutouts are okay as long as they're not too grown-up. Forget the high-on-the-thigh cut for *any* child! Classic tank styles, the type used for team swimwear, are always appropriate. When made by manufacturers such as Speedo in the current season's new colors, they are a great alternative for a child who prefers sleeker, singular lines, but still wants to be trendy.

The Bloomer Bathing Suit. It fits over diapers. This, at Biobottoms.

Summer Baby Wear. This lightweight hat protects not only the head but the shoulders. Not all babies tolerate hats, but if yours does, this is the number one choice to protect her. Use other protection such as sunscreen, or limit exposure to the sun if she won't wear a hat.

The onesie or bodysuit, already part of her wardrobe as an undershirt in winter, now performs double duty: in summer, it's a simple hot weather outfit.

For Boys

1. *Fabric.* The best fabric for boys' bathing suits of the boxer shorts type is a cotton/polyester blend, which dries faster than 100 percent cotton. Supplex nylon, a 100 percent synthetic fabric, that was first used by California surfers, is another popular choice. It dries even more quickly than cotton/poly blends, yet feels as soft as cotton because of the finishing process. The breathability of 100 percent cotton is not as important in a boy's suit as in a girl's since usually the wide leg opening provides room for enough air to circulate. Another popular nylon resembles a crunchy taffeta: it's a more active fabric developed for hard play on sand as well as in the water. All these synthetic nylons hold the brilliant neon colors that kids love so much far longer than 100 percent cotton. Avoid 100 percent knitted cotton in suits. Because you want quick drying, this is one time a synthetic makes sense. Otherwise, your child will end up sitting and playing in a damp, clammy suit. After swimming, you can replace the suit with a garment made of soft, dry 100 percent cotton.

2. *Comfort.* The longer leg shorts have taken over as the most popular shape for boys' swimwear. They look great and can double as shorts *or* suits. A nylon inner lining tells you that the shorts are bathing suits. They are roomy and comfortable, with a wide leg opening. Check that the "rise"—from crotch to waist—is long enough. An inside drawstring is better than just an elastic waistband, because it helps to fit individual waists.

3. *Style.* Styles change from area to area and from year to year. The most consistently popular boys' suits are jams, which come to just above the knee; surfer pants at mid-knee length; trunks with elasticized waist and a drawstring—a classic style in a mid-thigh length; and swimmers' nylon bikinis, for the boys on the team. Bikinis aren't so great for running around—they're too skimpy. Bicycle pants are also popular these days as swimwear.

. . . .

"White bathing suits with appliqués look so good in the store, but they end up looking cheap when they're wet, no matter how much I paid for them and at about six Lauren started to realize they were see-through and refused to wear them."

. . . .

SUMMER CLOTHES

Summer is the cheapest time of the year to clothe your kids, so go ahead and buy lots of inexpensive t-shirts in every color of the rainbow. Cut up outgrown winter jeans, sweats, and turtlenecks to make shaggy, cool-looking summer cover-ups. Shorten t-shirts to make crop tops, or cut t-shirt sleeves in strips for fringe. Go to the flea market and pick up Hungarian and Mexican embroidered peasant blouses, Greek gauze dresses, and African bloomer pants. Use winter cotton slips as skirts and dresses. Dress infants in the bloomers from dress suits and terrycloth diaper covers without the shirt.

This is the season when outlet or discount stores such as K-Mart, Woolworths, and Caldor's shine with fabulous adaptations of fashionable brightly colored summer clothing for a fraction of what you'd pay in boutiques and

Jams: History of a Trend

"Back in the sixties, surfers from Santa Monica, California, actually had their regular tennis shorts custom tailored to achieve the wider, comfortable fit for this new sport. Regular bathing suit brands like Catalina and Jantzen were not made for the flexibility required to straddle a surfboard, or for the rigors of riding it. David Rochlyn, a champion surfer and stuntman, noticed a young boy early one morning surfing in pajamas he'd cut off at the knee. David asked the kid about this look and he responded 'I just can't find anything loose enough.' At about the same time, David saw a *Life* magazine spread on Russian vacationers in the Crimea, and *they* were sitting around sunbathing in their pajama bottoms.

Something clicked, and in December 1964, the first pair of 'Jams' (from 'pajama') hit the stores. These shorts were cut more amply for the needs of the surfer. They had a wider leg for straddling, and a drawstring waist to loosen or tighten depending on whether [the surfer was] sitting across the board or standing. Made in fabrics that dried quickly and could stand up to salt water, with a back pocket to hold the wax for their surfboards, Jams were totally functional. Living in tropical Hawaii, Rochlyn adapted the colorful prints of the island he loved; they are still a Jams trademark."

—Jack Hyde, Fashion Institute of Technology, N.Y.C.

"My kid, unfortunately (or fortunately), has really expensive taste. I took him shopping for summer clothes and of course he picked out two pairs of $25 shorts. I mean, summer is supposedly the cheap time to shop! We finally compromised and I bought him one pair of the expensive shorts. The rest were from the discount outlet."

department stores. It's so satisfying to put together a great outfit for under ten dollars. And in the summer, it's especially easy. Here are some of the summer basics you can find in any of the low-price stores. (Surprisingly, many are to be found in 100 percent cotton.) If you see an appealing outfit in 50/50 cotton/poly, feel the fabric before you buy it. Summer is the one season you want to try to dress in 100 percent cotton.

➤ tank tops
➤ t-shirts
➤ baby bubbles
➤ rompers (short or long one-piece jumpsuits)
➤ cotton circle skirts
➤ elastic waist and pleated shorts
➤ cotton shirts
➤ knit polo shirts
➤ oversized sweatshirts
➤ surf shorts
➤ fly-away crop tops
➤ cotton bike pants and capri pants
➤ jellies, sneakers, thongs, and sandals
➤ sleeveless t-shirt dresses (see also the Smart Shopping chapter)

Pretty cotton underwear as a bathing suit for a diapered toddler. This mother solved the problem of her daughter's skin rashes. They were caused from sand being trapped in her regular bathing suit: "At eighteen months all they do is sit in the sand and play. Her regular suit fit perfectly, but I found out that 'perfectly' is too tight when there are plastic diapers involved. There should be extra room for the suit to drop down a bit." Right now, she's giving diapers a rest with a walk down the beach. (If your child is still in diapers, and you're going swimming at a pool, check the pool rules ahead of time. Often an extra pair of plastic pants is required to be worn over already existing cloth or plastic diapers for extra protection. Check catalogues that specialize in layette for good-looking opaque, printed ones.)

The Ubiquitous Summer Dress. This drop-waist design in cotton knit is a favorite of young girls and their parents. It fits any growing shape and can be pulled off and on like a t-shirt. Prices range from $8 at the discounter to $32 at the specialty store. On the far right, the party dress version. Two summer tips: Avoid frequent use of cheap cartoon character sunglasses. If your child is sensitive to glare, choose sunglasses that filter out UVA and UVB rays. Check labels! And encourage your child to go barefoot. Unless you live in an area where Lyme Disease is a problem (then feet, legs, and shoulders should be covered), feet and arches develop most healthily when left alone. Unless the ground is unsafe—broken glass, or poison ivy—the best condition for the foot is to be bare.

Summer Shoes

Yes, summer is a good time for inexpensive children's shoes as well as clothing. Of course you can spend $30 or more on a pair of really fine leather sandals, but most kids prefer to wear shoes that are easy to get on and off: jellies, thongs, slip-ins, and between-the-toe-with-elastic-back-strap sandals. Make sure your child wears socks with all plastic shoes (though this may be difficult). Limit the use of between-the-toe thongs or blisters may occur.

Summer is the season where most shoes get left behind. It's warm enough to go barefoot, and it's the rare child who doesn't have to be constantly reminded after play at the beach or pool: "Do you have your shoes?" For an especially forgetful child, don't even consider expensive shoes. Or if you need to purchase a more expensive pair to accommodate orthotics or fit, felt-pen his name in large visible letters in the shoe, on *both sides* of the inside.

And, most of all, stay on top of your child's shoe fit: Check the big toe for redness. Avoid the slip-on sneaker with no laces for the younger child. They often don't stay on well till the child reaches size 1. And because the slip-on sneaker has to be fit more snugly than a laced one (there is no lace to securely anchor the heel), he'll grow out of them faster. You may need a new pair before summer is finished.

"I bought three pairs of those cheap slip-on canvas sneakers for $3.99 each—all in white. They're easy to dump in the wash and when one is lost, I'll find one from another pair. No more morning fights finding shoes, and the stray always turns up. When they get really grungy by mid-August we have a paint-in to pep them up."

"Which dress is more expensive?" On the left, Shayna has on a $25 dress with a detachable lace collar added. Jessie, on the right, wears a dress with its own collar at five times the price. Large collars and longer lengths are a European tradition and give dresses an expensive look. The wide collar is also flattering to a young child whose head is still proportionately larger than her body.

PARTY CLOTHES

W hen I was growing up in the 1950s, there wasn't much variation in getting dressed for parties. Little boys sported their short-pants suits with knee socks, and their hair was properly parted and combed. Little girls wore starched organdy dresses or pinafores with slippery Mary Janes on their feet and a stiff bow in their hair. Today, this traditional approach to dress-up may be still pretty much the same when it comes to larger, more formal family get-togethers or celebrating the season's holidays.

However, the nineties birthday party is a totally different matter. The modern birthday get-together is no longer a children's version of a grown-up party. Whatever form the party takes, active play and organized chaos are the byproducts. After watching kids play in a padded gymnasium and eat pizza and birthday cake on a paper tablecloth on the floor, my attitude about party clothes has relaxed considerably.

Every family has its own approach to dressing up. It's a reflection of the family's lifestyle and in many ways the parenting style of the parents. How important is it to look good to the world? Is it a command performance or just a last-minute rush to look presentable? You can't predict a family's attitude on dressing up by their income. Some very wealthy families may value a casual, sporty life and purposely take a utilitarian approach: "Can we get by with last year's dress?" or "Okay, if he won't wear the blazer jacket, his school cardigan is just fine." Other families with less income but a more traditional lifestyle may place great importance on the formality of a dressy occasion. For them it's a welcome opportunity to reaffirm tradition. A sashed puff-shouldered party dress or a sailor suit are their standbys. And if they can't afford the designer versions, they'll search in less expensive stores or in catalogues to find a well-bred interpretation. Still other families might view dressing up as an enjoyable creative outlet and an opportunity to look different from their everyday appearance. With their off-beat approach, they might dress their toddler boy in a cotton embroidered pajama set from a Chinese gift shop, or their baby girl in satin overalls.

Except on rare occasions, kids don't see their parents in very dressy clothes. With the more casual lifestyle of today's family, why would a youngster understand the tradition of uncomfortable dress shirts and ties, stiff shoes, or starchy dresses? After all, since birth they have been living in clothes which have actually been designed for their comfort and movement, such as cotton baby

Other Traditional Party Dresses for Little Girls—Pros and Cons

1. *Toddler Smock Party Dress:* This is also called a "float" dress. This silhouette is number one for comfort. There is virtually no restriction. This is also flattering to a stocky child: If you need to buy it larger, the length will still look fine, in fact it will look elegant.

2. *The Bloomer Dress or Party Pants:* Great for an active child—it's both pants and a dress. Bloomers are an adorable answer to a somersault-party. Be sure the waistline is raised slightly. If it's set in there will be no give.

3. *Smock Dress for the Thin or Average Child:* The most well-bred look you can buy. Only catch: It is always designed in more muted colors, so a little girl with strong coloring may look dull.

4. *The Traditional Sailor Dress:* This always looks right. But if your child is uncomfortable in tight-fitting clothes, avoid it in the classic cut because of the set-in waist, and often tight arms.

5. *The Drop-Waist Dress:* This is a more adult look, and has become one of the most popular choices. It mimics adult designer shapes and is surprisingly flattering to a child with a stocky build—the ruffles at the hem balance her wider chest and waist, and the smooth line down the front elongates her. However, for the child with the protruding baby fat tummy, this shape is not flattering if the seam at the hip is too low. Check cheaper versions (which are often cut more skimpily) to make sure they're cut wide enough through the middle.

1. Toddler Smock
Party Dress

2. The Bloomer Dress
or Party Pants

3. Smock Dress for
the Thin or
Average Child

4. The Traditional
Sailor Dress

5. The Drop-Waist
Dress

A Black Reebok Sneaker. An alternative to the stiff dress shoe.

overalls or sweats and t-shirts. If your child is only used to casual knit clothing, don't be surprised by his resistance to more formal outfits, even if they're great-looking. Prepare him ahead of time for the new clothes and introduce the new clothing a week or two ahead of the event. Put it in his closet and let him get used to it. Or, take your children on a special shopping trip. Let *them* pick out the party outfit. (And choose a store with looks that *you* like. The expedition won't be fun if you have to say no to their choices.) Try not to buy a party outfit on sale too far ahead of the occasion: it may not fit (or may now be out of favor!) on the day of the big event. However, a classic such as a navy blazer or a smock dress in a light-weight cotton is always useful—even if it's in

A traditional dressed-up look for an active boy. Read is wearing his favorite pants to play in the park and then go to a party. Some classic accessories changed the whole look while keeping the comfy pants. Consider short pants and high socks as an alternative to long, stiffer pants. Rugged cotton drill Bermuda shorts at play.

The same Bermudas dressed up. An extra ingredient: a little gel added to just the front and sides of his hair.

a bigger size. It can always be worn later. This kind of quality clothing is often handed down on the party clothes circuit. Phone calls around the neighborhood, or church and school bazaars, are the best way to connect with some of these items.

No matter what the approach, dressing a child well has less to do with paying high prices than with ingenuity. When a child looks and feels his best, it's not because he's the picture of perfection of a designer's concept or because he fulfills certain of society's dictates. When parents take into consideration the clothing likes and dislikes of their child, along with his temperament, and combine them with comfort and what works for the family style, they create a

The Knit Cardigan Sweater. An alternative to the stiff jacket. Add a Superman patch for fun, or find one with his favorite motif.

The new dressed-up look for the nineties. Two brothers in nontraditional party clothes. Good looking roomy cottons one step up from sweats. Teddy, three, in his mom's playful choice of contrast dots and stripes, with a cute bow tie. Gilbert, six, more grown-up in his cool belt and toned-down pants.

successful party outfit. With the help of a few fashion tips and some tried-and-true parenting techniques you'll find here, plus a dose of imagination, any parent can get a child to the party on time, feeling and looking great.

Styling Tips for Boys

➤ Use suspenders. When the boy's jacket comes off, as it inevitably will, he'll still look dressed up.

➤ Take regular pants to the tailor and have cuffs made for a few dollars. Cuffs make pants look finished and expensive.

➤ Use a little of daddy's hair gel on the front of your son's hair to make him look well turned out.

➤ Dress up an inexpensive blazer or cardigan sweater with new gold-toned, dome-shaped buttons: Put three on the sleeve—it won't matter that there are no real buttonholes; no one will notice. Replace the front buttons also. Now a $20 acrylic-blend jacket has the look of an $80 wool designer one. Another upgrade: Iron on a heraldic crest from the notion store for a dressier, prep-school look.

➤ Use accessories: dinosaur suspenders, cowboy bolo ties, belts with cartoon characters or astronauts on the buckles, bright primary-color argyle socks, and animal ties.

Styling Tips for Boys

Little boys aren't fans of getting dressed up formally. And who really is these days? However, there are those occasions when a dressed-up look is appropriate and necessary. Don't despair. Here is a list of what may strike an adult as the "ideal" boy's dressed -up look. Next to it are alternatives that are perfectly acceptable. Substitute one or all, and he'll look great.

	The classic well-bred dressed-up look for boys	The alternatives, for boys who hate to dress up
1. Jacket	Blue blazer	Cardigan or nice pullover sweater
2. Shirt	Button-down oxford shirt in blue or white	Knit collar-shirt; plain or solid-colored t-shirt
3. Pants	Gray flannels, corduroys, long or short	Clean, pressed jeans or khakis; short pants
4. Shoes	Slip-on penny loafers	Black Reebok-type sneakers
5. Tie	Red stripe or club motif	Colorful bow tie, suspenders, or cowboy bolo

➤ Let him wear his superhero t-shirt under his dress shirt. No one will know and he'll feel like one!

➤ For the boy who doesn't like wearing a tie but must: undo the top button of his dress shirt. No one will notice it open under the tie, and he'll feel a lot more comfortable.

Styling Tips for Girls

➤ If your daughter has straight, thin hair, braid it in tiny braids the night before the party. Undo the braids the next day and brush for a fluffy, stylish hairdo that's easy and fun. If hair is thick, use fewer braids and start them lower down. For the shy child, practice this hairdo ahead of time, or forgo it.

➤ Design a simple but elegant hairdo that will withstand an active child's play. Use lightweight hair ornaments such as plaid or satin ribbons and decorative barrettes. Take time to bobby pin or elastic band them securely.

➤ Headbands with oversized satin bows, inspired by the classic taffeta Victorian bows of yesteryear, are usually found in smaller specialty stores and range from $10 and up. Though expensive for an accessory, they add unmistakable class to any outfit. Even a sweatshirt dress will look dressy with one of these.

➤ If there is a headband or bow in a fabric or print that matches your child's party dress perfectly, buy two. Party headbands often get lost when they're pulled off in vigorous play. (Catalogues often have this added fashion feature.)

➤ Look for a ruffled or tiered dressy skirt. You can pair this with either a t-shirt or blouse and still have a dressy look. This is a good alternative for a child who hates dressing up because she gets itchy under her arms or across the chest. If you find colors that coordinate for both top and bottom, the effect will be more like a complete outfit or even a dress.

➤ All white for summer always looks dressy, even if it's a t-shirt and a skirt. And matching white accessories, frilly socks, hair bow, even fake pearls, will reinforce the dressy look.

➤ If your daughter is making her debut as a flower girl, and you have a stiff cotton or taffeta dress she has to wear, try hiding a soft sleeveless undershirt or light-colored leotard underneath. These, along with some nylon tights or cotton leggings, will prevent itchiness better than most slips can, and help remove some of the strangeness of the outfit for her.

➤ Parents love to dress up baby girls. Often their closets are filled with adorable miniature dresses, most of which may never get worn. When they do get worn, baby is likely to grab the skirt and pull it up to her mouth, and in essence, end up wearing nothing. Buy only one or two dresses for infants, and for active babies, party pants (a full-length or short-length

The Detachable Lace Collar. If you like the idea of using a detachable collar, invest in a quality, ready-made lace collar available at adult accessory counters and notions stores. You'll be able to use it as your child grows. The wide adult size will be suitable for a child with lots of contrast between her skin and hair. Evaluate if your child has more muted coloring. She may need a less exaggerated shape.

The Party Slip. This is useful to extend the length and life of a party dress. In the summer, let her wear it simply as a pretty skirt, or layer it under a cotton dress for a festive note.

Instant Family Tree. One-of-a-kind antique Victorian summer cotton dresses from the fleamarket, so twin girls could be alike but different. Look in your parents' attic for hidden treasures or in an ethnic neighborhood for inexpensive modern-day copies.

bloomer jumpsuit with a full feminine collar) are a great alternative and easy to find in any department store. For active toddlers or preschoolers, party pants or dresses with bloomers are mostly available in catalogues.

➤ Buy dressy-looking knit sportswear—the kind of fabric she's used to playing in—with dressy ornamentation such as ribbons and appliqués. There's a whole category of decorated sweats available in stores and in catalogues. If it's a pants outfit, use the top and substitute a skirt on the bottom.

➤ Your little girl's favorite, comfortable cotton t-shirt dress can be glamorized with inexpensive accessories such as lacy tights, special party socks or headband, a lace collar, or a pretty sweater.

➤ If you're buying a dressy cardigan sweater, make sure it can easily fit over the sleeve of the party dress. Classic party cardigans are often cut narrow. You can offset this by buying it a size larger. Or a light-weight white sweat jacket may do the trick.

The Classic Girl's Party Dress.

The details of the well-bred party dress for girls:

1. Puff shoulder.
2. Special large collar. Lace, cotton, pique, or satin. Any are fine as long as they are large enough to be festive. Avoid cheap fabrics around the face.
3. "Tea-length" (mid-calf) skirt.
4. Wide sash tied at back.
5. Lace or plain tights or dressy ankle socks for summer.
6. Black patent leather Mary Janes or ballet shoes.
7. Dressy headband or hair bow.

Inexpensive alternatives to the classic party dress:

1. Summer: To a basic cotton t-shirt dress or sleeveless floral print dress, add a lace collar and wide lace sash at hip or waist. Also, use the lace as a hair bow or headband.
2. Winter: To a basic velvet, taffeta, or satin dress that is *plain* on top, add a piece of satin or lace as a collar *and* matching sash. Also use a three or four-inch piece for the hair. (*Note:* Double-faced polyester satin ribbon, available at notions stores, looks exactly like real satin. Make sure it is double-faced so you don't have to worry about tying the shiny side to show. It can be washed easily and all told will probably cost under $2.)

Special Note: This party dress with a lace collar and sash is the traditional silhouette that flatters every child. But before buying, run your finger over the seams *inside the sleeve that crisscross under the armpit.* Make sure they don't feel thick or scratchy. Most party dresses that bite the dust because your child won't wear it haven't passed this test. To assure longest use, check the *outside bottom of the sleeve.* It is usually finished in piping, self-fabric, or elastic. It should be comfortably wide, not at all tight on the upper arm, to accommodate growth.

Proud older sister Fia dressed up Carlie, her new baby sister, her new "little doll." She dressed her just like herself, using her own stretchy headband and bright socks. Clothes can help bridge the sibling gap.

ACCESSORIES

Y ou can really encourage your children to express their personalities by letting them choose and wear accessories that they love. The kind of accessory the child chooses often reflects how he is feeling about himself. However, since accessories are sold at checkout counters and presented at the child's eye level, they are impulse, emotion-packed purchases. So supporting the child's choice at that moment is often a challenge for the parent who knows that the novelty might wear off by the time you get home.

Fortunately, accessories are an inexpensive way to give an old outfit fresh appeal. My preschool daughter was perfectly happy with the addition of a new headband even though she had to wear last year's party dress. For grown-ups, accessories are what marketers call affordable luxuries. If you can't swing a new dress or suit, a pretty scarf or new tie will often do. For children, a cute animal-face purse or a pair of suspenders with astronauts on them are not only inexpensive, but can be real outlets of creativity for you and your child. A friend of mine with three kids humorously terms accessories "shut-up" purchases.

Arlene Peller, a twenty-year veteran of the kids' accessory market, and vice-president of sales and merchandising for Rosecraft, the largest girls' accessory company in the U.S., has done much research on the subject of why and how little girls buy accessories. Much of this research applies equally to boys. She says: "As adults, we buy an outfit. Then we buy accessories to complement it: shoes, necklaces, bracelets all in colors to go with the outfit. Adults feel that if they're totally coordinated, they've done the job. But kids buy the accessory first. They evaluate it almost like a toy. It has *nothing* to do with being *part* of an outfit. It's looked at completely separately. Then they wear the clothes around it." And children do not wear accessories discreetly like most adults. Peller says they instead tend to "shout" when they dress. This is why you often see a little girl in a nice traditional plaid school outfit sporting a dressy hot pink tulle headband. What caught her eye was the beautiful headband, and so what if it doesn't match what she has on. I often hear parents say in vain to their kids, "But that doesn't match." I recommend relaxing this attitude and letting your child experiment for herself.

Matching an outfit perfectly—color to exact color—is not what concerns most parents. Instead, it's the apparent lack of rhyme or reason in the outfit that drives many parents crazy. But if you're the type of parent who's allowing your child choice in dressing, realize that matching clothes is a developmental skill that takes time to learn. Being able to correlate all the different parts that make up one outfit (shoes, socks, skirt or pant, top, jacket or sweater, etc.) and put them into a logical and harmonious whole is a skill that takes time to learn. It requires a certain mature visual sense and analytical thought. From what I've observed, most children tend to naturally start matching their outfits at about age eight, nine, or ten. (If a child is a first-born and the direct role model is an adult or has an early high spatial or logical intelligence, this may occur sooner.)

If you're relaxed about this issue, set your own example and ultimately the child will follow your lead in his own time frame. If you're of two minds about it—you want your child to have freedom of expression in dress, yet you also want guaranteed socially acceptable outfits at certain times—set up family guidelines of dress. And start them *as soon as* you begin to allow your child choice, so your child knows "this is how it is." (If you suddenly impose rules after the fact, the child will identify negatively with the situations that produced them, i.e., seeing grandparents.) Try to be consistent. And set up specific occasions and times when these guidelines apply, for instance, family holidays, restaurants, and visits with grandparents.

Accessories answer different needs for girls than for boys. First and foremost, girls use accessories to decorate. Headbands, necklaces, bracelets, serve to enliven the day's outfit. A new headband is rarely bought for purely functional reasons. Accessories are also an interesting barometer of the developmental stages a girl is going through. A toddler-into-three-years-old may spot a nice belt in her closet that's buckled and decide it's a perfect crown for her head, or pile everything on in doubles and triples to wear to the park. Actually just handling and manipulating the items like tools—a skill toddlers are honing— may be half the fun. The same child who adored wild experimentation as a toddler will probably prefer a single necklace or bracelet (though not matched) or a superhero watch in preschool. Her choice may now reflect the symbolic thought typical of three-to-five-year-old girls looking for their identity ("just like mom" or "just like sister" in one of her Berenstain Bears books). Many changing accessories will help her in the search for identity.

In primary school, the influence of friends and the desire to be accepted is just starting. Many psychologists feel that this starts a particularly challenging time for girls socially as they jostle for position and accessories often reflect that. These psychologists theorize that the aggression *not* shown by girls in preschool (we can see that they don't play with guns or as superheroes as vigorously as boys) comes out now, but not in a physical way. The kinds of things boys have worked out with guns, girls are now working out in relationships. Girls are shaping relationships and identity through friendships. Accessories are not only judged "fun" or "cute" now but also "cool" or "uncool" socially. Some accessories, for this reason, can wield surprising power among

. . . .

"We went to a theme park this summer and Jeremy got a hat from there he just loved. In fact, he refused to take it off. Sometimes he even went to sleep in it. It was so filthy it really got to me, so I tried to reason him out of it. But no way. Finally he agreed that when school started, he'd stop wearing it. Later my wife told me he had asked her earlier in the summer if his head shape was 'funny.' It was an off-handed remark and the only time he ever mentioned it. Who knows where he got that idea? But I'll bet it's why he was married to that hat."

. . . .

A preschooler's fantasy: the classic musical jewelry box with twirling ballerina that everyone loved in the fifties. A winning gift with a price to match. From the Lilly's Kids catalogue.

kids. One example is the two-halves-of-a-heart friendship necklace meant to be shared by "best friends." Unfortunately, developmentally, at the beginning of elementary school best friends are rare. A friend deemed "best" one afternoon may not be the next. It can be confusing, even heartbreaking, to a six- or seven-year-old when she's unceremoniously told so in front of others, even as she's proudly wearing her friendship necklace given to her the day before. And if these two do remain fast friends, the necklace can become a badge of honor, excluding others. Let your child wear this type of gift out of school, and explain to her how others may feel.

Girls' Accessory Tips

➤ Get a see-through plastic shoebox from the dime store for each category of accessory: one for ponytail holders and barrettes, another for larger items such as headbands. You will probably need to organize the contents often as the early morning rush doesn't always leave time for organizing. Keep the most functional items, such as covered ponytail elastics, in generous supply.

➤ Find a hook that extends out from the wall and set it up as near as possible to the door. Hang an inexpensive three-bin wire basket of the kind used for kitchen produce and organize all hair stuff in it. The smallest top basket is for elastics, etc. (line it so they don't fall through), the middle for stretchy fabric-covered ponytail holders, knit headbands, and even the hairbrush and plastic bottle of detangler. Reserve the largest for plastic headbands. Hang the basket at your child's height. What a help to get out of the house in the morning when all components for the hairdo of the day are accessible. (Don't use the wire baskets for jewelry or necklaces—they'll fall out.)

➤ Find a permanent place for the hairbrush and foster responsibility (not fights!) by having one for each child. If two siblings both like the same type of brush buy a second and use an identifying sticker initial to avoid confusion. (This hair-care issue is also a sanitary one. Preschools forbid children to borrow and lend each other combs and brushes to prevent the spread of head lice.)

➤ Avoid costume jewelry that mimics real jewelry. It's *always* too fragile. Chain necklaces with little hearts or "gold" name initials will disappointingly break almost immediately, no matter how careful your child is and no matter how much you paid.

➤ Buy very cheap hair accessories for everyday use. Get in the habit of picking them up whenever you see them. Splurge on nice accessories for parties and keep them separate.

➤ If you have a special accessory to be worn with a special dress, use this fashion stylist's trick: put it in a plastic baggy, punch a hole in the baggy, and hang it on the hanger with the outfit.

➤ Necklaces will last longer if they're hung. They won't get tangled and broken as they're picked over in a drawer with other jewelry.

➤ If your child has fine hair, and barrettes slip out, wind waxed dental floss around the underside of the clasp until it's thick enough to close tight. Or glue a strip of light-duty Velcro under the clasp. It will hold the hair but won't damage it.

➤ Invest in a glue gun for about ten dollars from the dime store. You'll save lots being able to repair accessories.

➤ If your child has pierced ears, have extra backs on hand—these always get lost. A note about piercing ears, if you're wondering when to do it: A good deal of maturity is required to take care of pierced ears. A child has to be willing to clean the holes as they heal, and to deal with an infection that may occur. She must take care not to lose them or remember not to wear them to bed. Unless your child started pierced earrings as a baby, my suggestion is to wait at least until your child is eight to ten. Any younger

Chris was heavily into G.I. Joe, but I forbade the camouflage stuff for school. I let him wear just the hat. Then he started having some trouble at school. When I came to pick him up I would get a look from the teacher that said 'Today's one of those days!' We finally figured out that whenever he wore his hat he'd get into trouble. It was as if it gave him permission to get away with things. Then I remembered a class exercise an old acting teacher had required—we would rehearse our scene all week in jeans but one day a week we had to wear a dress. I remembered how different I had felt in the scene when I wore that skirt. I thought it might be the same for Chris so I forbade the hat for school. His behavior calmed down.''

When "more is more." Some little girls can never have enough accessories and some attach themselves to only a few cherished ones. An old outfit can be recycled with a new headband or pair of socks. Brightly colored cotton leggings are the most recent clothes accessories that have real function: warmth plus a color accent.

1. Use two inexpensive lightweight plastic headbands together to add color.

2. Yellow socks and a polka dot hair bow pep up this two-color outfit.

3. A wider, sturdier headband is best to hold thicker hair.

4. An oversized t-shirt is a cool summer dress by itself and a comfortable top for cold weather when a turtleneck can fit under. Add leggings, hair stuff, and she's all set. (Note: If she wants to wear her dressy shoes other than for parties, buy rubber-soled ones.)

5. Bright grosgrain shoelaces are sturdy and can refurbish a well-used but not yet outgrown pair of shoes.

and you're really the one responsible for proper care, and after the initial excitement, girls often just plain forget to put the earrings in and the holes close up. Children who've worn pierced earrings since babyhood have grown up taking care of their ears and earrings so it's natural for them to remember everything.

➤ Avoid hair ornaments or other accessories for the under-two set that can be pulled off and swallowed. Grabbing at hair bows may start at six months for some babies.

Boys' Accessories

Boys' accessories also tend to be used as symbols of identity in preschool or for connections to peers in elementary school. In these ways, boys' accessories follow a similar developmental pattern as girls'. The difference in boys' acces-

How to make "princess" hair: Braid it wet at night—start just above your child's ears, no higher, otherwise it will come out looking too unruly. Undo it dry in the morning. Brush lightly. This hairdo is the secret many kids' fashion stylists use to make fine hair look thick. Try it.

Accessories to Encourage Autonomy

A backpack is a fashion accessory with a purpose. A young child can carry her own toys, snack, and sweater, experiencing an early sense of responsibility. Belt packs can be worn all day to hold a protein snack if school doesn't provide them. Later a backpack transports bulkier, heavier items such as textbooks and after-school sports clothing, not to mention sticker books and baseball card collections. Primary school kids may have strong opinions about the color and style of their backpacks, which are now considered "cool."

Tips on Backpacks and Bags

- A simple single-zippered nylon backpack with no added pockets is both lightweight and sufficient for the very young child.
- Prices vary wildly for the simple nylon backpack. They may range from $4 at the discounter for a solid brightly colored one, to $23 at the department store for a fashionably printed one. Both backpacks are the *same* in durability and practicality.
- Use the nylon duffle bags for overnight or sports equipment. They are too bulky for everyday use on the run. Because they're not strapped on to the child, like a backpack, they're more likely to get left behind.
- Sew or glue the child's name tag on the *outside,* facing the straps—for safety purposes—where it won't show when he wears it.
- A backpack with quilted padding on the shoulder straps is best for carrying heavy books. Make sure the backpack can fit wide, bulky items like loose-leaf folders and piano books, and that the straps are wide enough for the sleeves of thick winter jackets.
- Avoid elaborate backpacks that feature bodies of cartoon characters built in. They're cute, but the fascination will wane when the kids realize how cumbersome these bags are, and how little room they have.

"Jake could be sweating bullets and he wants to wear this certain hat. It's like a thing, it has to be that hat, and, yes, his dad does have one too. But God forbid I'd have to wash it. I went and bought two more so there's always a decent one. I think the mesh insert on it makes the hat 'cool' literally and figuratively."

*Who says boys'
clothing has to be
boring? Nobody can
resist a little boy in
bow tie and
suspenders. Mixing
patterns and using
lively motifs and bright
colors are sure ways to
avoid an overly serious
miniature grown-up
look. The second boy
from right is wearing
an unusual shirt in a
patchwork of stripes.
This is the classic "fun
shirt" invented and
always available at
Brooks Brothers.*

sories is that they are used primarily for functions, rarely for simple decoration. Suspenders, shoelaces, hats, and belt packs are mainly items of function that not only attract attention but serve a purpose. Belts are one accessory where comfort is key. Kids are not drawn to belts, no matter how cute, if they're stiff—elastic stretch belts are most useful. The only decorative exception, at this point in time, would be surf bracelets, pin and button collections, usually worn on jean jackets, and of course ties and bow ties. To the complaints of mothers of infants and toddlers that "boys' clothes are no fun," I offer bow ties with polka dots, cartoon suspenders, and elasticized belts with fun buckles, for starters. Any of these can turn a basic outfit into an upbeat ensemble that reflects your child's personality.

The majority of preschool boys' accessories usually involve some kind of association or identification with a larger than life hero or important person in their life. Boys may attach themselves to a watch with their current favorite superhero or to a baseball hat with the favorite baseball team of an older cousin. Or a boy may wear a different hat to school every day, testing what it's like to be a fireman, policeman, or football player (see School Days, page 70). Or he

Roey has had to wear prescription eye glasses since birth. Her parents have turned what could have been a negative into a positive. Her parents treat her glasses as an accessory and buy them to match her clothes, a luxury, they choose to treat as a necessity. "We wanted to develop her self-esteem," they say. Her varied fashionable glasses never fail to attract compliments.

The Cool Surfer Look. Surfing is the most important sport to influence boys' sportswear in recent years. Accessories are key! Of utmost importance to the primary school boy is to feel comfortable and be cool. Surfwear has brought in a flamboyance of color not seen in traditional male sportswear since the wild colors worn by golfers in Palm Beach in the fifties. Accessories are an essential part of this look and if the surf clothes aren't being worn at the moment, the laces, belt packs, neon watches, haircuts, and high tops are (see page 79). The obsession with pockets in the toddler years continues into primary years. Though pockets are rarely used now, workable details—like flaps that Velcro-shut over pockets—are symbols of adult competence. Be cool but be safe when skateboarding: add helmets and knee pads.

may simply practice matching his kid-sized ties to different shirts, to look just like daddy. When it comes to accessories for identification, hats of *any* kind are the number one choice for boys. Psychologists often link this ferocious attachment to traditional male symbols—sports figures, superheroes, firemen, fighter pilots, etc.—to the fact that boys are separating from their mothers' early nurturing (boys and girls are still primarily raised by women). To do this, boys deliberately turn to male figures for self-definition. Hopefully, as more and more men participate in parenting, sometimes taking primary responsibility, we should see a loosening up of stereotypes and a more relaxed attitude about gender roles (see School Days, page 72) and "Guns and Dolls," *Newsweek,* May 28, 1990, p. 65.

Sometimes kids get really stuck on an accessory. Your three-year-old boy may refuse to take off a particular hat. Maybe those socks with the frogs on them that you have to keep washing all the time remind your five-year-old girl of her favorite baby-sitter who gave them to her before she left for college. Dr. Stanley Turecki says that some children often form a "linkage" between an article of clothing and what it represents to them. The persistent wearing of that pair of socks becomes linked to your daughter's emotion toward her beloved baby-sitter. "Getting temperamentally 'locked in' to a piece of clothing may be frustrating to a parent but is not unusual for a child," Dr. Turecki says. "It may even signal a positive trait when in later years, he turns that persistence into a dedicated pursuit of a school subject." Try to be as sensitive to your child's attachments to certain accessories no matter how annoying it may be, to help keep track of them day after day. Let your child wear them with the same joy as you bought them. We can learn a lot about the inside of a child through how he chooses to present himself on the outside. Enjoy his myriad concoctions as an expression of his uniqueness.

Markers of growth, by Tobias, aged four-and-a-half: "Nursery is when I got to wear my hat all day. Pre-kindergarten is when I had to put my hat in my cubby."

. . . .

"Willie is three-and-a-half and has a hat collection of at least fourteen—a policeman, fireman, Mickey ears, even a Santa Claus hat with his name on it in sequins—that he'll actually wear around. I have them all at eye level on a special shelf in the closet on the way out. He doesn't seem to be able to focus on putting his toys or clothes away yet, but he's great about his hats. And he takes such pride in his collection, he'll often wear two at a time!"

Samantha's Suitcase: How a Three-Year-Old Uses an Accessory for Self-Definition

Samantha's suitcase made its first appearance right after the birth of her baby brother. She simply picked up an old overnight case, stuffed it with as many toys as it would hold, and announced her plans to leave home. Two-and-a-half years later, Samantha is still here . . . and so is her suitcase. Samantha carried it around for the first six months after his birth. She filled it with clothing and insisted each morning on choosing her outfit from it. Then we noticed that the case was coming apart at the seams. So we bought her a new one with cartoon characters on it, and she packed for our summer vacation that day. It was February.

I once bought her a book that I thought we would read over and over. I read it to her once, and then it disappeared . . . into the suitcase. At first I was disappointed, but then she explained that only her most precious belongings went into the suitcase. Every now and then, I catch her sitting quietly beside her case, "reading" this book to herself.

Samantha has gained a sense of autonomy through her suitcase. Come wash day, she reaches into the clean-clothes basket and pulls out her favorite garments. These she stores in the suitcase, and in the morning when she gets up, she quietly dresses herself.

Other treasures go into the case as well. A pack of gum is almost always stored inside; when Samantha feels generous, she opens it up and, without prompting, distributes the pieces among her siblings and friends. Birthday-party invitations also find their way inside. In addition, the case serves as a repository for pictures of friends, and these Samantha brings out often.

We have five children now. The most recent two are foster children, whose introduction into our home has temporarily unbalanced the existing order. Our other three children, feeling a bit threatened and perhaps slighted by the new demands placed on my time and theirs, have been expected to share toys and meals with these young newcomers. Some days, the levels of resentment have been surprisingly high. Samantha, however, has been the least resentful of all. Perhaps this is because she has one thing that no one else is allowed to touch: her suitcase.

Last night, I almost tripped over the suitcase, and for the first time ever, I was tempted to break one of my maternal rules and invade it. But I overcame the temptation and waited till morning to ask Samantha if she would show me the contents. Proudly, she brought out her umbrella; some toys she won at a fair; a small, stuffed bear; a package of gum; her photos and books; a bowl of rocks (I had wondered why the case was so heavy); her clothes; and my hole punch (I had been looking for that). Then I thanked her, whereupon she admonished me to put the zippers together in the exact middle before closing the case.

Samantha's suitcase symbolizes her ability to sustain a strong, healthy ego and to retain a sense of identity and entitlement. We adults speak of unloading the "baggage" carried over from our childhood. Perhaps some of that baggage should be carried into adulthood— protected from desiccation, aired out as needed, and shared with loved ones.

—Tracey Crocker, Mothering Magazine #58, Winter, 1991

Who's "wearing the hat"?! In American business the person in charge is the person who wears the hat. It's no different with little boys who would like to be. Hats are their universal accessories and an instant way to experiment with identity in their early years. Take one off, put another one on: some boys wear a different one every day. Don't be surprised if your little boy loves one so much that he wants to wear it while he's sleeping. It doesn't matter what type of hat it is, as long as it's on his head. They range from fantasy like fireman and policeman hats, to "cool" baseball caps, to macho army fatigue and G.I. Joe hats, to favorite cartoon characters and animals, to sports teams. All signify mastery and competence and a first vision of how he'd like to be and where he'd like to go. (See the School Days Chapter for further discussion of role identification.)

Accessories without the "Gimmies"

What if your school-age child really puts pressure on you for the latest accessory, driving you nuts?

Parents may worry that somehow it's their fault and they've spoiled their kid, or that they're raising a follower, not a leader. If a few readings of the Berenstain Bears book *Get the Gimmies* doesn't work, here is advice from learning specialist Judith Schneider, who tends to give children the benefit of the doubt: "When youngsters seem obsessed about needing a new 'something,' it may be their assumption that having this thing will change how they feel. When it doesn't, they think that magically something *else* will do that. Instead of responding in irritation ('I just bought you something two days ago!'), objectify the problem, and bring in the idea of making choices, such as: 'Gee, that is so great. Too bad we didn't see that before we bought such-and-such. But we didn't. Next time let's not settle. Let's hold out for something we really like, not the easiest thing.'" She goes on: "And if you have a child with learning disabilities, the situation may be even more intense. Learning disabled kids feel so different from others, and they have a desperate need to fit in. One way to be like everybody else is to look like everybody else. Parents who fight their L.D. child on having the 'cool' shapes, colors, accessories—of course, within reason and budget—is really making an error. In the sense of confirming of their okay-ness, and normalcy, they need support. They don't want to be unusual. They feel unusual enough!"

One parent says, "It really presses my button when the kids start to whine for more stuff or say 'You never get us anything.' So I have a list I've put up noting any little tchotchkes we're buying along the way for each kid—no matter how small. That's the hardest—not to forget to mark it down ourselves! Then we can point to the list and remind them without criticizing. Often, my youngest, who's especially forgetful, will get so excited that she'll run to find one of those treats lost in her room to play with it. I figure kids live in the present and often just forget what they've been given. They just need to be reminded."

A general rule of thumb is: the time to buy your child a treat is when *you* decide to, not when your child is pressuring you into it. If you give in and buy it, it'll only be harder to say "no" the next time. And your child will be in the scary position of having overpowered his parents. With a particularly persistent child who tends to get "locked in," give a definite "yes" or "no" right away (even if you're ambivalent sometimes): this will sidetrack long negotiations. Acknowledge the feelings of frustration he may have of not getting what he wants (at that moment the need is very real to him). Explain your reason later (if needed) calmly so he can begin to understand the decision-making process.

Keeping it in the family. This mother buys basic traditional clothes that can be exchanged among her kids. The emphasis is not on color or knitted fabrics. The unisex factor here is in classic shapes and sturdy sportswear in woven cotton. Kelly is wearing older brother Sean's shetland sweater with her own lace collar blouse. Timothy is wearing his favorite piece of clothing, older brother Sean's old tennis sweater. Shannon is wearing Kelly's plaid dress, and Sean looks like he's wearing one of dad's shirts.

HAND-ME-DOWNS AND SECONDHAND CLOTHES

T he value of hand-me-downs goes beyond thrift and conservation. Each time a piece of clothing gets handed down to another child, it becomes more interesting and more historic. Hand-me-downs are a record of a family, sometimes of generations. Often, clothes passed from one child to another become a thread connecting the children of friends and of friends' friends. My daughter always calls certain hand-me-downs by the name of the previous owner: "I want to wear Taryn's pants today." Among only children, handed down clothing can even create the feeling of an extended family.

Of course, hand-me-downs that make these prolonged rounds have to be of pretty strong fabric and design. Since kids tend to outgrow good clothing long before it gets worn out, a well-made tweed jacket can last through fifteen years of seven-year-old boys and still look fine. I was surprised to find that even among the more well-to-do of my friends, very little was spent on their younger children's clothing. Hand-me-downs constituted a large percentage of their kids' wardrobes. Then I realized that, of course, they were exchanging items of superior quality and craftsmanship. A beautiful and timeless Laura Ashley party dress or a well-made pair of flannel dress pants may be expensive, but those who can afford them can get a lot of mileage out of it by passing them down. Of course, you don't have to be a millionaire to give—and get—hand-me-downs with pride. Here's what to look for when accepting or packing away outgrown clothes as hand-me-downs:

1. *Durable Fabric and Make:* Levi jeans and jackets, corduroy pants, OshKosh overalls, are just a few of the indestructible clothes that get handed down again and again.

2. *Classic Design:* Oxford shirts and cotton striped shirts, smocked dresses, embroidered French school blouses, twill pants, and navy blue blazers will probably never go out of style. Some of these classic children's clothes aren't worn daily so they have a better-than-average chance of making it through more than one family. However, some of these classic clothes (especially the expensive designer types) require a certain amount of extra special care, such as frequent dry cleaning. Evaluate how much time and effort you want to put into your child's wardrobe. You may decide that wash and wear is your priority. If so, pass these items on to parents who'll enjoy them.

3. *Universal Fit:* Play clothes fall into this category—t-shirts, sweats, elastic-

"My oldest child is really savvy about hand-me-downs. She knows that her clothes—no matter how funky and beat-up—carry a lot of weight with the younger ones. I've seen her barter shamelessly with her little sisters, getting huge favors, like maid for a day, in exchange for some skirt that she doesn't even like anymore!"

"I have to admit, I feel like the cat that ate the mouse when I see my younger kids passing down pricey ice skates to each other. We personalize them with bright laces. Now with neon laces, even boys' black hockey skates can be used by girls."

A hand-me-down with history: an embroidered OshKosh bib overall started in 1979 by Mary Kay Dillon McKenna. Worn by: Ellie, Charlie, Conor, Max, Peter, Maureen, Evan, Claire, and twins, Nina and Maura. All children are cousins or close friends and live in Wisconsin and Illinois. (PHOTO BY: Mark Salisbury)

waisted shorts and circle skirts, stretchies for babies, and blanket sleepers.

4. *Unisex:* These are mostly play clothes in primary colors: t-shirts, sweatpants, sweatshirts, sweat jackets, flannel shirts with great patterns, snowsuits, winter coats and jackets, layette items (except possibly blue or pink) and blankets, even ice skates, can all be used by members of both sexes.

5. *Sentimental Value:* Here are the hand-me-downs that are really fun: fringed leather jackets, antique pinafores, sweatshirts with beautiful appliqués. Any of the clothes that you or your child really loved demand to be handed down, either from child to child within one family or from family to friends. A lot of the items mentioned—especially blue jeans and sturdy cottons—are even better the second (and third and fourth!) time around. Jeans get broken in, cotton dress shirts get softer—everything feels more comfortable after a few dozen washings.

6. *How many hand-me-downs can you deal with?* Some lucky parents have many friends or relatives with older kids and hand-me-downs are plentiful. This is not always a benefit. Some people are just not comfortable handling large amounts of clothing in their home, even if it's free. If you feel "less is more," choose what you love and send the rest on to friends, or Goodwill.

As the prices of children's clothing rise, a parent's ingenuity becomes more and more necessary. A new popular solution to the problem of clothing kids on a strict budget lies not only in your friends' closets but in consignment shops, secondhand shops, thrift shops, and tag sales. Resale shops catering especially to children are springing up all over in response to leaner times. Resale shops carry only clothing that is in excellent condition at reasonable prices. These shops sometimes resemble pricier specialty shops or boutiques because they are usually run by a single owner, and the merchandise reflects the selectivity and taste of that owner. It's not unusual to pick up a 100 percent wool boy's navy blazer for $15, or a practically unused snowsuit for $20. Thrift shops have better prices but are far less selective and you have to work harder to find the good things. Tag sales are completely hit or miss. They are a favorite haunt of mothers of twins who buy in bulk, especially when they hit gold (e.g., ten decent t-shirts at a quarter apiece). Other places to find secondhand clothes include fleamarkets, family swap meets (start them yourself!), and Salvation Army stores.

Of special note: Cartoon and TV character clothing are immediately accepted as valued hand-me-downs by kids. But they also ride the trends of the times. Strawberry Shortcake and Smurfs aren't nearly as popular as they once were because some kids wouldn't even know who they are. There are some perennial favorites, however, such as Superman, Batman, and the Muppets, that seem to prevail no matter what the trend. It's not only because of their inherent appeal but also because of the persistent, long-range licensing and advertising budgets that keep them in the public eye, and on morning TV shows. Mickey Mouse t-shirts will probably be worn by kids a century from now and still look au courant. Some shirts, though, will not see the next year. T-shirts that are too personal, carrying logos or inscriptions that mean some-

When Hand-Me-Downs Don't Work

1. *Doesn't Fit:* Not all siblings (or age group peers) are built alike. For boys, pants, jeans, khakis, and corduroys can be a problem. One size 8 pants might fit your first son fine, but the next child in line may have a completely different body shape in size 8. Retailers tell me that pants are the item most often returned in boys' wear.

2. *Wrong Sex:* Perhaps ruffles can't be handed down if your second child is a boy. But hold on to them—someone you know is bound to have a girl someday. Maybe you!

3. *The Child Hates the Clothing:* It is rare for all the kids in one family to prefer the same clothing unless it has universality, like a great-looking jean jacket. The hierarchy of preferences shaped by birth order can come into play here, along with family politics. Preference has to do with aesthetics, comfort, and a child's self-image. You can tell a lot about a child's priorities by what he accepts or rejects, especially when compared with his siblings.

   Often school-age children are sensitive and if they think their friends wouldn't like an item, they'll reject it. On the other hand, if neighborhood teenagers hand down some of *their* cool clothes, these same kids will probably be thrilled. These attitudes can't be talked away, nor should they be discounted, as frustrating as they can be to parents who just can't afford a brand new winter jacket, or lots of new outfits. You can encourage a child to make a hand-me-down his or her own by decorating, changing the buttons, or altering it in some personal way. This can be done only if you're certain that the donor doesn't expect the hand-me-down to be handed back. (See the Clothing Art chapter for ideas on how to decorate and personalize all kinds of clothes.)

   Not to be underestimated is the fact that your child may reject hand-me-downs in hopes of buying new clothes. On the other hand, if your child loves the myriad of choices made possible by different hand-me-down donors, all the better!

4. *Any Item in Acid-Washed Denim:* Any jeans that have been specially bleached or garment-washed to get the fashionable bleached or stone-washed look have had their fabric treated in professional machines as if they'd been washed at least twenty times at home. The worn look is achieved by breaking down the fiber so it looks as if you'd worn it a long time. These jeans, though great looking, will not last like regular blue denim. This is one case in a child's wardrobe where the item may wear out before the style does.

5. *Out of Style:* This is not too common a problem for kids' clothes. Except for outdated superheroes, boys' clothes for the most part remain standard issue. If air force was in last year, and this year it's motorcycles, the change in motif won't matter. It's still in a boy's range of interests and the silhouettes of the clothes—blouson jacket, pleated pants, jeans, won't change. For girls, an appliquéd sweat top that looked great last year with a jean skirt will mix in fine with this year's capri pants (as long as it covers her backside in a flattering proportion. If not, add a mini-skirt).

6. *Worn out or Hopelessly Stained, Faded, or Pilled:* Reject completely.

7. *Underwear, Worn-in Shoes, and Synthetic Nightgowns:* Some things every kid deserves new. Evaluate. On the other hand, a pilled character nightgown may look unusable to you but be coveted by a younger sibling.

thing only to the buyer and recipient such as "My Grandmother Went to Hawaii and All I Got Was This Lousy T-Shirt," don't usually make a graceful transition to another child.

ORGANIZING   When your child outgrows something you love, put it in a small shopping bag or corrugated box labeled with the *size* and the *season*, for instance, "size 4, Fall." Always label *sizes* on your storage boxes. *Don't* give in and label when

Keeping it in the family. This mother buys cheerful unisex knits and sweats for her four kids. Everything gets shared by both boys and girls. Baby Karol is wearing older brother Mickell's outgrown jumpsuit with a "girl" bow. Older sister Asiya is getting her older brother Glenn's striped top when he's finished with it, to wear with leggings. Second brother, Mickell, will soon graduate to Glenn's separates. The unisex principle here is primary colors, shapes like sweats and jumpsuits, in knitted fabrics that both boys and girls can wear. At about five, Asiya did ask for skirts.

you're in a hurry with the next child's name and when you think he'll wear it (e.g., Michael, next summer). Kids grow at different rates. He may be out of the size range of those clothes by summer, or not even near it. When and if you have a second boy or girl, or if someone close to you has one, with this kind of organizing, you can easily find the perfect hand-me-down. If you have two or more kids, or if there are several years between kids (when clothing piles up waiting to be worn), many parents simply divide the clothes into *categories* and *weather (not sizes)*. For instance, sweats, shirts-winter, shirts-summer, short-sleeved shirts, long-sleeved shirts; then just combine the smaller items into one box, such as socks, gym leotards, undershirts, cotton leggings. This is another way for parents of many children to deal with the growing volume of outgrown clothes, and the different fit needs of each child. If you spend only a half hour or so packing and labeling, you'll save tons of money. As a parent you'll have a great time rediscovering these poignant little clothes.

Tips

➤ If you have very little room to store future hand-me-downs, buy shallow boxes from the dime store that can be put under the beds.

➤ Find a permanent place out of the way to store your first child's outgrown clothes. There may be a several-year time lag till your next child can use them. Once your second child closes the gap, move them to a more accessible place—you'll be sifting through them now every three or four months.

➤ Dye pink or blue layette items a primary color to make them unisex.

➤ Use name tags instead of marking pens to identify clothing. Ink can't be removed from fabric, which makes handing down clothes difficult. Or just use your family's last name.

➤ Plan ahead. Buy clothing—especially the big-ticket items like snowsuits and jackets—in unisex styles and colors. Stripes, plaids, and blue, red, green, and yellow are appropriate for either boy or girl and can be handed down without any problem. The new unisex color for infants is turquoise.

➤ Especially good-looking hand-me-downs from past seasons can become treasured wardrobe items. They're not to be found in any stores and your child will look distinctive.

➤ Make handed down boys' clothing more feminine for girls by decorating with ribbons, lace, and appliqués (see the Clothing Art chapter).

➤ Get together once or twice a year with all your friends and neighbors who have children for a swap meet. You can pick up and get rid of a lot of clothes quite effectively by bringing all your kids' outgrown clothing to exchange. Don't forget to bring costumes!

➤ Avoid monogramming. Once it's outgrown, no other child will want to wear it. (And you don't want to advertise your child's name to strangers.)

"Hand-me-downs were really emotional for my first-born. Giving them up to her younger sister was like giving away part of herself. Plus she felt that her sister would look 'cuter' in them than she herself had, or that it 'wasn't fair' that her sister had her hand-me-downs plus the few new clothes we do buy her. Her reaction also had a lot to do with growing up and suddenly having to shop in grown-up areas where she fit the sizes but didn't think the clothes were 'cute' anymore. So, now we go through the clothes she's outgrown, alone, first. Just asking her what she'd like to keep 'for sentimental reasons' is enough for her to feel heard and she'll usually say, 'Oh, that's okay Mom.'"

"But I love them!" Boys' sneakers are their first wheels and the more beaten up they are, the better. It's almost impossible to separate kids from their favorite sneakers. Even in this kind of dilapidated shape, parents find they have to either ease their exit—relegate them to the back of the closet—or perform a disappearing act. Any sneaker, no matter what you paid for it, will start to go in three or four months if it's worn with frequency, and especially if it's used as a toe brake on bikes or skateboards. If you choose to spend a lot, do it for summer, when they'll get real use out of them. When the careening rush through sizes of the toddler through the preschool years tapers off, cheap sneakers are no longer a great buy. Depending on size, older kids don't grow out of shoes as quickly, and cheap sneakers are likely to disintegrate before they're outgrown.

SHOES

A wareness is a parent's best ally in the campaign for healthy feet. Most adult foot and back problems are a result of poor foot health when young. Keep an eye out for knock knees, bow legs, toeing in or out. These problems can be corrected with ease, but the problems that stem from long-term incorrect foot posture can be serious. Body posture and correct placement of the spine depend on the child's ability to walk and stand properly with the knees directly over the ankles. And good foot health is grounded in the proper fitting and use of shoes.

Signs of Foot Problems in Children

1. Child's feet toe in or toe out.
2. Child's feet roll in on ankles.
3. Child walks on tiptoe all the time or holds feet further apart while walking.
4. Child tires easily, doesn't like walking or running games, or gets leg cramps.
5. Child shows incorrect alignment of knees and feet; knees should be directly in line with the foot.

Nearly all babies have flat feet because the bottoms of their feet are covered by thick pads of fat. By six to eight years of age, most children develop arches; by three years of age, the arches usually become visible.

"When my child hated walking, being health conscious, I assumed he was having a low-blood-sugar problem or just tired, or even worse, spoiled because I'd used the stroller for so long! In fact, I found out his feet were not comfortable, and he couldn't communicate the problem."

Dr. Virginia E. Pomeranz, pediatrician and author of *The First Five Years*, writes: "I have had parents bring babies to my office fully shod at the age of six months. I have discovered that [parents]'d gotten the notion—a mistaken one—that forcing a child's feet into shoes will benefit them in some way. The fact is that there is no real need to put shoes on a child until the time comes to walk outside."

So what do you do with all those adorable miniature Nikes, baby ballet shoes, and tiny sandals for your newborn that well-meaning friends gave you at the baby shower? Keep them for show. When baby starts "cruising"—walking while holding on to furniture for short periods of time—he should be able to feel the floor with his entire foot. Give him plenty of time to practice indoors—

Feet were made for walking. Bare feet grip the ground more easily without shoes. This helps to develop balance. When your young baby has used his feet to propel himself to roll over in the crib for the first time, he has discovered the joy of motion.

free of shoes—to encourage the development of the gripping and balancing skills needed for walking. The little toes need to grip the floors and the muscles need to have the freedom to flex for balance. *There is no need for a "pre-walker" shoe.* Once he walks outdoors, he will need shoes to protect his feet. Most experts agree that the time to shoe your child is two to three weeks after your child starts walking.

When it is cold indoors, booties and socks are fine for babies, but be careful that they aren't too tight. Avoid the booties or socks with very thick, tight elastic at the ankles. Don't assume that the baby's feet are cold—check to see if her stomach and thighs are warm. If *they* are warm, the baby is not chilled. Many parents are overprotective with socks and clothing. Remember that *we* feel the cold a little more than the baby, whose tiniest movement amounts to quite a workout.

Buying Tips for Shoes the First Two Years

➤ Start your child out with a soft shoe, preferably one that laces up. Pliable sneakers, soft leather shoes that breathe—all with rubber soles of course— are good beginner shoes. Kenneth Meisler, D.P.M., director of the Preventive and Sports Medicine Center in New York City, says: "Avoid hard-soled shoes for the first two years. They're too hard for a twenty- to thirty-pound child to bend. The children will end up adjusting their gait to the shoe."

➤ Don't buy by size only. There are as many variations in shoe sizes as there are shoe manufacturers. You should regularly get the child's foot fit by an experienced shoe salesperson during these critical first years. Word of mouth is usually the most reliable recommendation. Check with parents of older children in your neighborhood. Avoid buying by catalogue, except to order soft fabric shoes for house use.

➤ Buy less expensive shoes. You'll be more likely to update the size for a correct fit—the cardinal rule of good foot care. Expensive shoes are not necessarily better, especially if you buy them infrequently.

➤ Buy to fit now! Children whose shoes are too large will either curl their toes to hold the shoes on or else shuffle along, neither of which will promote good posture or easy walking.

➤ Don't wait for your child to complain about tight shoes. Children's feet are *not* miniatures of adults'. The front of the shoe should be squared off to conform to the real shape of a baby's foot. According to Penelope Leach, a British psychologist and child-care expert, "Shoes or socks that cramp your child's feet will not cause him any pain; the bones are still so flexible that they will squash up quite comfortably, causing damage without the child [realizing it or] complaining." There are a lot of kids whose love for a particular pair of shoes outweighs any trouble they may have stuffing their

"Courtney is two-and-a-half and crazed for party shoes. I didn't want to fight over it every morning before school, so I just let her wear them to school and left a pair of sneakers in her cubby. By the time she got to school she realized she had to wear her sneakers."

feet into them. Check your child's feet at the end of the day for the first few days of wearing a shoe to see if there is any redness or soreness indicating a shoe is too tight. If the shoes are too tight, return them for incorrect fit. Once shoes that initially fit well get too small, hide them, bronze them, throw them out!

At some point in the early years, your child will form some amazing conviction—backed up by intractable behavior—about footwear. Your daughter may insist her grubby sneakers are the correct accessory for her party dress, and that party shoes are perfect at the playground. And if you can crowbar your son out of his favorite sneakers, even for bed, you're a miracle worker.

What is it about kids and their shoes? Marguerite Kelly, author of *The Mother's Almanac* and mother of four, believes that "shoes, like wheels, are symbols of freedom, and although clothes sometimes may not matter, shoes always do." Ongoing testimony to this are the actions of uniform-wearing private and parochial school teenagers after school. The only non-uniform accessory usually allowed them are shoes, so it's not unusual to see cowboy boots or funky ankle boots mixed incongruously with demure school uniforms. Very young children are no less opinionated.

A very common preference in preschool is illustrated in the example of a little girl who tantrums to wear her party shoes to school every day. Most child development experts would link this obsession to that little girl's task of discovering her own identity in the three- to five-year-old range. (See School

Fit Tips

The child must be standing to get the right fit. Compare how your child walks in the shoes with how he walks barefoot. The gaits should be similar, if not exact. And check if he has difficulty getting up from the floor.

1. The shoe should not gap at the heel; the heel should stay firmly in the shoe, especially as the child is walking.
2. The widest part of the foot should be at the widest part of the shoe.
3. The shoe should extend a quarter inch longer than the longest toe.
4. Run your finger across the top of the shoe. The canvas or leather should ripple slightly. If it doesn't, the shoe is too stiff.

For further information see: Roberts, D.P.M., Elizabeth H. *On Your Feet,* (Rodale Press: Emmaus, P.A., 1975, 1980.) and Porretto, Denise. "Care and Feeding of Baby's Feet," *Mothering Magazine,* #60, Summer 1991.

"Party shoes were really a social issue in my child's kindergarten. I made the mistake of letting her wear them to school for a few days when I was just too tired to argue anymore and we were going to be late. I really incurred looks of wrath from the mothers who'd forbade them and who had to deal with their girls' complaints about my child being allowed! The whole thing actually caused friction in the classroom too. As a first-time mother I was shocked that just a pair of shoes could be such an issue! A dress code would have been such a help."

Days chapter for more on this.) Feeling "dressed up" may also make her feel more grown-up, more powerful.

Another example of shoe preference is that of some little boys who won't wear a new pair of sneakers—they're used to the pair they have. For one boy, it may be a temperamental issue—he has a hard time making transitions even if they're positive. For another boy, it may be that he likes the superhero image printed on the canvas and doesn't want to give up his "power." Whatever the preference and whatever the reason, it is the rare child who has *no* opinion about his or her shoes!

Luckily for parents of girls, most party shoe manufacturers are putting rubber soles on all fancy footwear. If you do end up buying shoes with slippery soles, rough the bottoms with sandpaper or an emery board for traction. Or, have your child scrape her feet on the pavement. Patent leather and synthetics don't breathe or give with the foot and when worn without socks, promote blisters. Try to limit their use, or have a sock rule. If your child goes through a phase of wanting to wear them every day and you indulge her, buy a second pair to alternate with. Because patent leather doesn't breathe, it tends to build up perspiration while being worn. You need more time than overnight for the shoe to dry out.

I've been told that handing down shoes is not a good idea, that a pair of shoes that have been molded by one child's feet aren't good for another child. However, I know that many of the shoes I handed down from my eldest to my younger daughter had hardly been worn at all (and cost a fortune). Two months' wearing by a person who weighs about thirty-five pounds could hardly "mold" a shoe. Be reasonable about secondhand shoes, especially in the early years. Check the shoes. Feel around with your hand: If the inside sole as well as the inside of the uppers are still smooth and the sides hold up well, by all means, save a buck and pass them on.

Some of the best tips I've gotten on shopping for children's shoes have come from experienced salespeople. They've told me to get my kids' feet checked by a podiatrist; their support has saved me from arguments with my kids about what shoes to get; they've taught me—often at some cost to the sale—that price is not a criterion, only fit.

Shopping Tips for Shoes

➤ Try to keep one salesperson, if possible: one who knows your child's foot.
➤ Don't offer your child free choice in the store ("You were such a good boy today; pick out any shoe you want!"); the one he chooses may not fit, or it may not be in stock.
➤ For your own sanity, avoid the 3 P.M. after-school shopping crush. Avoid, too, possibly the worst time of the year in a shoe store: the week before school opens in the fall.

➤ If you have more than one child with you, bring snacks and toys.

➤ For a more accurate fit, buy shoes in the afternoon when your child's feet are enlarged. This applies especially to boys' dress shoes or girls' patent leather party shoes that have little give. You'll be able to avoid a return visit to the shoe store for the next larger size.

➤ Go to a podiatrist if you suspect any foot problems. The best investment you can make is in your child's health.

➤ If a salesperson comes up to you and says your not-yet-walking child "needs a pre-walker," you know that this store's main motive is profit, not your child's foot health. Also, avoid stores that are loaded with expensive designer shoes and "cute" looks, with obvious minimal emphasis on the basics. The styles *are* enticing but fitting expertise may be questionable. You know you're in a dependable store if a shoe size is in stock, but the salesperson won't sell it to you because it doesn't really fit.

➤ Look carefully at the shoes in a store, ask a salesperson to explain why one shoe costs more than the other, or how one brand of the same style can fit differently on your child than another brand. Then you can make informed buying decisions, e.g., "The only canvas slip-on that fits my daughter so her heel doesn't come out is the expensive version. Okay, I'll spend more than I thought I would for that shoe because she's going to wear that all the time. The party shoe is fine from the discount store, because she's only going to wear *that* a few times."

Tip to secure a narrow heel: Tie shoelaces differently on the last hole: outside in. Shoelaces will end up being crossed together directly on top of the tongue of the shoe, not on top of the shoe itself, as is usual. This provides more direct support on top of the foot, while pulling the shoe forward slightly on the heel. Tip to secure flailing laces: Use shoe boppers available at shoe stores and from the Right Start catalogue. Thread laces through and pull. Or, simply use this parade marcher's tip: Tuck ends of laces down inside laced portion.

Velcro vs. Laces

Velcro is considered by most parents to be one of the major kids' clothing inventions to save time and arguments. For parents, Velcro speeds getting out of the house; for kids, it's one more step they can take to be independent. For an older child who's taking his time learning to tie laces, Velcro saves the embarrassment of a parent doing it for him. Velcro is also a boon for learning-disabled kids who have a hard time tying laces because of fine motor skill problems. For children who have to wear orthotic inserts and can't wear laced low-top sneakers because they are too shallow for orthotics (the insert pushes the foot up too high inside the shoe and the heel "walks" out) the Velcro on the upper part of high-tops adjusts to keep both the shoe and the orthotic comfortably on the foot and speeds the dressing process.

Velcro's only drawback: If your child has a narrow or slim foot, it's best to reserve Velcro closure for the "second best" pair of sneakers. Despite their convenience for everyone, the foot may slide around inside the sneaker because of the less precise fit that a Velco closure provides. The lace-ups do hold more securely because the sides of the shoe pull together to hug and support the foot. (See illustration at right).

At four and a half, Chris discovered a way to identify his left shoe from his right. Out of frustration one day, he dipped each of his feet into paint, then stepped on some paper and imprinted them. He cut them out and tried to fit each "foot" into his left and right shoe. Two years later here is the result: "My Little Footsteps" stickers that are placed directly in the shoes. Even kids as young as two can recognize right and left by seeing which direction each big toe points. Available in most smaller shoe stores, and from the Right Start catalogue.

"Puzzle" shoes: This mom discovered an intriguing way to learn how to tell left from right. Here, a smiley face. Why not a train with the front car on one shoe and the caboose on the other? Or a dinosaur with its head and tail on each shoe? (Why does your child constantly remove his or her shoelaces? It turns any laced shoe into a slip-on.)

➤ Don't give in to piteous appeals or even tantrums by your child to buy a shoe that doesn't really fit. Enlist the aid of a friendly salesperson—let the salesperson explain why your child can't have them. Your child is likely to take an explanation more easily from the "expert."

➤ As your kids grow, keep an open mind about fads and must-haves. You can often compromise without destroying your budget.

Teaching the Difference between Left and Right

Understanding the spatial sequence of left and right is a skill used, of course, in being able to put a pair of shoes on correctly. It is also a skill needed to learn to read. Learning specialist Judith Schneider says: "How can you expect a child to read if he or she can't yet understand left and right in such tasks as dressing?" It's the same task. Here are some tips from Judith Schneider and others to encourage competence in both activities:

1. Start early in life by naming the pieces of clothing and your infant's (or toddler's) parts of his body as you dress him. When you ask him to lift each arm or leg to slide through the shirt or pants, touch each and label whether it's the left or right side. This will start him "feeling" his left from his right physically, through touch, not just through hearing.

2. Try the "happy feet" game. One learning specialist I know of has developed this wonderful game for her very young learning disabled students. Try it! Put the pair of shoes together the wrong way, with the toes arching away from each other. Tell your child "See these feet? They're looking away from each other. They don't even want to talk to each other! They don't look very happy." Then switch them back to the correct position. "Now, look at them! They're facing toward each other. Let's make them touch—for a little kiss. They look happy now!" Whenever this teacher gets her class ready to go after nap time, she says "Let's put on our 'Happy Feet.'"

3. Lay out your child's clothing for the next day in *spatial* sequence—left to right—on the floor, desk, or table. Put the first item to be worn, underwear, on the left, then the rest of the clothes, as they'll be put on, left to right. (*Before*hand explain to your child the *temporal* sequence of dressing—the *order* in which clothing is put on. This way, the sequence of dressing is also in the head.) Your child will not only *remember* the order of dressing but physically *see* the order on the floor in three dimensions. (This will also reinforce the reading skills the child is trying to master in school.)

4. Use your child's own hands. Say to your child: "If you're confused, hold up your hands, palms down, and touch thumbs together. Your left hand will say 'L!'"

5. Use shoe stickers: parents tell me they really work! Paint "puzzle" designs on canvas shoes, as shown on page 178.

"I have two girls and when we go shopping for shoes, we always buy at least one matching set. Usually it's the sneakers. There's six years difference between them, but they seem to love wearing something identical."

"I only bought two pairs of shoes at a time until my kids were five years old. Any more pairs and there was no hope they'd be broken in before they were outgrown. And I found that the fewer the shoes, the fewer the arguments."

"When Jenny wants to go out in her snowsuit wearing her party shoes, I offer the alternative of carrying them with us in a little purse, and she seems to be as happy as if she were wearing them."

Shoe Tips

➤ Slip-on sneakers are hard for very young children to keep on. Because they are cheap to make, you'll find them being sold everywhere at every price. But even an expensive version doesn't guarantee that they will stay on. Stick-on padding under the tongue will help prevent slipping. The store

Locked into Her Shoes?

The highly persistent *child who won't give in, the* poorly adaptable *child who doesn't tolerate* change, the low threshold *child with strong preferences,* can get locked into a ritual with the parent that may escalate into a full-fledged struggle. For example, the child says, "Mommy, tie my shoes." "Okay," says Mommy, and she ties them. "Mommy, they don't feel right. Tie them again." "Okay." "Mommy, they feel horrible, tie them again!" The technique here is simply to **bring it to an end.** Every time the child asks and the parent does it again, you are pushing the situation into a higher level of difficulty. A child can start out with a threshold issue (such as shoes not feeling right) and then become locked into the "do it again" cycle. And once this happens, the more you try to please the child, the more the sneakers or hair barrettes don't feel right, the more she complains, and the more both of you get locked in and upset. This kind of interaction also fosters the doormat mentality in mothers who go to any extreme to please their child. The cycle has to be brought to an end.

You must recognize that after a certain point you are no longer providing relief. Realizing this, you could say to your child before you begin to tie his shoes, "I know it's hard for you to get just the right feel of your sneaker laces. But if I tie them over and over, you will get more and more upset. So from now on, I will retie your sneakers twice, and if they still don't feel right, you'll wear something else." If it is essential that the child wear sneakers (for gym class, for example), you could end by saying, "Then it's too bad, but you'll have to wear them."

The critical issue for parents locked into power struggles with stubborn, difficult children is to recognize that repeatedly going back and forth on any issue is not only ineffective, but also actually perpetuates the struggle.

A lot of parents persist in these endless routines because of the temper tantrums that result when they don't. You can't be sure that your child won't tantrum after retying number three versus number ten, but if your child tantrums after number three, you can be sure that he would have had a tantrum after number ten anyway. In the meantime, you have eliminated ten minutes of the vicious circle and reasserted, kindly but firmly, your position as the leader. By stepping away and recognizing the underlying temperamental origin of the problem, you will make it considerably easier on yourself and your child.

—Stanley Turecki, M.D., The Difficult Child

See the Fussy Dresser chart, page 90 for more tips.

should have these on hand. Or, avoid them till your child can keep them on when the salesperson asks him to run a little inside the store to see how they fit.

➤ Keep your child's toenails clipped. An almost outgrown shoe may still have a couple of more weeks of use once the toenails are trimmed to allow more room in the front.

➤ Improve the look of your child's grubby sneakers that still fit: adorn them with new bright laces. You'll give his shoes a new lease on life till they no longer fit.

➤ To extend the life of new white sneakers, "treat them with a stain-repellent silicone product (it should be labeled 'all fabric') when you first buy them, even before they're worn," says Gwen Levy, District Manager for Stride-Rite Children's Group in Cambridge, Mass. Similar to applying Scotch-gard™ to rugs and furniture fabric, "this [repellent] will keep [the sneakers] from getting dirty as quickly; the silicone provides a wall between the fabric and dirt. This works equally well on canvas sneakers or the new machine-washable leather ones. There are many brands on the market and they all work equally well."

➤ Toddlers love to remove their shoes. Some mothers buy them high-tops which are too difficult for them to untie. Resist the temptation. Toddlers are still learning their stride; high-tops are stiff and don't allow their legs to bend naturally. If your child is constantly taking off her shoes and throwing them from the stroller, etc., your nonverbal young child may be telling you they don't fit.

➤ Name-tag (try glue) or ink in your child's name inside the type of shoes that are common among his friends, slip-on or laced canvas sneakers, dock-siders, party shoes. Put it on one of the inner *sides* of the shoes; *not* on the inside sole, it will be worn away. If they're lost at school or camp (after a uniform change, or trip to the lake), or left behind at a friend's house, they're more likely to be returned. When it comes to popular, sometimes expensive, styles of shoes, take steps to avoid loss.

· · · · · · · · · ·

"Henry insisted on wearing his sneakers untied, 'cool' like all his friends. That ended when he ran for the school bus late one morning and actually walked out of them!"

· · · · · · · · · ·

Socks

- If your baby has chunky (but cute!) legs avoid bootie socks with thick cuffs. (See page 33 in the Layette chapter.) They're uncomfortable and may affect circulation.
- Watch for bunched up socks inside the shoe; these can cause blisters as well as discomfort. Children often think their shoes are too tight when the problem is really the sock.
- Socks should fit snugly, but not too tightly. You should be able to put them on and take them off with relative ease. Most parents prefer a little synthetic in a sock for very young children because the fabric is softer and more pliable than 100 percent cotton.
- Patterned Japanese socks are adorable but are often too tight on the leg, and tend to shrink. American copies are sized wider and looser.
- The best, most useful, children's socks are the classic ribbed type made by Trimfit and others. These are available in many solid colors; white is still the best seller.
- If you lose a sock from a bright-colored pair, don't throw the other one away. Make a lively fashion statement by using a different solid-colored sock on each foot, as some primary school children do.
- Always have more socks than you need!
- A pair of fun socks is a perky, inexpensive gift that is always useful.

And now. The last word on all those socks "eaten" in the washer-dryer!

"I have five kids and I keep a policy of white socks only. They're in two drawers. The older kids pick the larger sizes from the top and the younger kids, the smaller ones from the lower. We never have to search for a missing partner. I focus on their individuality with their clothes."

DEAR ABBY: This letter is for all of those frustrated housewives who wonder if they've gone off their rockers when they find only one sock in the washing machine. You dealt with this problem some time ago by stating that washers and dryers do not eat socks.

Sorry, Abby, but the washer is, in fact, the culprit. I have worked in customer service for General Electric Major Home Appliance Repairs for many years, and we were instructed to tell our customers that the washing action of the water will sometimes push a lighter item, i.e. a sock or washcloth, over the top of the inner tub into the space between the inner and outer tub — and during the pumping cycle it can be washed down the sewer.

I have scheduled hundreds of service calls for socks to be removed from the pump of a washing machine. So, women, take heart, and tell your husbands to go yell at the washer!
NEW ORLEANS WOMAN

DEAR NEW ORLEANS WOMAN: I'm sure that many who have thought they were going crazy after discovering an odd number of socks in their washing machines will appreciate your explanation. Here's suds in your eye!

First-time parents are often so excited about their new arrival that they may splurge "just for the fun of it" on items like expensive Japanese itty-bitty socks with adorable graphics of planets, "smile" faces, or baby blocks. Each design is knitted into the yarn, a costly process. What a disappointment to lose them, from the point of view not only of investment, but of fun! Now that you know about the eating machine, be sure to enclose *all* small-sized clothing in a nylon drawstring lingerie bag before throwing it into the machine. If you have a machine, keep a magnetic hook on the side of your washer so the bag's easily accessible. Keep the habit as your kids grow and use this as a remedy to the missing-sock-of-a-pair syndrome.

Designer Nicole Stevenson's Tips
for Little Girls' Tights

- Really cheap tights rarely last through one birthday party. This is one accessory on which you really should spend the going rate.

- Most American-made nylon party tights don't have a natural heel and toe woven in. Instead, they end up in what's called a "fish mouth" seam, which can bunch up and annoy a sensitive child. Japanese-made tights feature woven-in heels and toes. They cost more, but last a lot longer.

- Check the size ranges on the back of the package and follow the size spread they describe. They are according to age and are almost always accurate. Tights are designed to fit in three-year groupings, for the normal build.

- On good tights, the first thing to give out is the waist band—the leg part can usually make it through four hand-me-downs. Put gynmnastic briefs over sagging tights. On thicker tights whose heels have worn through, cut the feet off to make leggings.

- Buy the wool/orlon ribbed tights for winter at the beginning of the season. Buy several pairs in the next size for growth spurts. This is a hard-to-find item midseason, and even if you can find a few, there won't be as good a color selection by midwinter. If they aren't used, put them away for next year. If you're caught short, try catalogues, which have a longer selling period. By first and second grade, your child will have probably graduated to leggings.

- Wonderful party tights that feature child motifs like bears, hearts, alphabets, bows, candy canes, and Halloween pumpkins are a great addition to any outfit, and make a terrific, inexpensive gift.

*Hand painting t-shirts
is an inexpensive way
for the Karrell family
to get together and
have fun.*

CLOTHING ART

F rom the time she was one, my oldest child Skye wore the same sweatshirt I'd decorated until she could hardly cram her body into it at age five. Then it was eagerly grabbed by her younger sister Piper until she couldn't even squeeze her fist through the sleeve—whereupon it was handed down to Raggedy Ann. Decorating clothing at home with your kids is a relaxing *and* exciting activity. Making a plain t-shirt sparkle with appliqués and rhinestones, or upgrading a graying pair of sneakers with puffy paint stencils is a wonderful way to let your children express themselves creatively as they add to the personal value of an article of clothing. There is something very important to your child about the shared activity of creating art you can wear and which will last beyond your time making it together. And it's so satisfying to spice up cheap basics if you can't afford a stop at the local chic boutique.

* * * * * * * * *

My kids end up wearing their personalities like a flag on whatever they've decorated.''

* * * * * * * * *

You don't have to be a perfect knitter or sewer to personalize clothing. You need only a vague sense of what you'd like to see and what would be fun for your kids to wear. When my kids were old enough, I started taking them along when I visited the trimming shop. They really enjoyed picking out their own trims and took such pride in creating their own look. Go to an art store or five-and-ten that sells machine-washable clothing paint and help your kids pick out a handful of hues. You can often choose from glitter, metallic, neon, or flat colors. At a notions counter, pick up trimming like rickrack, appliqués and buttons. Then get out the clothes that have sat unworn at the bottom of the drawer or back of the closet and transform their appearance. You'll have a great time with your children doing something that is at once artistic and constructive. You'll be teaching your children resourcefulness, invention, and empowerment. There's something magical and powerful about clothing when we (and someone else) have firmly imprinted it with our own personalities. And you'll be encouraging and seeing new dimensions in your children's tastes and personalities you never knew were there.

Here are some ideas: Glitter stripes and glued-on stop signs (one shoe "Stop," the other "Go," etc.) will suddenly get three more months of wear out of those "boring" old shoes. Your child's name spelled out in neon will turn the ignored turtleneck you spent a good amount of money on into your child's favorite shirt. You can improve a dowdy skirt by adding rickrack and a ruffle to the bottom (see the photo on page 188) or enliven a dull cotton shirt with pastel tie-dying. With a snip of the scissors, your toddler's favorite denim

Oshkoshes that are too short can become his favorite pair of summer shortalls, with an appliqué of his favorite animal. A simple t-shirt becomes a princess blouse with lace added at the neck and some rhinestones. Sweatpants with worn-out knees are reincarnated as cool surfer shorts for spring.

The possibilities for fabulous clothing revivals are virtually unlimited when you start thinking creatively about decorating your kid's clothing. In no time you'll be looking at your own wardrobe with an adventurous gleam in your eye!

· · · · · · · · · ·

"My first baby was only five weeks old when she had to switch to formula. I wasn't prepared for the stains and mess it made—I honestly didn't know to use a bib when I fed her! Formula really doesn't come out, so I got lots of little horizontal bow appliqués that covered the stained area below her chin perfectly."

· · · · · · · · · ·

Sneakers as art. Two-and-a-half-year-old Max didn't want to give up his old sneakers. His mother encouraged him to make the transition by painting the new pair. He did and he loved them. Her creative use of clothes was an effective parenting tool.

Art to Wear (left to right). How to give a basic top a little fashion magic. Have a boring jean jacket or sweat top? Decorate it in less than thirty minutes. The secret is in "Unique Stitch," a new fabric glue for about $3 which eliminates time-consuming sewing and which doesn't come off in the wash.

1. *Patches like these really appeal to an older child. Stiffer appliqués may need to be reinforced with thread, especially when applied to stiff fabrics such as denim.*
2. *Choose any ribbon or trim you love, remembering before you glue to bend back a little of each end under itself, so the edges aren't ragged. Lace is sewn onto the inside edge of hood.*
3. *Take any old buttons and sew them onto a pair of plain old suspenders. These, for an older child who won't bite on them.*
4. *This jacket, though bright and good looking, wasn't a hit until a few duckies and bow appliqués were added. Be careful that your designs aren't too perfect, too grown-up for the taste of your child.*
5. *One very simple ruffle around the collar of a jean jacket was just enough for this little girl. Her mom saved some for a matching headband. Be sure to follow ruffle all the way around the pointy part of the collar. Don't end at the point. All trims: M & J Trimmings, 1008 Sixth Avenue, New York, New York 10018. 212-391-9072.*

Dyeing Clothing

- Use a cheap plastic tub that you will always use only for dyeing, or use the bathtub, which is easy to clean.
- Try to buy anything that you're planning to dye in a larger size, because dye weakens and shrinks a fabric. Synthetic fabrics won't take dye as well as natural fabrics such as cotton.
- You don't need to strip a fabric (bleach to white) before you dye it, but if you don't, the color may not be exactly what the box says. Experimentation can be part of the fun.
- Cold water dye produces softer tints than the commercial hot water dyes.
- Save plastic nozzle-tip shampoo bottles. Use them for neat dye applicators.

Tips

➤ The best fabrics to decorate are cotton sweatshirting, cotton knit, and lightweight, pliable denim. The least successful fabrics are anything particularly delicate or particularly stiff—rayon, fine cottons, thick corduroys.

➤ Design your own t-shirts as a birthday party theme, or for rainy day fun. For a family reunion, use an identical motif on a t-shirt for each family member. Personalize the back of each with their name. Include everyone, grandparents, too! Why just the children? Use either puffy-paint pens from the dime store for a raised effect, or plain indelible poster paint on pre-shrunk cotton t-shirts.

➤ Supervise a very young child. Don't impose your artistic opinion, but do prevent too much paint from being used, otherwise the shirt would become too stiff to wear.

➤ Make a great vest from your child's old jean jacket. Cut off the sleeves slightly past the sleeve seam into the chest to make a larger armhole, and decorate it with appliqués and fabric paint. He'll fit into it again because the too-small armhole problem is gone.

➤ Instead of investing in a rhinestone stapler, you can simply poke the pronged backing used to enclose the rhinestone through the fabric from the back. Place the rhinestone on top (on the front of the fabric) and bend the prongs over the rhinestone with the back of a spoon.

➤ Cover stains and mend holes in favorite clothing with strategically placed appliqués, ribbons, or lace.

➤ If you are handy with a needle, let your child design his or her own appliqué for you to embroider onto a piece of clothing or an accessory.

➤ When children are very young, appliqués, ribbons, and lace are the safest because they can be sewn on flat and don't hang off. Trimming that can be grabbed at and pulled off by a baby or young child might be eaten, or

"A dear friend gave us a t-shirt in an awful yellow color. My son refused to wear it. We had a great time dying it purple—what a surprise, it came out a vibrant blue! Since then, we've doctored up lots of his clothes with dyes. We've become buddies on this subject and it's given us a more open kind of relationship—the opposite of the 'this-is-what-you're-wearing' thing that I see between so many boys and their mothers."

"My in-laws gave Johannes this stiff blazer as a gift. He hated it. (And, frankly so did I!) To solve matters, I glued a Superman logo on the front pocket and then we could get him into it whenever they visited."

sucked on and aspirated, causing suffocation. For baby's comfort, don't use bumpy decorations on the front of baby's clothing—it's uncomfortable when they sleep on their stomachs. Reserve rhinestones and pearls and other doodads for the time when kids are old enough not to eat them.

➤ To make cheap acrylic sweaters look more expensive and lively, invest in cute, character buttons that fit the buttonhole from the notions store to match the design or color.

➤ Turn a "boy" OshKosh hand-me-down overall into a "girl" one: sew an inexpensive ruffle on the outside of the straps, and along the pockets.

Using clothes to distinguish identical twins. Instead of buying basic navy or gray, this mother opted for a more dynamic look—brights in oversized sweats she bought from the dime store for $5. For safety purposes, she used only one letter instead of their full names. Slanting the letters to the side with two colors for a three-dimensional look gave the shirts the look of offbeat graphics. She used water-based fabric paint that is machine washable from the hobby store. Tip: Turn the shirts inside out to wash.

The Best Catalogues for Great Clothing Decorating Kits

If you're too busy to go out to find paints and trims for decorating clothing, several catalogues have put it all together for you in neat packages. The Toys to Grow On catalogue, for example, has at least six full pages to choose from, including neon plastic surf jewelry, puff painting for t-shirts, rhinestone decorating kits, and hat decorating kits. If you can't find it here, it's nowhere. Honorable mention goes to Childcraft. Also, the Cockpit has an unbelievable selection of authentic aviator badges, pins, flight insignias, and t-shirts, even replicas of medals to decorate a jacket. All are listed in the costume catalogue section.

A comfortable start to any costume. Little girls often use a bathing suit as a base for a fantasy outfit. Alexandra, two-and-a-half, felt her pearls matched her suit perfectly with her Mexican fleamarket sandals for the beach. Her mom thought up a cute hairdo that was also a practical solution to all her toddler growing-in hair.

COSTUMES
AND FANTASY
DRESSING

When I was a child, my favorite rainy day activity was to put on the Little Red Riding Hood cape my grandmother had made for me and go downstairs to see her. She would pretend to be the wolf, and I would end up with candy! Or sometimes my twin and I would play "grown-ups," going to parties, dancing, hailing cabs, doing all those exciting things we thought adults did when the children weren't around. Today, few grandparents live downstairs from their grandchildren, and adulthood has been demystified by kids who already dress a lot like grown-ups, and grown-ups who dress a lot like kids. Can you imagine a child getting a big thrill out of traipsing around in his or her parents' Reeboks and sweatshirts?

However, if you listen to a group of three- and four-year-olds playing, their little productions do continue to star the original cast of most children's earliest "let's pretend" games: the mommy, the daddy, and the baby. Mixed in with these archetypical games are also games that involve pure fantasy television or movie characters. More intense and exciting than the mommy and the daddy or the fairy princess or the fireman are often Batman, Ghostbusters, Superman, and Barbie. It's unfortunate that so many of the characters that our kids play in their pretend games come prepackaged to them through heavy commercial exposure. I think this robs them of the use of their imagination and the excitement of their own creations.

One Teacher's Answer to Classroom Gunplay: Shaving Cream and Courtesy

The first year I started teaching preschool I was very strict about not allowing the children to bring play guns to school. But after a few months of finding them trying to turn anything into one—Legos, paint tubes, their own lunch boxes—I decided to allow them. But with two rules: they have to ask the person before they can point it at them, and they can't shoot "bullets." It's really worked out. They always do the asking and we have a great time hearing about what they're "shooting"; anything from pizza to shaving cream to gummi bears.

—Marigrace Gaughan Walker, preschool director, Armonk, New York

Fantasy Dress-Up Box at Home

"Preschool boys and girls (age three, four, or five) often try on outfits that are usually identified with the opposite gender, such as a little girl trying on a man's hat like daddy's, or a little boy trying on grown-up high heels like mommy's. Parents can feel perfectly comfortable about this—it's a way of exploring what it's like to be someone else, even someone of the opposite sex," says Jan Miller, director of the Calhoun Lower School in New York City. "Why not include capes and firemen's hats in your little girl's dress-up box or shawls, old scarves, and wands for your little boy?" Parents should be relaxed and encourage the many ways their children are creative.

- Shawls and scarves
- Mom's and Dad's old jackets
- Old hats from thrift shops, Grandma's or Grandpa's, fleamarkets
- Old boots
- Old towels, sheets, blankets, or anything that can be used for capes, gowns, and forts
- Funny masks and add-ons like animal ears, tails, or noses
- Pieces of beautiful fabric remnants, tulle, and bandanas in lots of colors
- Lacy slips, old shirts
- Cowboy hat, hard hat, police hat, sailor's cap, mouse ears, baseball cap, football helmet, fireman's hat, crown
- Football jerseys and shoulder pads
- Old pots for helmets
- Old clothes, ties, fake fur stoles
- Lots of cheap jewelry
- Wands, scepters, cheerleading batons, dance canes

"Elio hates costumes of any sort. This year he was happy just arranging his NASA-type stickers symmetrically all over his favorite sweater. That was enough for him to 'be an astronaut.' "

So what can we parents do to encourage our children to pursue creative and enjoyable fantasy play beyond what is fed to them by TV? I recommend a box of dress-up clothes and accessories that will reflect the child's ever-changing interests. My own children used to veer madly between wanting to dress up as a doctor and a ballerina, so I made sure that both of these noble professions were represented in their dress-up box. You can always buy dress-up kits at a toy store or from a catalogue that have all the components necessary for dressing up as a fairy princess, a bride, a cowboy, Batman, Spiderman, a nurse, and so on. However, many of these products are expensive and some won't withstand many playing hours. Start with a few items. Children seem to need only the barest of clothing props to become whatever they imagine: most can inhabit whatever role they choose to play with a key minimal item such as a cape, a clown's hat, a stethoscope. Sometimes just pieces of colorful fabric are enough to get them going.

Howard Gardner, professor of education at Harvard University in Cambridge, Massachusetts, has studied children's play and found two general styles. The patterner is a child who has a tendency to focus on objects. And once the object is designated to be a certain way, for instance, once a wand and a crown means she's the queen, it stays that way. The other, he calls the dramatist. This child has the ability to take an object and transform it into anythings he wants at will, no matter what it looks like. The same wand could start out as a microphone, progress to being a fence, and even end up as a flag. The object isn't as important as the fantasy, it's a take off point. One is not more "creative" than the other. Some children prefer to play with small scale objects they can manipulate in their hands, others become so involved in the play, that they play to the maximum, going all the way to actually putting on a costume. Temperament can come into play here too. A child could be a dramatist, idea-wise, but dislike wearing costumes because of a low-sensory threshold. A child who is a patterner and has assigned one "job" to an object in play may be exhibiting a temperamental quality of "getting locked in," or she may be playing according to birth order, the opposite style of her sister. The elaborate schema she develops with her stationary wand and crown could be as varied and "creative" as all the outlandish characterizations of the dramatist. A patterner may be the little girl who refuses to wear any Halloween costume, but is happy to carry a plastic pumpkin. A dramatist may go through twenty ideas for a costume until she settles on one the day before. Who's to say which is more "creative"?

> . . . .
> *"Every year we do Halloween with the same two other families and their kids. We're always changing costumes back and forth. My 'only' loves being the youngest and getting all the attention, and it takes a lot of pressure off me."*
> . . . .

HALLOWEEN

Halloween can be daunting to well-meaning parents eager to please. Their child may have grandiose ideas of going as a piece of pizza or their favorite candy bar, when the parents can't even draw a straight line! Or another child is so excited she can't make up her mind—she'll go wild with the possibilities and drive *you* crazy deciding she'll be a bride, no, a cat, no wait, maybe a witch, no, a ghost, I know, *Frankenstein!* no wait, maybe . . . and on and on it goes. The smart parent sits back and lets children go through their frantic changes of mind, keeping on tap the costume basics from which you can build any costume, (while monitoring the local card shop and dime store for what's still left)!

The best antidote to parents' Halloween willies ("How do I *do* this?!") is to talk to other parents. I've discovered that dialogue and companionship are the key to really enjoying Halloween (and parenthood). If you're wondering what to do, start networking for ideas and actual costumes. You'll probably find that other parents are as pressed as you are and have surprisingly simple solutions. Sometimes the pressure just comes from ourselves. Don't use the cleverness of your child's costume as a yardstick by which other parents can measure your child's or family's creativity, or, perhaps more importantly, your own fine parenting skills. Remember to take into account your child's temperament. I've seen parents who've had visions of making their child into a pair of dice or something wildly creative become very disappointed when she only wants a plastic mask from Woolworth's. But to this little girl, who usually resists new clothing in daily life; prefers to wear the same thing over and over, and finds most costumes uncomfortable, a plastic mask may actually be a great solution for her to join in the Halloween fun. Then there's the mother who works for days on the sewing machine developing a dinosaur costume her child had sorely wanted. When the day comes and her child gets raves from everyone he sees, it can be bewildering when he demands to take it off immediately. Being "on stage" is something he can't quite handle (*this* year anyway).

When kids reach primary school, they may not especially want to excel at dressing up; they don't see themselves in a creativity competition. More to the point, they want to know "What *is* my best friend going to wear? Can we both be clowns? Or a two-headed monster?" They would be mortified to turn up dressed as a bright red tomato when all their friends are Batman or witches. Don't think the child who wants to dress up exactly as his best friend does isn't "creative." He is only underlining the value of his friendship. This is a time when children are developing their own identities by aligning themselves with their peers'.

What children want to wear on Halloween can reveal where they are in the various stages of social development. The child who refuses to dress up at all, as most seem to do at different times, should be shown as much respect as the child who will only wear what the other kids are wearing. And don't read too much into your kid's choice to dress up as Freddy Kruger or a witch. While you may not be too thrilled by your little girl dressing as a red devil with a plastic pitchfork when all the other little girls look like visions of sugarplums, realize that your child's take on the costume and what it means is not necessarily the same as yours. To children, dressing up as a scary monster can take the sting out of their real fears of the bogeyman. Or it may simply be a perfect excuse to get away with poking people with a pitchfork.

All that said, let's make some costumes!

Qualities to Look for in a Halloween Costume

1. *Comfort:* If you stuff your kid into a box designed to look like a TV, he's going to be uncomfortable, unable to move with the pack, and most importantly, unable to reach for the treats! If it's a cold night, your little girl wearing a tutu is going to freeze. Take all the weather and easy movement factors into consideration when designing a costume.

"My best allies in the search for the perfect costume are catalogues and Toys 'R' Us. Believe it or not, I start looking around August. With four boys and my schedule you can't leave it to chance. My oldest has very strong opinions on what he wants to wear; my second is more easygoing but he has to have something as good as his brother; the third tells the rest of us what to wear."

The Princess Ballerina Bride. Dressing up is a major play activity for the three-to seven-year-old girl. Children's play styles vary widely and no one style is better or "more intelligent." Rather the style of play is a very interesting way to observe our child's temperament, learning style, and talents. We invited these ten little girls to come in their own costumes and put themselves together. They shared their stuff with each other and used some of our things too. Here's what happened:

1. *The traditional bride costume. It's beautiful, rather expensive, but miracle of miracles, not scratchy, the major complaint from a child about any costume, no matter what the price. And what is a bride without at least two twirling fairy wands? This dress, Childcraft.*
2. *Maribou stoles are available at different prices and different stores all over. This girl's mother sewed inexpensive ones onto the hem of two cheap nylon dance skirts she's used for jazz class. Extra maribou went around her topknot at her request. She picked our wand and sweater.*
3. *Inexpensive tutu from Jacques Moret, a leotard with a built-in circle of tulle. She added another separate circle of tulle over comfy cotton leggings so she wouldn't itch. The crown comes with the added circle, and a piece of fabric was the perfect stole.*
4. *For a child who gets itchy, or for making Halloween rounds in cool weather, add the costume on top of warm clothing. Here, her favorite sweat top and leggings, only*

minus her pull-on jean skirt from the mall. Of course our hair elastics made perfect ankle and wrist bracelets.

5. For the child who hates to wear costumes. She came in her own party dress. Her mother made it special by ordering a child-sized bouquet of flowers with streamers from the neighborhood florist—a memorable accessory for only $10. She chose our crown, a fleamarket find.

6. Her mom's crinoline from college went under her tutu and her favorite lace-trimmed party sweater. A perfect after-school ensemble.

7. Her own ballet skirt is the Pierrot collar around her neck! Free-form pieces of cloth make her gown, and streamers her crown. Her favorite jeweled sandals her godmother brought her from India are fit for a princess.

8. She wasn't sure about dressing up, but she was definitely sure that ponytail holders are perfect ankle and wrist bracelets. One crown wasn't quite enough.

9. One item can make a costume, in this case, a jeweled felt crown. The rest is her own leotard and pieces of fabric. Scout down beautiful pieces of fabric for your child's dress-up trunk in your local fleamarket.

10. Her ballet dancer mom went all out and made her authentic tutu—she stitched a tuck in the front just like real dancers do, and spray-glued sequins to the top layer of her skirt, not to mention the ribbons on her ballet slippers. She decided it wasn't quite enough. She added a rose, pearls, and the item of the day, ponytail "bracelets."

2. *Sociability:* Is your child an extrovert who wants to stand out in a crowd, or is he a shy guy who hates to be singled out? Halloween is for *fun*, not a time to change your child's personality.

3. *Creativity:* While all children are creative, some of them may not be at a stage where they can just dream up a costume. Offer your child a choice between two or three ideas. And don't put pressure on yourself to make the best costume a devoted parent has ever made. If necessary, spend the money and get one from a store or catalogue.

4. *Safety:* Will your child be getting on and off a bus in her costume? Going up and down steps in the dark? Avoid trailing skirts, overly baggy pants, large unwieldy capes, and sight-impairing masks. (Face paint is preferable to masks and much more fun.) Forget the high heels, and add reflective tape from the hardware store if the children will be outside after dark.

Why Is My Child Crazy for the Joker?

A lot more children talk to me since Batman and they all love the Joker, they're crazy over the Joker, which might worry someone—he's after all not a really nice man. But if you ask the same child who they want to be, they want to be Batman, which I think is the way that works.

—Actor Jack Nicholson, in an interview with the French television network, Le Cinq, after being named Commander of Arts and Letters, France's top award for excellence in the arts, September 1990

Bryan's home-made costume for his sixth birthday robot party. Bryan's mother, Bonnie, combined all the elements for a successful costume. The effort to dream up the costume was the hardest part.

1. *Comfort—He's got on his regular sneaks and his own bike top and pants underneath to prevent itching.*

2. *Borrowed—This robot tunic "is the top of a costume owned by my friend." The bottom was "too bulky." Who says you have to use the whole costume?*

3. *Creative—For a lightweight helmet, Bonnie found a plastic light fixture in a local hardware store. To keep it on, she glued a cheap hat mold under the top and attached scraps of silver acrylic fabric to tie under the chin. (She sewed them to the hat mold first.) Last finishing touch: a piece of mirror from her used-up powder make-up case glued on as a mysterious reflector.*

4. *Cheap—Total cost: Helmet, about $7.*

5. *Safe—Nothing hanging off to get caught when he's running and nothing to obstruct his view (often worn for effect, the "reflector" helmet can be tied on backwards).*

One-Step Costumes

Using a plain or hooded sweatshirt and pants outfit (which is warm and comfortable, perfect for cool weather climates) or a solid-colored t-shirt and leggings as a base, you can make any number of great costumes just by adding a couple of touches. The Franne's Kids catalogue is a great source for all colors, especially hard-to-find colors, such as turquoise or fuschia, in sweats. See the chapter on catalogues.

"A zipped-up hooded sweatshirt jacket is the start to any costume in our house. You've already got half the body covered. One year I pinned pink ears to my daughter's pink jacket—voilà, a bunny! Another year I sewed big felt "scales" from the top of his hood down his back—voilà, a dinosaur!"

For example:
Football jersey and helmet
Angel wings and halo
Tutu and slippers
White sheet or pillowcase for the body of a ghost and white face paint
Dracula fangs, cape, and face paint
Tiger tail and ears
Raincoat and fire helmet
Paint spots or stripes to mimic tigers, zebras, etc.
Baseball cap and bat
Fright wig and face paint
Witch hat
Indian headdress and war paint
Feather boas and jewelry
Cowboy hat, chaps, and gun
Iron-on stars, red boxer shorts, and cape
Plumed hat for pirate
Top hat and cane

Tips

➤ Buy flame-retardant pajamas in a superhero, crayon, or bunny motif and have them double as a costume. If you can't find them locally, they are always available in the Brights Creek catalogue. See the section on catalogues and the photograph on p. 72 for examples of these pajama tops used as t-shirts.

➤ In cold climates, buy the costume a couple of sizes too large so the child can wear a turtleneck, sweats, or a warm woolen sweater underneath.

➤ Store-bought, ready-made costumes are wonderful. However, be aware that your child may change his or her mind a half an hour before going out and refuse to wear it. Keep a lighthearted attitude and avoid a fight. The excitement of Halloween actually arriving is often too much for some kids. Buy the costume in a couple of sizes larger—for this year and next. If they don't love it *next* year either, swap with other parents.

➤ It's smart to have ready an easy back-up costume on Halloween. If your kid is tired of the fairy princess costume she wore to the school party, switch around what she already has on hand. Add bunny ears to her fairy princess outfit: Now she's a bunny princess. Or add her fairy wings to her ballet costume: Now she's a ballerina fairy.

➤ Buy face make-up or hair color spray that is easily removable and nontoxic.

➤ Make sure that the costume won't fall apart five minutes out of the house.

➤ After Halloween, keep all costumes in one place.

The largest selection of dress-up clothes will be found in the fall/winter issues of catalogues, because the Halloween season is the peak period for business for these items. However, all of the catalogues or stores listed below offer dress-up clothing and costumes year-round. All catalogues listed below can be obtained by calling the company directly, free, unless otherwise noted. If you use a catalogue ordering company to obtain the catalogue (these usually appear in ads at the backs of magazines) you will be charged a handling and shipping fee. A note about prices of the merchandise offered: I have picked each catalogue for the intrinsic value of the merchandise and have noted whether the catalogue's range is "inexpensive," "moderate," or "expensive." If I've noted "inexpensive," you'll get a good deal. If I've listed "expensive," and you want to splurge, the merchandise will be worth it.

TERRIFIC CATALOGUES FOR COSTUMES

Childcraft, 20 Kilmer Road, Edison, NJ 08818. 1-800-631-5657.

The classic children's catalogue with the widest selection there is of costumes for boys *and* girls. Extensive and expensive accessories for girls, such as wild, Dynel wigs, lace-trimmed ballerina slippers, the quintessential bride's dress (the most beautiful and least scratchy available anywhere), a do-it-yourself hat kit, cowboy gear, outfits for astronauts and race car drivers, a complete line of NFL jackets, scarves, etc., and a collection of hats are among numerous fabulous costumes. The most recent fall issue featured thirteen full pages of costumes. Moderate to expensive.

Hearthsong, P.O. Box B, Sebastopol, CA 95473. 1-800-325-2502.

A beautiful color catalogue with simple dress-up accessories and an arts-and-crafts approach that emphasizes creative play. Goodies include decorated felt crowns and wands to keep in the family as heirlooms; gauze and Chinese silk scarves in divine colors; colorful "dancing ribbons" to attach to a bangle bracelet for dancing and twirling; a hard-to-find friendship bracelet kit, and crystal pendant necklace. Moderate to expensive.

Toys To Grow On, P.O. Box 17, Long Beach, CA 90801. 1-800-542-8338.

A good choice of dress-up clothing and costumes. A phenomenal dress-up

. . . .

"I find one major piece can make a costume, like a black cape and Dracula fangs. The only hard part is if I have to find sweats in unusual colors. I'll order from the natural fiber catalogues like Franne's Kids or look in the girls' sections in department stores for those."

. . . .

trunk for girls that features thirteen "grown-up" pieces plus a doll-sized version of the trunk with a matching dress-up doll, and an exciting "masters of disguise" kit for boys with ten pieces. The "Hollywood prop box" has enough pieces to imagine any action adventure movie, including tickets, a clapboard, and cue cards. An exclusive doctor's office is a huge set that includes 110 pieces, including an authentic bag, medical instruments, X rays, rubber gloves, and even a fake cast, all for $30. This creative catalogue comes up with new exciting ideas every season. Moderate to expensive.

Taffy's Showstoppers, 701 Beta Drive, Cleveland, OH 44143. 1-216-461-3360.

> *"I think of Halloween as the best family holiday. I even plan to take off work way in advance so I can be with them that day. We have a wonderful parade in our town and it's a big deal, but not competitive—just a lot of fun."*

If your little girl is a born performer, she will die for these amazing Broadway costumes based on original Rockettes shows and musical extravaganzas. Cheerleader, cowgirl, figure skater, dance, exercise, and ballerina costumes in an authentic style and cut. Includes complete accessories. For girls. Moderate to expensive, but not exorbitant. Catalogue available for $5.

Brights Creek, Bay Point Place, Hampton, VA 23653-3112. 1-800-622-9202.

This collection of children's wear is famous for its huge selection of sweats and pajamas in superhero looks. This is where you'll find Superman, Ghostbusters, Batman, My Little Mermaid and all the latest cartoon character trends, in pajamas and sweatshirts. If it's not here, it's nowhere. Inexpensive.

Johnny Jupiter, 1185 Lexington Avenue, New York, NY 10021. 212-744-0818.

This is not a catalogue but a store that specializes in over-the-phone orders for kids' costumes. I include it in this compendium of catalogues for its year-round commitment to inexpensive yet extremely appealing, hard-to-find-anywhere-else costumes. Authentic American Indian headdresses start at $5.99. Fringed vest/pants and American Indian–style skirts and tops for boys and girls are all made by Cherokee Indians on the Qualla reservation in North Carolina exclusively for this store. They have a Hawaiian "grass" skirt with a little halter of real coconuts and poly-silk leis, plus many more. Inexpensive to moderate. Call early in the season. UPS service.

The Wooden Soldier, North Hampshire Common, North Conway, NH 03860-0800. 1-603-356-7041.

Charming fabric costumes for dressing up as characters such as those from the *Wizard of Oz*, as well as unique costume concepts such as ice cream cones or pumpkins. Expensive.

Lilly's Kids (Lillian Vernon), 510 South Fulton Avenue, Mount Vernon, NY 10550-5067. 1-914-633-6300.

All the hot accessories and costume trends at the best prices, plus exclusive items not anywhere else: a whole two pages are devoted to a ballerina theme with a watch, book, necklace, dress-up table, and gown. The catalogue offers cheerleader and gladiator outfits, and cowgirl and cowboy outfits in real suede with authentic tassel and all-over fringe. Usually 20 percent less than other catalogues. The "dress-up trunk" here is an excellent cheaper version of more expensive ones, offering everything from a corsage and gold evening purse, plus thirteen other items, to a corrugated trunk, all for a little over $30. An exclusive pirate costume includes nine pieces with a red bandana, gold earring, eye patch, money pouch with tie string cord, plus clothes and sword. Inexpensive to moderate.

Troll Learn and Play, 100 Corporate Drive, Mahwah, NJ, 07430. 1-800-247-6106.

The dress-up costumes in this catalogue feature lots of dinosaur items, plastic animal noses, cloth animal head masks, and a walking pencil. Inexpensive to expensive.

Just for Kids!, 75 Paterson Street, P.O. Box 15006, New Brunswick, NJ 08906-5006. 1-800-443-5827.

Clowns, turtles, dinosaurs, and dalmatians with firefighter's gear. The selections in this catalogue are unusual, like Dorothy's red shoes, a magician dress-up trunk to cartoon suspenders. Moderate to Expensive.

The Cockpit, 47-10 33rd St., P.O. Box 019005, Long Island City, NY 11101-9005. 1-800-354-5514.

All the accessory badges, pins, and patches that mimic aviator pilots' wear. Replicas of medals, t-shirts, some hats. All authentic. Moderate to expensive.

One mom's creative solution to a dress-up problem. For $6.50 she found another wedding veil at the fleamarket. Now two best friends can go to the same wedding—no more fights over whose turn it is to play bride. Of course, you can't always go out and buy duplicates of every coveted item. In that case, a timer is invaluable for turn-taking.

SMART SHOPPING

The smartest shopper I've ever known was my mother. She had very specific ideas about what constituted quality. She would wrinkle her nose if the design on a sweater "didn't continue from the front to the back." She would drag us downtown to Ohrbach's, a department store that featured good knock-offs, overruns, and reduced designer goods. My sisters and I would try on clothes for what seemed like hours, griping all the time. But we knew that, thanks to my mother's tenacity, we would come out looking great and just as well-dressed as the children whose parents spent a fortune on their clothes.

My mother was unusual in the fifties. She taught us that the smartest shopper wasn't the one with the most money, but the one who was eclectic, and not afraid to buy clothing that was different from what everyone else had. She knew she had to stick to a clothing budget, but she also had a sense of joy about clothing. By buying our regular clothes for us at discount stores, she was able to indulge us with Parisian velvet dresses with satin sashes that we remember to this day. But these days, who has that kind of stamina, patience, and—especially—the time to be such a smart shopper?

The good news is that with a little understanding of the ebb and flow of retail, you can still get the most for your money. In some cases, you don't even have to leave the house. In the past few years, catalogue shopping has blossomed, along with parents' interest in and sophistication about their kids' clothing. Catalogues offer busy parents the chance to see what's out there and to choose almost the entire wardrobes for their children from the comfort of their homes. With so little time, catalogues are a very popular, reliable way of shopping. I've included a list of some of the best catalogues in the next chapter.

These days good design is available at *every* price level. It used to be that you'd get well-priced but badly made clothes from the cheap stores, and be forced to patronize the expensive boutiques or department stores for a special outfit. Now, you can find good design, perfectly adequate knock-offs, and natural fabrics for extremely low prices even at the low-priced stores.

As a fashion coordinator for a major department store, I've learned a few tricks to shopping wisely. For example, in large stores, there are different buyers for every department. The buyer for sizes 4 to 6x might have fabulous taste. A different buyer for the *same* store, but in the next size range, 7 to 14, may pick clothes that neither my kid nor I like. This explains why large stores, depart-

"With my first child, nothing was too good. She had an outfit for every day of the week. With my second, I'd gone back to work and didn't buy nearly as much. If she wants to wear the same thing four days in a row, fine."

Michelle's velvet party dress that cost $19 looks like a million with lace tights, a satin hair bow, and pearls. Her bracelet from designer, Wendy Gell, is a family heirloom—brought out only for "special—special!" A smart shopper knows how good accessories improve the look of any outfit no matter what the price. (Note: Make sure obviously cheaper fabrics such as polyester lace, are away from the face.) Dress is from K-Mart.

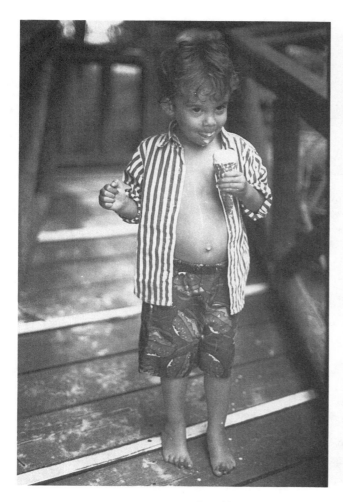 

The versatility of a classic wide-striped shirt. A smart shopper looks for clothes that can be dressed up and down.
Left: Max at the beach in the summer.
Middle: Max on a swing in the fall.
Right: Max rarin' and ready to go to the party.

ment and mall stores alike, can't be counted on to deliver a consistent level of style and taste. The trick here is to know your store.

If you are observant you can spot good deals. Certain major lines of clothing have separate manufacturing divisions that interpret their own high-end fashions and sell them for much, much less in the mass market chain stores. The name will usually be different, but the hangtag graphics and design may be identical. You (and your child) may even prefer the inexpensive version which has fewer costly unnecessary details which may actually be more comfortable. Fashion trends travel like lightning. You may also be shocked to see an *exact* duplicate of that imported clown sweater that your mom splurged on in Europe selling for a fraction of the price in an acrylic blend in the discount chain store. A sweater can be bought in a pricey boutique anywhere in the world and copied in months.

Some of the most useful shopping tips are those I've learned as a mother (and from talking to other mothers) about venturing into a store with your child or children in tow. When shopping with your children, as with any other adventure, it helps to be prepared.

Tips: How to Survive and Even Enjoy a Shopping Trip with Your Kids

➤ Whether a child enjoys shopping has a lot to do with temperament. Don't expect an excitable child to love shopping, even if you do. Most children can get overstimulated in department stores and some may even find a shoe store too much. If your child is excitable, stick to smaller specialty stores where a quick exit is possible and which have an atmosphere in which you both can relax. Small boutiques often provide space and toys for your child to play with while you're shopping and let you still keep an eye on them.

The higher prices of the smaller store may be worth it for the calmer atmosphere. Just buy less to offset the price difference. Limit the time he spends shopping, if you can, until he's older and can enjoy it. (However, always figure out a good time to bring your child shoe shopping—proper fit is a matter of health.)

➤ While your child is trying on clothing, avoid complaining that it fits badly or is overpriced. And avoid changing an outfit too often to "get it right." Young children are egocentric and also don't understand what's wrong with what they put on. They can't help feeling there might be something wrong with *them,* not the clothes. If a series of try-ons will be required for, let's say, a high-ticket item like a coat, or a difficult-to-fit pair of pleated formal pants, explain to your child *beforehand* why it's necessary.

➤ Avoid the "trophy child" syndrome by dressing your child too perfectly. Kids will instinctively feel that the clothes are more important to you than they are, undermining their growing self-esteem.

➤ Avoid bringing your child shopping if you're really not planning to buy anything that day. *You* may be used to "window-shopping" trips in which you browse, try things on "just to see how they look," and return home with nothing. For you, shopping may be a fun and a creative outlet—an end purchase is not always the motivator. Your child won't feel this way: for him or her, *trying clothes on is not fun, it's work.* There will be no payoff except wasted playtime, having to stand still, and there will be a nebulous result: "What did we come for anyway?" Be honest with yourself. Does your child really need the clothes? Do you have the money? If you find something "right," are you prepared to buy it? Or, is this shopping trip just an

Don't Buy Clothing for a Birthday or Holiday Present

The smart shopper knows that the only real presents are toys. Clothing (except, of course, if it has a logo or picture of the current superhero on it) is not considered a present, *especially* when it comes from parents, grandparents, or relatives. In fact, most kids are *very* disappointed to open what is wrapped to look like a delightful toy and find clothes. Protect your relatives and friends ahead of time from *their* disappointment at a possible lukewarm reception to their gift and alert them to this fact if they really like buying clothes as a present. Or let them be the winners when you clue them in to what your child *really* wants to receive! Or, let them take your child with them to go shopping for exactly what *the child* wants (a rhinestone top and leggings, not the new functional jacket that the relative thinks they should have). Birthdays for very young children are for "wants," not for "needs." Let the needed jacket be a gift for the parent.

excuse to get out of the house? If so, find another inexpensive hobby or activity you can enjoy with your child. Perhaps fleamarkets?

➤ Avoid going shopping after a long day at school, or after a full weekend. Saturday morning bright and early or rainy vacation days are the best bets.

➤ *Always* bring a good snack to tide them over and raise sinking blood sugar. Toys, crayons, and paper will also help occupy them.

➤ If your child hasn't had enough sleep the night before, leave him home or go some other time. Tantrums are less frequent in a well-rested child.

➤ Decide before you go what you're going to buy. Announce it to the kids, or else decide with them. They need to know the limits or they'll want everything. Be disciplined and stick to your plan no matter what else appeals to *you!* (If you really love something, you can put it on hold for later.)

➤ Avoid shopping in big crowds. Find out from salespeople when the store is the emptiest. This is crucial when shopping for kids' shoes.

➤ Limit how many items you ask your child to try on. You may have better luck if an older, experienced sibling is trying on clothes, too. The younger one will probably follow the leader.

➤ Young children love to please their parents. Even eight- or nine-year-olds—really! Be sure they aren't accepting your suggestions only for that reason—those are the clothes that'll stay in the closet. This compliance is also often found in a distractible child who says "yes" to anything so she can go and play.

➤ Kids' tastes can be as changeable as their moods. Don't be surprised at "out of the blue" choices. Respect these new tastes, within reason. And observe them. A new predilection in clothing may provide an interesting message.

➤ If you need to get a lot done and have more than one child to bring, it may be worth it to go ahead of time to big stores and set things aside. Most salespeople will hold things for you.

Okay, suppose the selection of big-name stores near you is boring and you want to take a road less traveled to find good buys and neat stuff? Read on.

1. *Fleamarkets:* Brand-new high quality clothing heavily discounted is not uncommon. You can find inexpensive basics such as tube socks, underwear, cotton shirts, pants, sweats, and t-shirts. However, check the discount store in your neighborhood before you shop the fleamarket. It often happens that those great off-price deals you get at the fleamarket would be still cheaper at home. And if you have a problem with merchandise quality, you can return it to a store, but not a seasonal fleamarket. Fleamarkets *are* still great places to find antique children's clothing. The clothes are not in as good condition

· · · · · · · · · ·
"I usually take the children with me to go shopping because they're so picky. I have four children, so to make it easier, I go myself first and pick out a few outfits for each of them. This way when I bring the kids back, it's not so overwhelming. The salespeople know me and they're great."
· · · · · · · · · ·

GREAT PLACES TO HUNT BARGAINS AND UNUSUAL CLOTHES

Perennial summer favorite: Guatamalan embroidered smock dress. As the child grows, this little dress with its wide drawstring sleeve can become a blouse under her overalls. Classic bright-flowered hat in hard-to-find baby and kids' sizes by Carole Amper at Shoofly, New York City.

as you'll find in specialized antique clothing stores, but are well priced. Items from the fifties are usually available, such as felt Mexican jackets and cute Shirley Temple dresses. They are easier to find and therefore not so expensive.

2. *Resale Stores:* Well-heeled customers who buy top quality kids' clothes give their outgrown clothes to these shops on consignment, or for charity. An $85 designer navy jacket can go for $10 to $15. Check the Yellow Pages or ask other parents for resale stores in upscale areas.

3. *Outlet Stores:* The unsung heroes for the consumer who wants quality, knows the manufacturers that work best for his or her family, and doesn't mind an extra car trip. Major vendors often have "overages," that is, clothing in styles that stores didn't buy, or "mark-downs," that is, clothing returned by a store that did buy it but couldn't sell it. In both cases the manufacturer or store over-estimated the popularity of a style. It does not mean there is anything intrinsically wrong with the clothing. Many manufacturers have set up retail stores to make some profit on leftover goods by selling them directly to the customer at greatly reduced prices. Overages from the manufacturers appear at the start of the selling season, and returned merchandise from retail stores comes in at the end. These types of stores are all over the U.S. and are found through word of mouth or local neighborhood newspaper ads. You can also try calling the manufacturers directly—they will often give you the location of their outlets. If you aren't near any of them, you may even be able to phone up and order with your credit card and have the items sent. It helps to have seen what's in the stores so you'll know what to ask for.

4. *School Fairs and Church or Temple Bazaars:* Good places to find party dresses, winter coats, and ice skates.

5. *Antique Clothing Stores:* For something really special, nothing has the same appeal as a fifties boy's sharkskin suit and plaid bow tie or a white hand-embroidered Victorian day dress. What you are paying for in an antique clothing store is the owner's expertise and taste level, and the work needed to sift through what's available and present the best. You are guaranteed quality and well-designed clothing. This kind of clothing is harder and harder to find, since the antique clothing fashion fad of the seventies and the lack of availability has driven the prices up to a staggering degree. If you do splurge for one of these items, relax and enjoy (but do take care of) what will probably rank as a family heirloom.

6. *Ethnic Neighborhoods:* Parents *and* kids are crazy about 100 percent cotton Chinese underwear and leggings, nylon Latin ruffled party dresses, and hand-embroidered Mexican dresses and sweaters. Network with friends and school teachers to find these items.

7. *Foreign Countries:* Savvy shoppers hit Prix Unic, the Woolworth's of Paris

. . . .

"I have four boys. I never take them shopping. I go on my lunch hour and buy a selection of things from a department store. I bring everything home and then we sift through. I feel like a delivery man, and I wish I had other time to shop, but this is the only time. I can shop calmly, the crazies occur at home, and I can return the rejects in peace!"

. . . .

for acrylic versions of the Chanel look and flannel-lined raincoats. In Italy, you can find a simple navy cardigan in the local dime store that would cost you an arm and a leg at the European specialty store at home. London's Marks & Spencer's boasts the finest quality cotton underwear and the original proper smock dresses. Japan offers kids' clothing with lots of color and creative designs. No one can match their upbeat translations of the preppy look or the ruffled dress concoctions in the Shirley Temple mode, but don't look at the price!

8. *Exotic Lands:* If you hear of any friends traveling to a country in the Far East, ask them to bring back folk costumes of that country. In Northern Europe, you might pick up adaptations of Austrian folk dress like lederhosen or rickrack-trimmed jumpers. For the sensitive child, however, stick to summer versions of European clothing, as the cold weather clothes are heavy weight (European homes are rarely as well heated as they are in the U.S.) and often too scratchy. Hong Kong is a mecca for great kids' clothes from China: embroidered shoes or dresses, quilted satin winter jackets, and white appliquéd pajama sets that double as adorable summer outfits. Moroccan bloomer pants are as comfy as sweats around the house or as part of a pirate costume.

The Map and Calendar of Smart Shopping. Here's my guide to all the stores and catalogues that are out there with the advantages and disadvantages of each. Use this as a map to seek out the best places to get the clothes you need when you need them, according to your budget, lifestyle, and time factor.

Now that you have some ideas for out-of-the-ordinary shopping options, let's look at the more standard places to buy kids' clothing. I've devised a chart that'll help you to understand the types of stores that are out there and what they do best.

No doubt many of you wonder why you can't find a decent bathing suit in the department stores in June and why the best-looking warm coats are sold out before winter's even started. No doubt many of you have also puzzled over the irrelevance of sales to season. It's not just to keep you on your toes that department stores have this seemingly bizarre schedule. Stores usually follow a very orderly, logical (to them!) cycle of shipping, selling, and sale-pricing. Unfortunately, the cycle has very little to do with the season we're actually in. For example, if you want the widest selection of bathing suits, you need to look in March and April. While this is okay for adults, your child may have grown a size by June or July. During the summer, stores stock winter wear and discount what's left of the bathing suits. The only stores trying to stock in-season clothing are the mall and specialty stores. One way to combat the seasonal problem is to shop in terms of light-weight layers that can be added or subtracted according to weather changes. And often catalogues may be the answer. See the chart on page 217 to get a better idea of which stores "rush the season" and which stores will have current seasonal choices available.

Fortunately for the consumer (but not for the stores), sales are now de rigueur almost every week in the fight for the market share. Even most cata-

The Map and Calendar of Smart Shopping

	Specialty Stores Such As the Gap, Locally Owned Smaller Shops, Mothercare stores	Department Stores Such As Macy's, Nordstrom's, Dillard's	Mass Merchandisers Such As J.C. Penney, Sears	Discount, Off-Price, & Outlets Such As K-Mart, Caldor's Kids "R" Us	Convenience Catalogues Such As Sears, J.C. Penney, Brights Creek	Unique Catalogues Such As Hanna Andersson, Biobottoms, After the Stork
Price Range	Expensive, some moderate	Moderate to expensive	Inexpensive to moderate	Lowest price	Moderate to expensive	Moderate to expensive
Selection	Tightly focused: usually offer one defined point of view (for example, American sportswear at the Gap, or handmade clothing and novelty basics at a boutique). Comparison shopping isn't possible in this type of store.	Provide most variety possible: there are more buyers for larger space, thus wide range of views and prices.	Large variety of basic brands (OshKosh, etc.) plus value-priced quality merchandise.	Surprisingly good quality for the price, and some brand names.	Best selection of brand merchandise.	Tightly focused. Certain tried-and-true basics carried through each season in new colors. Emphasis on 100% natural fibers.
Service	Usually provide the best service possible: personal help by salespeople who know how to put a child's wardrobe together.	Little sales help.	Ample sales help.	Self-service.	Professional sales help on telephone only.	Knowledgeable and even personable telephone sales help, plus further help from catalogue staff if needed over telephone.
Quality quotient	Should be highest quality clothing for the price.	Good quality.	Surprisingly good quality for the price.	Quality items are available if you shop thoroughly.	Usually good to excellent.	Excellent quality overall: check with friends who know about strong points of individual catalogues. Also, see catalogue listing, pages 232–236.

	Specialty Stores Such As the Gap, Locally Owned Smaller Shops, Mothercare stores	Department Stores Such As Macy's, Nordstrom's, Dillard's	Mass Merchandisers Such As J.C. Penney, Sears	Discount, Off-Price, & Outlets Such As K-Mart, Caldor's Kids "R" Us	Convenience Catalogues Such As Sears, J.C. Penney, Brights Creek	Unique Catalogues Such As Hanna Andersson, Biobottoms, After the Stork
Basic vs. Fashion Merchandise	Best for unique fashion items or European-inspired quality clothing.	Store brand basics are well-made and well-priced in season's new colors; coverage of fashion trends depends on each store.	Best bet is quality basics and all types of licensed merchandise (McKids, Mickey & Co., Garfield, Batman, etc.)	Best bet for trendy merchandise and value-priced basics at lowest prices.	Some fashion trends covered: best bet is brand name basics.	Not so concerned with fashionable items as with great-looking basics in natural fibers.
Time & Accessibility	Less time needed to shop. May not be easily accessible.	More time needed to shop. Longer waits at registers.	No long waits at registers, but more time needed to shop because of store size.	No long waits at registers. More time needed to shop to cover large areas and to find a salesperson if you need help.	Fastest way to shop. Look, choose, call, and charge or send check. Possible obstacle: receiving package.	Fastest way to shop! Look, choose, call, and charge or send check. Possible obstacle: receiving package.
How Much Can I Get Done?	Usually only a part of a child's wardrobe.	Can shop for total wardrobe needs in one place.	Can shop for total wardrobe needs in one place.	Possible to do whole wardrobe except shoes.	Possible to do entire wardrobe except good, fitted shoes.	Possible to do most of wardrobe except good, fitted shoes.
How Often Are There New Items?	Frequent shipments but often behind major department stores, which are usually given priority from brand manufacturers for first deliveries of the season.	Frequent shipments but not as often as smaller stores. Here is where you'll find newest fashions first.	Similar to department stores.	Constant flow of new items.	Complete offerings.	Choice of all is available at beginning of season, only.

	Specialty Stores Such As the Gap, Locally Owned Smaller Shops, Mothercare stores	Department Stores Such As Macy's, Nordstrom's, Dillard's	Mass Merchandisers Such As J.C. Penney, Sears	Discount, Off-Price, & Outlets Such As K-Mart, Caldor's Kids "R" Us	Convenience Catalogues Such As Sears, J.C. Penney, Brights Creek	Unique Catalogues Such As Hanna Andersson, Biobottoms, After the Stork
When Are the Sales?	There are usually two major, knock-down, drag-out sales, but at the very end of the season. Continuous small amounts of items on sale during the year. Put yourself on the smaller stores' mailing lists to receive postcards of sales.	Major sales often! One after each season, and planned promotional sales (check newspaper), such as Columbus Day, etc. Watch for sale catalogues.	Five times a year and frequent "special sale" days.	Look for weekly circulars in your newspaper.	Watch for after-season sale catalogues.	Watch for sale catalogues, often in January and June.
Who Always Has Clothes the Child Can Wear Right Now?	Smaller stores don't usually "rush the season." During the season, these stores still have full-priced clothing appropriate to the weather. However, big sales occur at the end of the season, so don't expect bargains till later.	Department stores do rush the season. During the season, e.g., summer, in June almost all summer clothes will have been marked down and cleared out. In July, you'll find only fall clothes and probably not a trace of wear-now summer clothes.	These stores do rush the season, but you may still find sale merchandise on the floor along with next season's new offerings.	You can expect a good balance of new full-price wear-now clothes and the next season's clothing. You'll also find sales promotions and markdowns.	Check sale booklets.	These catalogues stock natural fiber basics year-round. Check each catalogue for best-sellers and carryover items. Check sale booklets.
What about Returning Clothes?	Usually only store credit is offered, in some cases charge card credits. Only in season.	Store credit, cash credit (with receipts), check credit (if receipt is lost).	Store credit, cash and check credit. Only in season.	Will accept only with receipt in season for money back.	Check policy of catalogue.	These catalogues often feature unusually generous time and quality guarantees on their products. Check stated policies of each catalogue.

Unisex in the 1990s

It's not unusual to shop for a girl in a boys' department. It's more unusual to scout the girls' departments for boy things. The mothers of boys who do this are addicted. As Piper Smith, mother of twin boys, enthusiastically puts it: "Now that we don't feel funny walking over to girls'—I had to admit the first time was a little embarrassing—I can't wait. We go there *before* boys'. The reason? The colors. And lots of times, when the store doesn't know where to put a grouping of those great unisex pull-on clothes in bright colors, they'll stick it in girls', because it doesn't quite fit into boys'. I walk around stores now scouting every single area. It takes two minutes to pop into girls' to check—who knows what I'll find?" Here are some suggestions for boys under five (only) gathered from some of the most creative shoppers I've met. Keep in mind that by age five, most boys will reject anything that could possibly be read "girl" especially if it's in some motif or print from a store in the neighborhood that he could see on a girl in his class at school.

Parents who shop by catalogue are already used to this open way of buying clothes as many catalogues use a unisex theme to merchandise their books: it's easier for the parents and it's economical for the catalogue, which can then stock fewer items. If you are intrigued by this eclectic approach, small boutiques in your neighborhood often display girls' and boys' things together because of space. This fosters a grab-anything-that-works mentality and the sales-people in those stores often have wonderful, offbeat suggestions on how to mix girl and boy clothing together that will make the difference between a merely nice outfit and a really great one.

1. *Socks:* Try the girls' department for bright colors and lively motifs not available in traditional boys' departments. Best-sellers in boys' are consistently white and blue. Because brights don't sell as well, retailers are loath to waste time on them, even though they will pick up the look of the display. If a store does stock some colorful socks to pep up the presentation, you're not likely to find a full size range. Why should little boys be offered only cars and sports motifs? How about frogs, houses, cartoons, ABC's, even polka dots?

2. *Accessories:* Try the girls' department for suspenders in brighter colors and less predictable motifs. Why should little boys only have navy or plaid or Superman? What about polka dots (see Accessories, photo on page 156), and brighter colors like turquoise? Look there for belts with cheerful motifs. Why should boys be limited to a web belt or at best an Indian beaded belt? Why not a belt with a pencil buckle or animal face? And how about an umbrella with animals, brighter stripes, or a map of the world?

3. *Bib Overalls:* This is especially good for babies. Colors and prints are often more lively in girls' departments, even in so-called "boy" primaries. How about a turquoise bib with a red shirt?

4. *Basics:* Try the girls' department for better colors: t-shirts in solids and stripes, pull-on shorts, turtlenecks; sweats in unusual colors; and knit-collar shirts.

5. *Cotton Leggings and Footed Wool/Acrylic Cold Weather Tights:* Who says only girls can have the benefit of warm tights under their snowsuits? Or how about cotton leggings under sweats if the blends are too itchy? Leggings also make a good substitute layer under the snowsuit when sweats are too bulky. Both are useful for layering and the cotton leggings are a way to introduce some vibrant color too. Also, colorful leggings and tights bought in the girls' area are the secret to many a successful and inexpensive costume. Boy parents tell me that thermal underwear with a fly front isn't really necessary until they've been toilet-trained for a while. Many younger boys are too much in a hurry to stop and use the fly—they just yank pants and underwear down together. And most are not even aware of the opening till they are three or four years old. (Wash leggings inside out for less wear and tear.)

6. *Outerwear:* Why should boys only wear simple solid bright raincoats? Or only with blocks of color? There are loads of bright motif raincoats that work for both girls and boys in the girls' area. Zip-front cold weather sweater jackets are offered in more creative color-blocked combinations for fall.

7. *Cardigan and Pullover Cotton or Wool Sweaters:* Girls' departments have motifs such as ABC's, stars, polka dots, animal characters, and snow scenes. Why should boys only wear sports, argyles, and firemen? Shop for these in girls' if only to find a color-blocked cardigan for your three-year-old boy who still hates things pulled over his head.

8. *Bike Pants and Shorts:* Bike pants are merely pull-on pants in nylon. They work for girls or boys; often the ones in girls' are more wildly colored. And boys don't always have to wear the shorts with the inner linings. If girls' are roomy enough, why not?

9. *Sleeveless Undershirts:* These are often not available in boys' departments after todder sizes, but are easy to find in girls'. Avoid lace trims and pastels and you have a nice answer to the winter chills without the bulk of sleeved t-shirts. Or stock up on unisex tank tops in summer.

10. *European Girls' Winter Clothes:* Imported girls' clothes from Europe are often brought into department stores for the "fashion look" of the season because of their more sophisti-cated tailoring. Yet the prints, colors, and shapes, though they may be inspired by folk outfits, are more somber than American designs. These often work better for boys. Wait till they're on sale (they will be) and get loden sweater jackets and preppy tennis V-neck vests. You might pick up a navy jacket with a skier embroidered on the pocket.

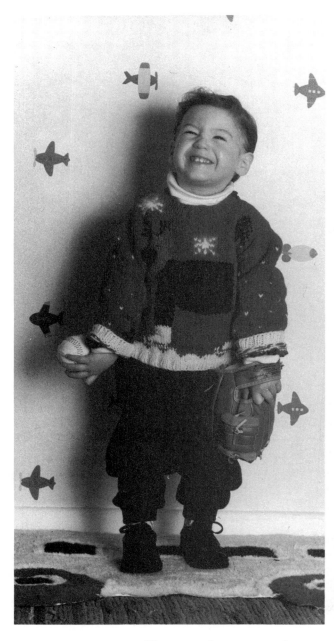

The patterned cotton or wool sweater as a pivotal wardrobe piece. Charlie's mother started knitting sweaters when she was home with her first child, Eddie. Now she's in business and you can find her sweaters everywhere. Left, Charlie dressed for winter play. One quality piece can improve the look of any basic. Whether you add sweats from the discount store or a boutique, they'll look great with an upbeat sweater. Right, Charlie dressed up. Mixing pattern with pattern gives a sophisticated, European look.

logues have end-of-season clearance sales. So the really smart shopper never needs to pay full price on anything but the absolutely one-of-a-kind, first-of-the-season items.

Tips

➤ Be prepared for overly sophisticated styles suddenly cropping up in the 7–14 girls' size range. The problem is that the manufacturers are trying to appeal to the older child with a pre-teen sensibility who still fits in that size range. Your bigger five-year-old may end up wearing clothing designed with a twelve-year-old in mind. You don't have to go along with this: your child can maintain her unhurried look in dressing for as long as you buy her clothes. Shop in more traditional stores that are known for classic design.

➤ Specialty stores like the Gap have a wider selection of a certain price and style range: they have targeted their customers and are serving those particular needs only. Department stores have a huge spectrum of prices, but fewer actual items in each price range. If there's a quality specialty store whose prices and styles are compatible with your needs, stick with it. But if you prefer a wider selection, a department store may be for you.

➤ If you've missed beginning-of-the-season basics in your local department or specialty store, check out comparable catalogues. Most clothing catalogues offer these items for a longer period of time than the retail store. However, don't dawdle over a really great, attractive piece of clothing. If it looks great in the picture, it'll probably sell out quickly.

➤ Evaluate the quality of each piece of clothing, no matter what the price. An expensive garment doesn't always guarantee quality. It may only indicate that a company is smaller and more creative than larger vendors (but may be less able to afford manufacturing resources for the best fabrics and construction. It's possible for a high-priced item in an expensive kids' boutique to be badly made, and a very reasonably priced item to be well made in a Taiwan factory for a reputable discount store.

➤ Keep an eye on those small, trendy children's clothing boutiques. They often have sales that discount as much as 70 percent, which means you'll pay a sane price for a really great item.

➤ Don't assume if something's on sale in mid-season that it's defective. There simply may not have been enough customers who understood that eye-popping color or balloon shape. Stores often buy designer, fashion articles to pep up their racks. Evaluate the item. If you love it, take advantage of the sale.

➤ Stores vie for exclusivity from certain popular manufacturers. If one of your favorite brands is always carried in your neighborhood specialty store, that brand reassures you as a customer. However, someday you may go in, and find it's no longer carried. This may be due to one of two reasons: (1) it doesn't sell, or (2) a larger store in the neighborhood promised the man-

"I always buy cheap party shoes on the theory that they'll wear them once and outgrow them. I spend a lot of money on clothes they tend to wear a lot, like really good sweats."

ufacturer very large orders if it could have the exclusive rights to sell those clothes in the area. For the clothing vendor, this kind of order from a big store is hard to resist. You, as the customer, can either go to the bigger store to buy the clothes, or stay at your neighborhood store to see what replacement appears. Sometimes it may be even better.

➤ The difference between sizes 6 and 6x in girls' wear is hard to pin down. One vendor says "it's a little bigger"; another says "it's a little longer"; still

The classic drop-waist dress that Alison wore for a year and a half. The smart shopper looks for kids' clothes that are trans-seasonal and can be layered more or less for the season's changes. The key is to buy big when you can. Look for wide armholes; avoid set-in waists. Left, Alison in the summer, in her favorite dress. It's roomy and long as she likes to wear them. Middle, Alison in cool weather, five months later, in leggings, sweatshirt jacket, and new moccasins. Right, Alison dressed up for a party in her favorite dress, ten months later. A lace slip adds the length she loves. A big-collared cotton blouse makes it dressy.

another says "it's only obvious in woven, not knits, and the extra length is in the leg, not the crotch." The bottom line, according to Carmen Nieves, a twenty-five-year veteran of kids' wear, is that "it's really just a gimmick of the manufacturer to keep the customer shopping in that department a little longer. No customer ever came in saying their child was size 6x. Most people think it's a chubby size, or would rather go up to size 7 for more mileage."

➤   Look for clothing that can "go forward." This is a retailer's term that describes how smart manufacturers of women's clothing ensure good business. They design adult clothing in groups that relate to other groups coming later. If the customer already has items that relate to the next group she will find it easier to mix and match with a new purchase even though it arrives later. This concept is used widely by manufacturers for adults, and applies more to color and fabric than actual shapes. When it comes to going forward for kids, parents should think in terms of *shape* only: matching colors is not as important in kids' clothing as it is in adults. Lightweight, layerable shapes stretch a kid's wardrobe. Buy roomy shapes so you can layer: add and subtract according to season. From infant wear on into the toddler years, keeping a color theme such as brights may be possible and practical. But as kids grow and their wardrobes and tastes expand, it's not as easy to keep such control (nor is it desirable). At that point, it's best to ask yourself, "How large can I buy this jacket and not have him swim in it?" or "Is this jumpsuit armhole large enough to layer something under it?" or "Are these pants cut roomy enough and can I roll up the bottoms?" or "Is the waist on this dress loose enough to accommodate growth or is it set-in, and guaranteed to be too tight after only one season?"

Don't Judge a Book by Its Cover!

Just how important is it to dress in a certain way? We have to educate our teachers so they can educate our children about the non-importance of how a person looks. Most people, even unconsciously, evaluate others by how they look. The problem is that this is based on subjective perception of what's attractive and not attractive. It often has nothing to do with the objective reality of who that person really is. Role playing exercizes would be a good way to make this issue transparent for kids. Have kids who are already friends dress up ugly and beautiful. Ask them first how they look to each other. Then, the important part, the debriefing. Talk about how they feel and ask questions like 'Did you not want to play with so-and-so because they looked ugly?' Or, 'Did it look like more fun to play with so-and-so because they looked cool?' Kids would be less likely to fall prey to these attitudes if they were exposed to them.

It's up to parents and teachers to realize how they're contributing to these social patterns. When we lavish attention on our children's appearance, we're enforcing the stereotype that 'I'm valuable because of what I wear and what I own.' These are values that come from adults. Let children stand up to trends and to their peers and say 'I disagree.' That's a value that can be encouraged in the area of clothing.

—Alfie Kohn, author of No Contest: Why We Lose in Our Race to Win

(Houghton Mifflin Company, Boston, 1986)

CATALOGUES
FOR GREAT
KIDS' CLOTHES

Here is my selective guide to the current crop of specialty catalogues for kids' clothes. What fun and convenience to shop at home without the cash register crush and all those overwhelming choices at the stores. How relaxing to cuddle up and thumb through bright-colored pages of smiling kids. Happy hunting!

Tips for Catalogue Shopping

➤ Measure your child before ordering. Key measurements to have on hand are: waist, crotch to ankle, waist to ankle, and around chest. Some catalogues that size in European measurements may only need your child's height and weight. If your child is squirmy, do what one inventive (desperate?) parent I know does; measure him at night when he's asleep.

➤ Feel free to really ask questions. Salespeople for catalogues are surprisingly knowledgeable. Many of them are thoroughly trained by the catalogue company. Smaller catalogues may even have their whole range of merchandise hung on racks right in the phone room so a phone rep can get up and walk over to the item to answer your question. (This is not true of larger catalogues that include other types of merchandise, such as gifts or household equipment.) Have confidence in their suggestions.

➤ Delivery of items may take from two to twenty days. Your child's size could change before the clothes arrive. Discuss this with the phone salesperson.

➤ Don't be swayed by a great price on a basic. Certain types of clothing, often the inexpensive ones, will look better in a picture. One way manufacturers make up for lack of quality in a cheaper garment is to use attractive fashionable colors. And they may pay a lot of people—art directors, fashion stylists, photographers—to make their clothes look great. As a result, that one item, say a basic t-shirt, will pop off the page. On the other hand, a more expensive, higher quality item in the catalogue of a smaller company with a smaller advertising budget may look great but not much better for the price. It may be difficult to tell just why it is more expensive. It is not as easy to spot triple-seaming, roomier cuts, and other high quality details of a more expensive garment in a photo. Take into consideration how much wear you want out of the item. Is it to last just for a summer, or is it a back-to-school basic you'd like to last the whole year?

➤ Don't wait if you see something you love! It's highly likely other shoppers love it too. If you can afford it, order it right away. It is a well-known merchandising fact that the color in which the item is photographed is the color that will sell the best, and most quickly, even if the item is offered in other equally attractive colors. The irony is that even an item that is photographed in a color that *isn't* the current hottest color (the first choice may be late from the factory and the only sample available in time for the photography shoot is the second choice) will still sell the best. In mail-order shopping, six weeks after you've received the catalogue is considered too long to wait to order a "hot" item. If a company has underestimated the popularity of this item, it may end up being out of stock by the time you order it, and you'll be put on a back-order list by the company. Four weeks is the longest you should be expected to wait for an item from the next batch.

➤ Keep a record of everything you ordered, and the date you ordered it. It's sometimes easy to forget if you're ordering verbally, so keep the catalogue accessible. If the merchandise is late, you can easily call the correct catalogue company back. After it arrives, keep all the paperwork from the item for a few weeks (or as a record for your clothing budget). If there is any problem, or you decide to order more of the item, you'll have all the necessary information.

➤ If you're trying a catalogue for the first time, do a "test order," just as big stores do for new manufacturers they are trying out. If you're satisfied with the clothes, next time you can have the confidence to order more items. Most catalogue phone salespeople are just as courteous whether you're ordering one t-shirt or a whole wardrobe.

➤ Liberal return policies are one of the advantages of catalogue shopping. The only problem is that it can be a hassle if no one is at home for UPS pickups. Mailing it back yourself may be the easiest. You can avoid most returns if: (1) you stick to ordering easy-fitting basics like t-shirts and sweats (clothing that requires a trickier fit, such as pleated pants, a blazer, or anything with a set-in waist is better bought with your child present to try it on; this definitely applies to shoes too); and (2) you take your child's temperament into consideration. Include your child in browsing through the book without having to worry about tantrums in the dressing room. If he's a school-age child and somewhat fickle, keep the catalogue around for a few weeks and see if he continues to like an item. If he still ends up changing his mind after the clothes arrive, return mail is a lot easier than dragging yourself to the store late in the season hoping to be credited the full price.

➤ When it comes to sales in the mail, names are often pulled at random from computer files of customers. Hard to believe, but catalogues for sales are often sent at random, without any merchandising research or records of what and how much their subscribers have purchased in the past. Make

Savvy Washing Tips from a Cotton Expert

If you order 100 percent cotton clothing that is hand-dyed or brightly colored, Franne of Franne's Kids, a catalogue of 100 percent natural fibers, suggests using these tips to avoid colors running and ruining other clothes:

- Always wash with cold water for the life of the garment.
- Before wearing any of the clothes for the first time, run them through the washer. Use a separate load for *each* color. Instead of soap, use just one tablespoon of white vinegar. If there was any chance of colors bleeding, the vinegar will set the colors permanently.

some noise to get yourself on these lists. Tell the phone salesperson "I want my name on whatever list comes up."

➤ Use catalogues for lessons in quality. The Land's End catalogue has only a few pages for children's clothing. However, the quality points are so carefully delineated on every t-shirt, overall, and sweat, that it is a virtual classroom on the subject. Selection is limited, but if you read *every* description you will become as educated as any top kids' designer as to why and how something feels and fits right. The same goes for the Patagonia catalogue. Every item and its description sounds as if it were designed and written by a parent of ten.

➤ Don't assume because you're ordering 100 percent cotton that you should get it two sizes bigger. Check the shrinkage rate in the front of the catalogue or ask the salesperson on the phone. You may be surprised at very low shrinkage rates in high quality catalogues; this means the size range may be more true to size.

➤ Many of the catalogues listed below are involved with environmental causes, e.g., Hanna Andersson. This catalogue has a return policy for used clothes, which they call "hannadowns": When you send back clothing you've bought and used in the past, and it's still in decent shape, you'll get a credit and the clothing will be donated to charity.

Two other catalogues come to mind as encouraging environmental awareness: Biobottoms, for the complete information service it runs to encourage environmentally benign cloth diapering; and Patagonia, for the costly color pages it devotes not to sales but to articles about conservation. Patagonia was the first children's and adult catalogue to convert to recycled paper for its catalogues, and it donates free winter jackets to the needy. Patronizing companies like these is one way parents can support efforts to better our kids' futures.

This working mother found a way to enhance her limited time with her daughter. Every so often, Courtney's baby-sitter would bring her to her mother's office for lunch. Off they would go to the coffee shop in their finery. Now their "private time" is even more special. Kids' catalogues often have adult versions of their kids' clothes or at least items that are very similar. In the fifties, "mother-daughter" dressing was very popular. But baby boomers have often viewed it in hindsight as a reflection of that stifling era. Now, the trend is returning for a more profound reason: With two-paycheck families who never seem to have enough time to see their kids, or for single-parent household heads with the same problem, dressing now is viewed as one way to bring busy families together. Catalogues specializing in both boy and girl versions of dressing alike are: Hanna Andersson, Biobottoms, The Wooden Soldier, Land's End, Patagonia Kids.

BARGAINS

After the Stork, 1501 12th Street, N.W., Albuquerque, NM 87104. 505-243-9100.

Casual, comfortable cotton clothes in bright colors and patterns. Lots of great printed t-shirts and funky prints. For boys and girls, from birth to junior. Famous for great buys on 100 percent cotton t-shirts and leggings, in ten colors. Use washing suggestions for 100 percent cotton. Inexpensive to moderate. The Wear It Now catalogue is a new offering from After the Stork to address preteen needs. Same address, 505-243-8022.

Brights Creek, Bay Point Place, Hampton, VA 23653. 800-622-9202.

Comprehensive catalogue for all children's clothing and accessory needs from birth to junior. Sports to dress-up, reasonably priced and trendy. Brights Creek carries an awesome selection of character pajamas not to be seen elsewhere. Their sale catalogues feature extremely low prices. A layette selection is extensive, offered in 100 percent cotton, and extremely inexpensive. Here is the hard-to-find mock turtleneck bodysuit with excellent coverage for cold weather: a snap-crotch for a smooth line, long sleeves, and a mock instead of a full turtle, so a tiny baby won't be crowded under the chin. Inexpensive.

The Company Store, 500 Company Store Road, La Crosse, WI 54601. 800-356-9367.

Down-filled goods, factory-to-you priced. Great value for outerwear for very cold climates, baby to adult. Famous baby bunting that converts to snowsuit with legs. Styles are more basic than trendy. Moderate to expensive.

Olson's Mill Direct, 1641 South Main Street, Oshkosh, WI 54901. 414-233-7799.

Eighty percent of the clothing is the OshKosh line; features hard-to-find OshKosh items for babies through adults. The most popular items are the famous overalls and shortalls in every incarnation. There is even a baby bibbed overall with feet in a lighter-weight denim and pinwale corduroy for the newborn in size six to nine months. At least one shortall or overall is always available with leg snaps in size 4—a hard-to-find item for the older or bigger toddler who is still diapered.

A new OshKosh overall shape is called the "Busy Body Bib" and is a feminized bubble shape in a European style with the same great price. A light-weight nylon jacket lined with fleece is a find for $20, sizes 2 to 16. A full selection in boys' sizes 8 to 14, hard to find in department stores, accommodates older kids who still want to wear OshKosh. They carry the traditional but classic hard-to-find flannel-lined jeans with matching shirt. High style for this catalogue would mean contrast colors or patches of solid or striped denim used as accents on some overalls. Moderate.

Biobottoms, P.O. Box 6009, 3820 Bodega Avenue, Petaluma, CA 94953. 707-778-7949.

The authority on cloth diapering and inventors of the original Velcro-closure diaper cover from which they get their name. Hard-to-find 100 percent cotton sweats; their own exclusive jumpsuits in comfortable, sturdy velour. Great beachwear. Hard-to-find cotton zip-front hooded jacket for baby and all-weather twill jackets lined in fleece for older kids. Exclusive mock turtle long-sleeved "tummy topper," a version of the onesie for baby in colder weather. Floral party dresses with matching elasticized headbands. Unusual boys' surf looks. Interpretations of kids' wear that cleverly combine trendiness with good taste. Moderate to expensive.

Franne's Kids, 8306 Wilshire Boulevard, Suite 7065, Beverly Hills, CA 90211. 800-526-KIDS.

One hundred percent cottons, wide selection of bright solid-colored clothing. From hats to socks to vests, to long- and short-sleeved shirts, to leggings to skirts to coveralls, bloomers, and bibs—all can be mixed and matched. Customers rave about the colors which they say are run-proof and stay vibrant. Offers a three or six pack of certain basics at a modest discount. Moderate to expensive.

Garnet Hill, 262 Main Street, Franconia, NH 03580. 800-622-6216.

The Original Natural Fibers Catalogue, features high quality under- and outerwear, wonderful flannel sheets and linens for baby, including hard-to-find cotton jersey knit crib sheets (so soft!), and other layette items. The children's clothing and accessories, many of which are imported, have an Austrian or Victorian mood. Expensive.

Hanna Andersson, 1010 N.W. Flanders, Portland, OR 97209. 800-222-0544.

Extremely well made, the crème de la crème of classic cotton children's clothing in clear, bright colors. The focus here is on quality and colors, not fashion. Made or designed in Sweden for ages birth to adult. Used Hanna clothing is of such good quality that it is often indistinguishable from newly minted. Telephone salespeople have complete specifics on measurements in inches for each size for every item that appears on their computer screen when you're ordering. Measure your child beforehand to eliminate the guesswork. Expensive, but worth it.

Land's End, Land's End Lane, Dodgeville, WI 53595. 800-356-4444 or 608-935-9341.

A sensible line of rugged playwear, focusing on durability with quality details such as double knees and reinforced side and seat seams. A large selec-

"Because I'm working, I use catalogues a lot. In June, I buy things from the sale catalogues when they get rid of their odd sizes. I stock up on sweatpants and t-shirts in the next size. Come September, for the first cool day, I'm prepared."

tion of bright colors or traditional color stripings is offered for their basic overalls, t-shirts and sweats. Pair their bright rugby shirts with overalls for an especially ebullient and durable play uniform. Overalls and shortalls are available with snap-crotch linings in hard-to-find size 4. Authentic wool baseball hats for $16, based on the originals worn by Babe Ruth and other legendary greats, are only to be found here. Moderate.

The Nature Company Catalogue, P.O. Box 2310, Berkeley, CA 94702 1-800-227-1114

Do you have a nature- or animal-loving child? This is a naturalist catalogue offering *everything* from binoculars, leaf-collecting albums, and dominos with insects on them to a ninety-pound, human-size penguin to safaris. I mention this catalogue for the incredible selection of t-shirts with every animal you can think of featured—from elephants, to frog families, to bugs, to dolphins, to tropical fish. The artwork is excellent on every shirt and there is even a black t-shirt with yellow bats on it that glow in the dark. Prices range from $9 to $18. Moderate to expensive.

Patagonia Kids, 1609 West Babcock Street, P.O. Box 8900, Bozeman, MT 59715. 800-638-6464.

A striking, full-color catalogue features photos of kids' clothes in action, sent in by customers from all over the world. Synchilla, a new insulated, synthetic fiber which the company developed for mountain climbers, is used for soft, cuddly buntings and snowsuits. (In other catalogues, it's called Polar Plus, or Polarlite, etc.) Sweat suits, rain gear, and sturdy pants with knit cuffs are clothes to rely on. They carry the best bright-colored backpacks to be found anywhere as well as ingenious cold weather accessories, such as the neck gaiter, a substitute for a flyaway scarf, in a soft circle of pile. Moderate to expensive.

CLASS ACTS

Les Petits, 3200 South 76th Street, Box 33901, Philadelphia, PA 19153. 900-333-2002.

Traditional high quality clothing and accessories made in France. Crisp embroidered Peter Pan collar blouses, knit pleated pull-on skirts, and excellent boys' knitwear are surprisingly affordable. Dress-up for toddlers through juniors in well-bred European looks. Especially good for back-to-school fall clothes. Moderate to expensive.

Pleasant Company (The American Girl Collection), P.O. Box 112, Madison, WI 53701-0112. 800-845-0005; in Wisconsin, 608-255-6410.

Victorian dolls, their accessories, and books about their "lives" inspire these classic American clothing designs for girls. Many are copied from original period children's clothing. All clothing is exclusively designed for this catalogue. Parents rave about the quality and detail of the dresses with laced bloomers and aprons, and with high-button shoes to match. The long yellow rain slicker is a universal favorite and best-seller. Expensive.

TRADITIONAL

Talbots Kids, 175 Beal Street, Hingham, MA 02043-1586. 800-543-7123.
Complete wardrobing, wonderfully photographed, for girls and boys. The fresh attractive selection runs from play clothes to beautiful party dresses, even double-breasted jackets with hankie pockets! Their own make of quality basics at a good price and some well-known traditional brands. Great looking, but not trendy. Order fast—items go quickly. Expensive.

The Wooden Soldier, Kearsarge Street, North Conway, NH 03860.
603-356-7041
Elegant clothing for special occasions in an English mode: specializes in brother/sister outfits that coordinate, with all the accessories to match. Also features contemporary play clothes with unusual lively motifs. Expensive.

FASHION FORWARD

Maggie Moore, 29 West 57th Street, New York, NY 10019. 212-750-5001.
Clothes for boys and girls from infant to primary school. High quality fashion items in 100 percent cotton. Bright, upbeat, and unusual selection of hats and sweaters. Very well made costumes. Funny "fruit" buntings (but without arms for "handles"). Great quality and fashionable goods. Expensive.

Saks Fifth Avenue, Folio Collections, Inc., 557 Tuckahoe Road, Yonkers, NY 10710. 800-345-3454.
Quality traditional clothing with a fashion twist. Fall plaid dresses and skirts could feature big black velvet bows or scattered bright bow appliqués. Boys' surf looks, real leather bomber jackets, matching father and son sweaters, decorated sweats with matching tights or bike pants. Expensive, but especially worth it for back to school.

SPECIAL RESOURCES

The Right Start Catalogue, 5334 Sterling Center Drive, Westlake Village, CA 91361. 800-548-8531.
The only catalogue of its kind to feature unusual and useful child-rearing equipment; devotes at least one whole page to clothing accessories that help extend the life of kids' clothes. "Kneekers" (See Layette, page 42), stretchy terrycloth pads similar to adult tennis wristbands, fit over crawling babys' knees to prevent holes in clothing and scratches to bare knees. "False bottoms" (See Layette, page 42) are snapped cuffs that add three or four inches to any outfit that snaps at the crotch. Inexpensive Velcroed cloth diaper covers are available

in cute, hard-to-find all-over prints. Note the diaper bag with its own bottle-sized cooler. This catalogue was recently awarded the Parents' Choice Approval Award for quality, design, and value, the first catalogue to receive this commendation. Prices range from inexpensive to expensive.

Shoofly, 465 Amsterdam Avenue, New York, NY 10024. 212-580-4390.

Although this is not a catalogue, it is the best store of its kind in the U.S. for kids' accessories. I include it as a special resource because no other store (or catalogue) offers as large a selection of suspenders, bow ties, straw hats, and any other accessories you could think of. Ask for owner Roz Viemeister. Moderate to expensive. U.P.S.

Special Clothes, P.O. Box 4220, Alexandria, VA 22303. 703-683-7343.

Wonderful, colorful natural fiber clothing for kids with handicaps. Smart, subtle adaptive designs inspire self-reliance: Pants have side openings for leg braces; the back of a reversible poncho is cut to hip length so it doesn't bunch up in wheelchairs and the front is cut long enough to keep toes warm; shirts have flaps for feeding tubes; snap-crotches in pants allow for leg braces; and overalls drop down in front to hip level for easier dressing; even underwear is easy access. All adjustments are completely inconspicuous and colors are as trendy as any kid would want—black with turquoise, blue with hot pink. Owner and designer Judith Emens says: "Our goal is to offer the latest styles enhanced with adaptive features to help make dressing a positive experience for both the child and adult—to make kids as independent as they can be." Moderate.

Kids At Large, Inc., Building 32, Endicott Street, Norwood, MA 02062. 1-800-KIDS-FIT.

If your child takes a large size, this catalogue offers good-quality versions of all types of sportswear for both boys and girls. No more shortening the pants because you bought them big enough to fit the waist. All the trendy colors and attractive prints. Especially strong for back-to-school. Moderate to expensive.

For more catalogue listings, refer to *The Mail Order Shopper for Parents,* by Hal Morgan (Doubleday, 1990) and the advertisements in the backs of parenting magazines, such as *Parents* and *Child. Mothering Magazine,* especially, is a fund of excellent 100 percent cotton clothing offerings and other ads for kids' products in the back of their magazine. *Motherings'* address is P.O. Box 1690, Sante Fe, New Mexico 97504.

Kids' Territory. This space could be a magic kingdom, a private store, a hiding place when they're upset, even a closet.

CLOSETS

H ow often do we find ourselves trying to find tights to fit last week's unexpected growth spurt, or a quick change of those suddenly soaked overalls as we're trying to get out the door? My keen interest in closet organization came not only from the need and desire to streamline my life after my second child arrived, but also from what I noticed in my children's attitudes toward organizing their own things. I've seen how keeping on top of their own closets has really shaped my kids' attention to their personal territory. They've taken such pride in having their closets organized that I'll find them doing the same thing with their books or toys. And, practically speaking, an effective closet system for your children's clothing will improve your own life immeasurably and makes speed-dressing your kids more of a possibility.

Of course when your kids are infants and toddlers, it's not practical or possible to have a completely child-centered closet. But as they get older, gradually try to turn the closet over to them. Designing the closet space so that clothes are easy to reach, perhaps by installing a second lower bar, is a subtle way to let your child "own" his space and foster autonomy. You might even put shirts and over-the-head clothes on the *bottom* bar where they're easier to see and choose. Put skirts or pants on the *top* bar—they can be pulled down more easily than a garment with a neck. Sorting the clothes by category is a game that can teach and organize at the same time. And let your kids help organize in other ways, too.

Cleaning and organizing the closets about four times a year, by season, is a good schedule to bring order to a family's life. (For a disorganized child, or for a child with mostly hand-me-downs, more frequent organizing may be necessary.) Since cleaning out the closets is a real chore and really impossible for young children to do themselves, I recommend making it an enjoyable family project. But don't go overboard about the whole thing and drag your children into each phase of the job. Let them help you make a "yes" and a "no" pile—this is less tedious. The "yes" pile is for clothes that stay—they still fit, are appropriate for the season and in decent shape. The "no" pile is for clothes that go—to storage for the next season, for siblings, or to friends, or to Goodwill. They no longer fit, the season has changed, or they're too tired. Of course, at three or four years of age, your child doesn't care about whether something still fits. She just knows if she still likes it or not. So for the very young child, you only need a "yes" pile of favorites. (Observe her choices. Preferences are

. . . .

"I had an old hatrack that I hadn't used in years. I spray-painted it my son's favorite bright green and put it in his room right next to his door. Now every morning on the way out, he chooses the jacket he wants to wear off the rack and he's even started to put it back on the rack at night. We also use it to hang washed gym clothes that are due back at school."

. . . .

coming into play now.) Let her put some of the clothes into the closet by category. This mimics sorting games she's playing in school. Then finish up the job yourself.

If she's omitted some very useful clothes like sweaters or overalls, explain in simple terms why she may still need them, "but we'll put your 'yeses' right where you can reach them." As your child gets older, she'll become more objective about her clothes and the "yes" and "no" piles can be taken more seriously. At five or six, some kids really take to organizing their closets with your help. And by seven or eight, they will probably have definite opinions on where every garment should go, and will use this activity to tell *you* what they need. (See the School Days chapter for other learning and organizational closet tips.)

Okay, you've finally got that extra hour. I'm serious in saying that that's the most this will take. It's time to deal with those closets. Here's how to start:

1. *Decide what needs to be done.* Identify the most irritating problem. Do the clothes keep falling off the hangers? Maybe you need to replace small hangers with larger ones or wire hangers with plastic tubes or padded ones? Are there piles of well-folded t-shirts, of which the top two are the only ones

How to turn a grown-up closet into a two-kid closet: Just add a new shelf in the middle and another pole under it. Infant's clothing is on middle shelf within easy reach of adults, and the three-year-old's clothing is on the pole, hanging underneath, within her reach without help.

ever used? Do you need to store the winter clothes and hang up the summer wardrobe? Is the closet so stuffed, especially on the floor, that you can't close the door? Do you need to add a pole or some shelves? Do you need to turn a one-kid closet into a two-kid closet? Or kid-customize the closet to suit your child's growing independence?

2. *Get the right material for the job.* You need to get the right tool for the right job. Corrugated cardboard boxes from the dime store are great to store the out-of-season or hand-me-down clothes. You may want to invest in shoe bags, hanging pouch holdalls, hard plastic back-of-door closet organizers, even cedar sweater stackers, or any of the closet organizers illustrated here.

3. *Get going!* First, you must *pull everything*, and I mean *everything*, out of the closet. With all the clothes pulled out, you can see what kind of closet space you have to work with, and be refreshed with a clean slate. Then assess each clothing item: is it a "yes" or "no"? With your kid's help, put everything into piles. Put all the "yeses" into the closet and then organize them into categories: tops, pants, dresses, dress shirts, overalls. (Your child may have tired of organizing by now.) After you've done this, you'll be able to see what changes or updates you need to make in your kid's wardrobe.

There are many creative solutions for storage that are inexpensive and also encourage a child's independence. One mother I know had no closet space for

Alternatives to Heavy Bureaus

Most bureaus are designed to fit the spread of an adult's arms. Sometimes the only reason children avoid their bureaus is because they're just too cumbersome to open and close. Here are some good solutions:

1. Buy a bureau whose drawers pull out with center handles, or replace the wide-spread knobs with a single handle centered in the middle.

2. Make sure that adorable white-painted, small-sized chest you found at the fleamarket has drawers that pull out easily. Often the wooden drawers have warped with age and stick when you try to open them.

3. Buy a small put-together cardboard chest of drawers. This can be easily used by small children and costs a fraction of the price of a wooden one. These hold up surprisingly well, and they'll certainly get your child through the toddler and probably preschool years. For the six- or seven- year old, they're not as appropriate for bulky, cold-winter clothing—thick sweaters, sweatpants, and tops are larger in these sizes and the drawers aren't deep enough. Hang those in the closet.

4. Get plastic crates from the dime store and stack them in the closet. Your child can go in and get anything he needs and you might be able to eliminate a bureau entirely.

Closet Cubes. An extra closet in your closet that fits a child. From the Right Start catalogue. The Closet Extender. Extends a closet down to child's height. The separate spaces for each hanger help to organize him. From the Lillian Vernon (adult) catalogue.

her toddler's clothing in her tiny apartment. She put up a bar between the bureau and the wall and hung the A-list clothing on it. Her son could easily pick out what he wanted to wear each day. This simple fixture solved the space problem and helped him take a step toward responsibility. My friend Judy drew pictures of her toddler's shirts, pants, and underwear and taped them to the corresponding bureau drawers. When her daughter was dressing, she had the fun of knowing exactly which drawers to open. Another parent bought only easy knit clothing in colors that mixed and matched. She set up two plastic milk crates just outside her child's closet, one for dirty clothes, the other for clean. The clean bin held a choice of a few items, so her four-year-old could pick her own clothes with no problem.

I've noticed that in general parents allot less closet space to boys than to girls. Most boys' clothing—shirts, sweats, jeans—tends to be folded. Girls have more clothes that are hung up, such as dresses, skirts, and blouses. In some homes, the only boys' clothing that gets hung in a closet is the blazers, pressed pants, and one or two dress shirts. Then there's the unusual case of a friend of mine who has four boys: she keeps *nothing* folded! She hangs everything up in the closets, even t-shirts. She said that her boys would paw over all the neatly folded things in their bureaus looking for the *one* favorite shirt (which was probably still in the hamper). Instead, when each item was hung up, they could go right to what they needed without messing up the other clothing. She was lucky, of course, to have enough closet space to do this for each boy. Another

. . . .

"I didn't bother to readjust the closet pole height. I took an old fold-up bookcase, placed it in the closet below all the hanging clothes, and put all their folded clothes there. We can get at everything very easily, and the closet looks so neat, full, and well used. Plus, the kids have more room to play in their bedroom."

. . . .

. . . .

"My kids would come in the house and just throw their coats and backpacks on the floor. I knew they were probably too young to put their things away carefully, but I still wanted the hall neat. I bought a few sturdy, attractive brass hooks and put one up for each child on the back of the front hall closet door, right at their level. I taped their names over each hook. All of a sudden, they understood that the coats and bags had a place of their own. Now they get mad if one of them or someone else uses the wrong hook!"

. . . .

alternative is to forgo bureaus and closed drawers entirely in favor of open shelving as the kids get older. (Toddlers wouldn't be able to resist pulling everything off the shelves.) The advantage to open shelves is that clothing remains seen and not buried.

If a child's room or space in a shared room is her castle, so is her closet. Everyone can, with a little ingenuity, accommodate a tall person's closet to a little person's needs. Effective organization of your child's clothing will not only make your life a lot easier, it will also help your child appreciate order and become independent.

Tips

➤ Parents don't realize that cleaning up a room can be an overwhelming concept even to a capable ten-year-old. The easiest way to encourage your child is to break up the job into separate tasks, e.g.: "I'll put away your dolls; you do the animals. I'll put away your clean clothes; you dump the dirties into the hamper." Every once in a while, change who gets to do what. Your child will not only feel supported, but by dividing and conquering you will be teaching how to accomplish a difficult (to her) goal. And needless to say, the best teacher is example. Don't complain that your child is messy when your own clothes are all over the floor!

➤ Categorize everything in your child's closet. Make colorful dividers out of cardboard. Cut them to fit over the pole and then paint or decorate them together. When you mount them on the pole to separate pants from shirts, etc., make a game out of it. You will be reinforcing categorization skills that he's being taught at school. Caveat: Don't become so obsessed with keeping his room organized that it becomes inhospitable. He may not want to play in it because he doesn't want to mess it up if he thinks he won't be able to meet your standards when he tries to straighten it up himself. Always offer to get him started so he knows he's not alone.

➤ Since kids have so few pairs of shoes, you can put shoes on the shelf *above* the hanging clothes if the hanging bar is low enough to allow your child to still reach her shoes. This way, they won't get kicked on the floor to the back of the closet and outgrown before you find them again!

➤ Get a special, strong hanger for your child's winter coat so he won't get frustrated trying to wrap a heavy garment around a flimsy wire hanger. Or easier still, get a special sturdy hook.

➤ The back of a closet door is a gold mine of undeveloped space. Use shoe bags or buy over-the-door organizers. Customize a wall hanging out of heavy-duty felt with specific pouches to hold specific clothing or accessories. Or use *seethrough* plastic pouch hanging organizers.

➤ With contact paper, cut out a shadow of your kids' shoes and stick them to the closet floor, or wherever you store their shoes. Your kids can have fun putting their shoes away each night by lining them up correctly; they'll love seeing how fast they outgrow the contact paper size.

➤ Keep the size of the hanger consistent with the size of the clothes. Buy larger size hangers ahead of time so they're handy. At around age five, the sizes really shift and you may find that everything in the closet ends up on the floor. You can easily and cheaply replace baby hangers at any five-and-ten-cent store.

➤ Use those adorable but outgrown one-of-a-kind infant hangers to make mobiles or belt hooks.

➤ Keep a small, sturdy, light-weight chair or step-stool near the closet to help your child reach the shelf above the hanging pole.

➤ Cardboard boxes lined with a thin panel of cedar are wonderful for woolens. They give you the same exquisite moth-protecting scent as cedar drawers at a fraction of the cost. Make your own with a sheet or block of cedar from any lumber store and some cardboard storage boxes.

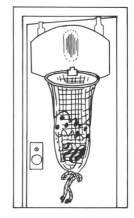

Dirty Dunk.
Heavy-duty drawstring empties clothing easily from the bottom. A fun way to start the habit of taking care of clothes. Get two, and even your three-year-old can sort lights and darks! An excellent organizational tool to build self-esteem is the inexpensive "Good for Me" chart offered by the Toys To Grow On catalogue. This is an attractive, effective write-and-wipe reward chart for ages three to twelve. Household tasks are termed "goals" and kids work toward coupons for rewards agreed upon by both parent and child. P.O. Box 17, Long Beach, CA, 90801.
1-800-542-8338

Catalogues with Great Organizers for Kids

Hold Everything, Mail Order Department, P.O. Box 7807, San Francisco, CA 94120-7807. 415-421-4242.

This catalogue focuses on making space more efficient. Primarily for adults, it does feature several items useful for kids, such as "Stretch-a-Closet"; hard-to-find clear sweater bags that can be used for travel as well as storage; sturdy, good-looking vinyl storage chests to take the place of cumbersome bureaus; and an inexpensive tension closet rod that installs in seconds to keep clothes at child's eye level (it can be moved up as they grow). Emphasis is on clean-cut modern or natural polished wood style and quality materials. Prices range from moderate to high but are worth the investment.

Lillian Vernon, 510 South Fulton Avenue, Mount Vernon, NY 10550-5067. 914-633-6300.

This is a gift catalogue for adults that happens to have a lot of great organizers useful for kids: exclusive large nylon net bags with heavy-duty drawstrings; vinyl-coated metal dividers to organize shelves; inexpensive vinyl hanging sweater bag shelves for the closet; and lots of curio cabinets that are perfect for kids' treasures. See the closet extender on page 241. Inexpensive to moderate.

The Right Start, 5334 Sterling Center Drive, Westlake Village, CA 91361. 800-548-8531.

Their Closet Cube turns a grown-up's closet to kid size, Dirty Dunk teaches kids in a playful way to put their dirty clothes away, and their changing table with pull-out wire drawers as shelves is hard to find anywhere else.

➤ Don't put costumes in the closet unless you plan to argue your kid out of his Batman outfit every day. The best place for dress-up and Halloween costumes is in a corrugated box under the bed. They should be accessible, but not in everyday places.

➤ Avoid large wood racks with numerous pegs or shoe racks with too many pockets. Kids tend to accumulate clutter, and these organizers—though great for adults—will only end up becoming one more area to sort out for your kids.

ON THE RUN

Today, children spend more time traveling than ever before, with or without the rest of the family. Many resorts, such as Club Med, are responding to this trend by making it easier to bring the kids along on vacations. They provide baby-sitting and all-day activities for the kids while the parents swim, scuba, or just take it easy.

For city folks, weekends and summer vacations are often spent in a second house at the beach or in the mountains. Whether the family rents, buys, or shares, they all have in common the packing involved in traveling between two places. Besides the Friday night packing, weekend travelers inevitably face the Monday morning "Where's my . . . !?"

Traveling is even an important activity for the young child. A major enjoyable activity is the sleepover. Packing a miniature suitcase with pajamas, toothbrush, change of clothing, and favorite book or toy, if only to go across the street (or across the hall!) for the night, is something most children really look forward to. And what would childhood be without visits to grandma and grandpa? One mother said that her own mom's favorite activity is shopping with her grandchildren for clothes their own parents would never indulge them. She packs them into the car and lets them run wild in K-Mart. Other parents I spoke to said that when visiting their own parents they felt the pressure to adjust their kids' wardrobes upward. Clean sneakers were always bought and the kids were dressed more neatly and conservatively. "Even though my mother's in the south now and wearing polyester wash-and-wear clothes, she likes to see her grandchildren as she remembers her own children looked in the fifties—proper dressy dresses to go out for dinner, good manners when she shows them off to her friends."

When it comes to joint custody, kids may go back and forth between mom's and dad's respective homes a couple of times a week. The organizational aspect of packing—bringing favorite clothes, getting laundry done, having second sets of basic items, and remembering special activity uniforms—is a complicated task. Each family has a system that works for them which they've developed through trial and error. Their primary concern is to keep the pressure off the kids and take care of the clothing exchanges themselves.

From talking with parents about how they deal with all their mobile children's clothing needs, I've put together some of their best tips and learning experiences. I hope they'll help make traveling *en famille* a more relaxed and joyous experience.

"I save those large, thick plastic zippered bags that new blankets come in. They're great suitcase packers! I pack my clothes in one, Kate's in another, my husband's in another, and put them all in one suit-case. The shoes and toiletries get stuffed in around them. When we arrive, each of us is all set, and we can unpack easily."

Bring:

➤ No-iron clothing in bright colors or patterns that won't show dirt.

➤ Sweats and light-weight clothes that can be layered for changes in weather and will save space in the suitcase.

➤ Clothes that are versatile and can be worn for play or dressed up to go to dinner.

➤ Comfortable broken-in shoes sturdy enough to walk all day in a park or theme park. Nice ones to go out for dinner.

➤ Lots of socks and underwear! If going south, view kids' bathing suits as *the* main part of their vacation wardrobe and pack several. You'll be happy to have many dry changes during the day. (Anticipate clothing needs for

Bridging the Gap Between Generational Clothing Styles

A word about grandparents: the dressing issue often holds special importance for some more conservative grandparents. Many parents tell me that their kids' looks are surprisingly important to their own parents. A pulled-together outfit on the grandchild seems to give confidence that everything else in the family is going okay (financial security, household under control, etc.). Some grandparents have a particularly hard time seeing their grandchildren "creatively" dressed. Autonomous dressing in kids was not a possibility or even an issue when they were growing up. They don't understand it. To them the child looks disheveled and they assume it's a problem and that it's the parents' "fault."

Here are some tips to alleviate these possible tensions between the generations:

1. Accessories, scruffy footwear, and grooming are the main culprits when it comes to outfits that look especially disheveled to grandparents. It's not that they prefer only matched outfits. Let your child pick her clothing, but monitor her socks, headbands, belts, haircare, footwear.

2. Find out your parents' expectations. If you're traveling to see them, call ahead to find out exactly where you're going. Are your kids going to meet their friends (this is grown-up show-and-tell!)? Is the occasion casual or dressy, conservative or relaxed? What does "dressy" mean?

3. Always have decent shoes on your children's feet for restaurants or other social occasions. For a visit down South, a fresh pair of white sneakers for a warm climate lets any child look "together."

4. Be on time. Lay the next day's **dressier, dinner** clothes out the night before, along **with** the next day's **play clothes.** Avoid clothing decisions at the end of a long day at the beach or theme park.

"The children have two bags each when we travel: one for toys and one for clothes. I oversee the clothing bag; the toys are up to them. I definitely pack a lot of underwear and socks. I try to pick out matching or complementary outfits so they can mix and match a lot. I don't like them to bring the everyday grubby t-shirts and pants."

holidays in warm climates. Buy bathing suits in the next size on sale at the end of each summer.)

➤ Nylon, plastic, or mesh bags to hold dirty laundry and wet clothes.

➤ Other necessaries: special toys and games, preferably new; paper and crayons (avoid markers which can stain clothes); one or two security articles such as a stuffed animal or special blanket; first aid kit; favorite snacks for train, car, or plane; portable tape recorder with favorite tapes (optional: earphones for plane travel), lullaby tapes; books for bedtime. *Note:* If a washer and dryer will be accessible, pack less. (And bring a pack of quarters.) If not, pack more. Cut expenses and avoid clothes that need dry-cleaning. Bring a portable inexpensive steamer to freshen knits and jackets.

Tips for Traveling

➤ Don't over-pack clothes; you never need as much as you think. The fewer things to keep up with, the more free you are for the kids and to have a good time. However, if there is no laundry service available, bring enough not to end up constantly washing things in the sink.

➤ Streamline your packing when traveling with an infant. Since you have to bring things like a stroller, carseat, and diapers, trim your luggage weight by bringing only the necessary baby clothes. You can always fill in with cheap basics.

➤ If you use cloth diapers, call ahead to your place of destination to arrange for service for however long you'll be there.

➤ Bring cotton and rubber crib liners to protect the mattresses of toilet-training toddlers away from home. (See the Layette Chapter.)

➤ Use one large bottom drawer in the hotel room for a dirty laundry catch-all to keep the room clear.

➤ Don't pack a new untried outfit for *yourself* for the trip. Vacations, though fun, are still stressful. Nine times out of ten, you'll end up wearing old standbys. Kids, though, adore new outfits, especially bought on vacation. Then, they can bring a little of the vacation home with them.

➤ Take advantage of the cheaper stores you may find and stock up on basics. And if you're anywhere near Freeport, Maine; Secaucus, New Jersey; Greenville, North Carolina; or any of the other clothing outlet areas, plan enough time to check their stores out, especially if it's time for the higher ticket back-to-school clothing.

Clothing Tips for Airplane Travel

➤ Be prepared for your baby to drink more fluids than usual. This will offset the dehydration that occurs in a pressurized cabin and his sucking will relieve the pressure on his ears at take-off and landing. That means, too, bring a *lot* more diapers than usual!

"My kids take their own backpacks when we go on vacation. They get to pack a change of clothes and overnight necessities like a toothbrush, pajamas, etc., and they feel very grown-up doing it. I take up the slack and pack the rest of their things in another bag. Then, if we arrive late at a hotel, I don't have to unpack the big bags. Those can wait until morning."

➤ Bring a change of clothing: several for an infant, one for an older child. If your child is toilet training, bring extra underwear and pants or skirts.

➤ Bring a change of clothing for *yourself* if you have a baby or are nursing.

➤ For cold cabin temperatures, bring a light-weight sweater for baby and a baby blanket. A few receiving blankets layered for warmth may be enough and not as bulky to pack. A soft cotton-knit cap that ties under the chin is enough for a baby's head. Your older child will be fine with a sweater or sweat jacket.

Tips for Weekend Homes

➤ Start packing in the beginning of the week. Don't wait till the last minute when you're too panicked to remember everything.

➤ Designate a place that is always the same where you put things you're taking with you for the weekend. It could be in the front hall closet, or next to a certain bureau. Items that can be put away ahead of time are: change of season clothing that you're taking to pack away, clean laundry basics from the previous weekend, dressy clothes and a birthday present for an upcoming party on the weekend, clothing that your child borrowed from her friend, or clothing her friend forgot at your home that has to be returned.

➤ Encourage responsibility: have a special personal piece of luggage that each child will own and can feel is really his or hers. Supervise their packing. Then check after, so nothing important is left behind. A feeling of success is important to foster self-esteem and responsibility.

➤ Create a generic packing list and photocopy it for future trips. When your kids are old enough, make one for them. This is an inexpensive memory aid that can be easily updated as the kids grow.

➤ Keep a separate list at the second home to write in items you need for the next weekend or that you've run out of, e.g., more turtlenecks, socks, etc. Bring that home as a reminder.

Tips: Other Spouses' Homes

➤ Name tags, especially the large kind, are essential. There is more travel between homes and that means more opportunity for losing or forgetting clothes. Large tags are easiest to spot, especially for outerwear. They can be ordered through catalogues or children's specialty stores.

➤ Keep a rough list of all the clothes your children own. This sounds ridiculous, but you'd be surprised at how easy it is to forget about certain items if you haven't seen them around for a while. When their wardrobes start thinning out, you'll know what to look for at your ex-spouse's home. One parent I know used one roll of film to photo his kids' clothes by category, and then posted the pictures on the back door of each kid's closet. What

. . . .

"One day I went out and bought them a duplicate wardrobe. It was really worth it. We almost never fight now. I didn't realize how many of our fights happened over what the boys packed (or didn't pack!) to come visit."

. . . .

"Each of them has a big, big bag. They live out of it and that keeps the clothes together that are going back and forth. It's less likely to end up stationary over at my ex's. It's the bag that becomes the bureau."

probably saved him hundreds of dollars cost only some time, effort, and $10.

➤ Keep an identical calendar of the kids' weekend or weekday events in *both* homes. The parent in charge will know what clothing changes are needed, and can make sure they've been packed. Post it where it's easy to see.

➤ Keep a set of dressier clothes at both households for unexpected parties or going out to dinner. And keep rainwear, including boots, for unexpected weather changes.

➤ Check the school's lost and found and their friends' homes regularly for stray clothing.

➤ Realize that it is usually only one of the parents who is good at this kind of follow-through, even though it's a matter of saving money. If you are, and your spouse isn't, don't use the clothes to complain. Focus on other positives, eg. how he/she *did* manage to get all the raingear/sports uniforms/turtlenecks back to you.

Acknowledgments

I wish to thank all the parents, friends, and family who participated in and supported this project. Because of the distances they traveled and/or the time they spent sharing their experiences beyond the call of duty, I'd like to thank especially:

Parents: Piper Smith, Jessica Mitchell Fleischer, Joanne Schwarzberg, Barbara Jacobs, Suzanne Matthau, Jenny Matthau Roman, Gail Pomers, Sarah Hardin, Elinor Greenberg, Margaret Karrell, Bonnie August, Liz Hock, Kathy Dorney, Claire Mullen, Karol Vickers, Ellen Silberman, Faye Brugger and Lois Watanabe

Also Susan Fisher-Diaz, Robin Mizrahi, Carol Lalli, Karen Von Etzdorf, Jane Flusser, Diana Bell, Sarah Holmbert, Teresa Hall, Elise Dunham, Kaye Ricciardi, Michi Raab, Patricia Pastor, B. J. Steifer, Peggy Cox, Kim Harris, Cathy Heller, Marie Evans, Tracy Amiral, Patti French, Robin Glicker, Karen Mook, Gardner McFall, Samudra Josepher, Silke Halajian, Ellen Gendler Salik, Zapora Weber, Roberta Goldstein, Gail Gleckler, Jill Long, Marjorie Gross Steinman, Virgil Doyle, Michon Ornellas, Eliza Ventura, Constance Lehman. Jannie Valickus, Terry Hill, Abigail Newman, Sabina Tompkins, Sydny Miner, Robyn Peterson Surprenant, Ralph Matinzi, and Trilby Schreiber.

The Day School mothers: Junie Mays, Beatrice MacDonald Barden, Chris Huette, Anne Herrmann, Suki Blutstein, Polly McCall, Ann Alter, Marcy Adelman, Patricia Farrell, Hilda Greenfield, Joanne Gerstel, Lucy Schraeder, Nommso Stubbs, and Lourdes Lynch.

The Gypsy Trail mothers: Priscilla Warner, Nancy Weber, Sally Norton, Vicki Rose, Carolyn Eckstein, Shawn Diaz, Gay Evans, Beth Olesky, Buff Penrose, Nancy Downey, Anne Heinemann, Lauren Burmester, Janet Calvo Friedman, Helene Gordon, Vera Hathaway, Kathy Rosenman, and Fritzi Bechard.

Children: Elizabeth Ackerman, Fia Aliotta, Charlie Aliotta, Chris Ammond, Noel Anderson, Stuart Anderson, Benjamin Atwell, Kristal Bernard, Rudy Bascomb, Stephanie Boldis, Steven Boldis, Cami Burmester, David Burmester, Albert Cahn, Alex Canas, Tommy Denniston, Nico Diaz, Shayna Diaz, Cole Dougherty, Elizabeth Downey, Alexandra Evans, Kaitlin Piper Flusser, Morgan Skye Flusser, Read Flusser, Gilbert Forsyth, Teddy Forsyth, Maui France, Alessandra Friedman, Jenny Friedman, Chaz Graves, Keivyn Graves, Eric Greenfield, Conor Hagen, Meaghan Hagen, Lucia Haladjian, Hilly Halstead, Haley Hardin, Patricia Harris, Ryan Healy, Christine Heinemann, Sara Heinemann, Julia Ho, Nicholas Hood, Alexander Horn, Nicholas Horvath, Jenna Hutchinson, Erika Isaas, Jamie Isaac, Eddie Jacobs, Charlie Jacobs, Helen Johannson.

Carolanne Karell, Victoria Karell, Patricia Karell, Michael Karell, Andrew Lawrence, Michael Lebensfeld, Eliza Lehner, Mathew Lesser, Tiffany Liu, Nora Logan, Lauren Lytle, Alyssia Mandel, Rebecca Marcus, Rashard Marshall, Jason Marshall, Willie Matthau, Graham McBane, Walker McBane, Crystal McGuire, Priscilla McGuire, Ross Metcalfe, Amanda Metcalfe, Bobby Miner, Jonathan Miner, Roey Mizrahi, Jessica Moldovan, Willie Moler, Sean Mullen, Kelly Mullen, Timmy Mullen, Shannon Mullen, Julie Mulligan, Alexandra Nelson, Gregory Norton, Jessie Norton, Olivia Oguma, Lizzie Olesky, Alexis Ornellas, Jacqueline Pomers, Nicole Przonek, Chloe Przonek.

Shaun Renna, Hilary Renna, Michael Restivo, Alexandra Restivo, Brian Rifkind, Courtney Rose, Douglas Rose, Molly Rosenman, Jonathan Salik, Mira Sacks Salomon, Wing Mai Sang, Sam Schneider, Alexandra Shaffer, Dylan Silbermann, Jesse Silbermann, Jake Silbermann, James Slattery, Taylor Smith, Raber Smith, Elisa Solinas, Tara Shanley, Alexandra Scott-Brown, Jacqueline Storr, Paul Stubbs, Duncan Stubbs, Mihiko Tanaka, Ben Tilghman, Katie Tilghman, Andrew Van Houton, Glenn Vickers, Asiya Vickers, Michell Vickers, Karol Vickers, Diane Vigilante, Bryan Van Brunt, Peter Von Burchard, Michelle Watanabe, Max Watanabe, Max Warner, Jimmy Warner, Karen Zimmermann, Alison Zimmermann, Julie Mulligan, Alessandra Friedman, and Jenny Friedman.

From the Assumption School in Wood-Ridge, New Jersey: Otto Clemente, Edward Mudzinski, Ashley Gaudioso, Brooke Bryant, Jennifer Newton, Keith Migliorino, Ian Janeczko, Saralyn Sendik, Danielle Gotha, Claire Follari, Daniel Nichols, Ariana Mendez, Nicole Altamore, Vanessa D'Amato, Georgia Homsany, and teacher Bonnie Talisse.

From Mirko Cavar's Friday Gymnastics Class at the Day School, 1990: Kate Barton, Kate Bogart, Julia Day, Tabetha Dobkins, Leslie Elwell, Carmen Epstein, Gillian Farrell, Eve Gutman, Kate Heinzelman, Marisa Herzog, Maisie Hughes, Jeong-A, Helen Johannesen, Stephanie Kim, Reina Kolman, Margot Norton, Alison Rapoport, Emmy Robinson, Simone Solivan, Jennifer Solomon, Rachel Tavel, Sarah Tavel, Danielle Teitelbaum, Alicia Van Couney, Lizzy Rosenshine, Laura Rosenshine, Caroline Smetana.

Few of the children photographed were professionals. However, there were times when there were special needs and difficult time constraints. Patty Fleischer at Close Ups and Cammy Scott of Wee Willy were extremely helpful and creative and never failed us.

FASHION ACKNOWLEDGMENTS

Special thanks go to these stores and for their generous loan of clothing when needed: Morris Bros., Shoofly, Chocolate Soup, Monkeys and Bears, Mothercare, shoes from East Side Kids and Tru-Tred (all in New York City). Also, these manufacturers: Jacques Moret, Schreiber and Co. and Jodi's Gym; bathing suits and sweaters from Hot Fudge; OshKosh; Jams World Inc., and Gap Kids; Rosecraft Inc., Shalom, Int. and Pelican.

Special thanks go to the Biobottoms catalogue and Hanna Andersson catalogue who lent their expertise and merchandise. Also Franne's Kids, Brights Creek, Childcraft, and Hearth Song.

I especially thank the following design and retail experts (not mentioned in the text) in the children's clothing field for their long, patient interviews: Barry Krumholtz of Morris Bros., N.Y.C.; Margot Holland, Fashion Director for Children's Clothing, Saks Fifth Avenue; Connie Carlson, The Company Store; Margot Jacobs, Vice President of Sahara Club; Julie Tarney of Oshkosh, Wisconsin; Steven Myers, President of Quiltex; Ronnie Scott, designer of girls' bathing suits, Hot Fudge; Janice Scott, designer of boys' bathing suits, Pacific Bay; Al Waldman, Sandra Aponte, and Charles Ferrante of East Side Kids Shoes; Jack Hyde, for Jams World Inc.; Eileen Baskin, designer, Mighty Mac; and Helaine Leskowitz of Pelican, Inc.

INDEX
....

MARILISE FLUSSER interviewed over 300 experts in various fields while putting together this first-of-its-kind guide. She also brings to it her own energy, enthusiasm, and expertise in children's clothing as a former spokesperson for The Gap; the children's fashion coordinator for Saks Fifth Avenue; and an image consultant to companies such as Reebok and Hush Puppies.

Flusser lives in New York City with her husband, men's wear designer Alan Flusser, and their two daughters, Morgan Skye and Kaitlin Piper.